# The Work of Theology

# The Work of Theology

Stanley Hauerwas

WILLIAM B. EERDMANS PUBLISHING COMPANY

GRAND RAPIDS, MICHIGAN / CAMBRIDGE, U.K.

Published 2015 by
Wm. B. Eerdmans Publishing Co.
2140 Oak Industrial Drive N.E., Grand Rapids, Michigan 49505 /
P.O. Box 163, Cambridge CB3 9PU U.K.
www.eerdmans.com

Printed in the United States of America

21  20  19  18  17  16  15        7  6  5  4  3  2  1

**Library of Congress Cataloging-in-Publication Data**

Hauerwas, Stanley, 1940-
The work of theology / Stanley Hauerwas.
       pages        cm
ISBN 978-0-8028-7190-9 (pbk.: alk. paper)
1. Christian ethics.   2. Theology,  Practical.   I. Title.


BJ1200.H38   2015
230.01 — dc23
                    2015005293

"Who Am I?" by Dietrich Bonhoeffer. Reprinted with the permission of Scribner, a Division of Simon & Schuster, Inc., from LETTERS AND PAPERS FROM PRISON, REVISED, ENLARGED ED. by Dietrich Bonhoeffer, translated from the German by R. H. Fuller, Frank Clark, et al. Copyright © 1953, 1967, 1971 by SCM Press Ltd. All rights reserved. "Who Am I?" is taken from *Letters and Papers from Prison* by Dietrich Bonhoeffer, published by SCM Press 1971. Used by permission of Hymns Ancient and Modern Ltd.

"Feeding the Poor at a Sacrifice" by Peter Maurin. From *Easy Essays* by Peter Maurin, Catholic Worker Reprint Series, Eugene, OR: Wipf and Stock, 2010. Used by permission of Wipf and Stock Publishers, www.wipfandstock.com.

*To*
*Allen Verhey*

# Contents

# *Preface*

*Approaching the End: Eschatological Reflections on Church, Politics, and Life* was, as the title indicates, a book primarily oriented toward the future. That is a little misleading. "End" is the eschatological end, which means the end in question determines the past, resides in the present, and makes the future possible. Yet *Approaching the End* was a book in which I tried to think thoughts I should think if what I have thought in the past has any claim to being true.

*The Work of Theology* is, however, at once similar and different from *Approaching the End*. It is more self-indulgent than *Approaching the End*. By self-indulgent I mean to call attention to my penchant in this book to return to some of my earliest philosophical and theological views. I do so not only because such a return may help me better understand the positions I have taken, but I hope those kind enough to read this book will better understand why I have had to say what I have said.

The retrospective character of this book means I have allowed myself to correct what I take to be some mistaken characterizations of my work. Some of those "mistaken characterizations" were made by someone named Stanley Hauerwas. One characterization that is clearly not by me is the depiction of me as a radical who is trying to convince Christians to give up on the world — or at least politics. That description of my intention some suggest is due to my having overstressed the Christian difference. I have tried to say what I think that difference to be but I have done so not as an end in itself but because I have assumed that by discovering the difference we might know better why what we believe is true. But all this adds up to the view that I am an edgy guy who has little good to say about anyone who does not share my primary convictions.

Needless to say, I am not fond of such characterizations of myself or my work. Of course I have been polemical, but I hope I've been so in a constructive fashion. I may be self-deceived, but I hope I have represented the general approach to theology I learned as a graduate student at Yale Divinity School in the sixties. Given the character of this book I think it appropriate to say what I mean by suggesting I am still working out what I learned at Yale from 1962 to 1968. Though I have never thought of myself as part of the "Yale School" — or better, I was never sufficiently sure about what the "Yale School" might be to know if I was or was not a member — nevertheless I have tried to represent an approach to theology I learned at Yale.

That approach has been wonderfully described by George Lindbeck's illuminating "Introduction" to Robert Calhoun's *Scripture, Creed, Theology: Lectures on the History of Christian Doctrine in the First Centuries* (Eugene, OR: Cascade, 2012). If you want to understand what the "Yale School" was about, there is no better description of that "ethos" than Lindbeck's "Introduction." Frei and Lindbeck were obviously crucial for defining what has become known as postliberalism, but the spirit that shaped them as well as the general ethos at Yale was that of Robert Calhoun.

In his "Introduction" Lindbeck quotes Frei's *in memoriam* for Mr. Calhoun in which Frei observes that Mr. Calhoun "taught us to use the time honored orthodox term 'doctrine' once again with ease." He did so, according to Frei, by helping them see that "orthodoxy" was a living tradition with wide perimeters. Frei observes that Mr. Calhoun's theory of knowledge was a form of critical realism — which means, although Mr. Calhoun never became a Barthian, he did think that God is "there" to be worshiped. The same critical realism that can be attributed to Barth was the decisive factor that facilitated Mr. Calhoun's transition from liberalism to a more traditional orthodoxy without abandoning all aspects of his liberalism.

According to Frei, however, Mr. Calhoun's account of Christian doctrine was distinguished from Harnack's because Mr. Calhoun thought the Greeks were right to see philosophy as an aid for Christian theology. Frei concludes his memorial by observing that Mr. Calhoun would have agreed with Schleiermacher that from the beginning Christianity has been a "language-shaping" force rather than a "shapeless receptacle" for every new vocabulary that a theologian might be tempted to use. Frei concludes by calling attention to Mr. Calhoun's great *History of Christian Doctrine,* which served as "the chrysalis of his generous, liberal orthodoxy" (pp. xix-xxi).

I quite realize I follow at a distance, but Lindbeck's and Frei's characterization of the spirit that Mr. Calhoun exemplified, I should like to think, has informed the way I have done theology. I think that is why I have always found it odd to be characterized as someone trying to isolate Christians from the world. I thought reading my footnotes would be enough to counter that charge. I have always assumed that if what we believe as Christians is true we should have no fear of truth that may turn up in strange places and may even take the form of important challenges to our faith.

To locate the tradition in which I understand myself may seem an odd subject for a "Preface." But I had to say it somewhere. So I thought I might as well begin *The Work of Theology* by calling attention to Lindbeck's "Introduction" to his edition of Mr. Calhoun's book on doctrine. I do so because I fear the significance of what Lindbeck has done to make Mr. Calhoun's book available can be lost. At the very least this should make clear how much I owe to my teachers at Yale Divinity School.

It will be obvious to the reader that many of these chapters were written in response to a specific request for me to address a particular topic. As I have often done, I used the opportunity to write for specific requests what I thought needed to be written for this book. The first thing I wrote for this book was "How to Write a Theological Sentence." That essay became the prototype for the book. I then wrote "How I Think I Learned How to Think Theologically," which was followed, I think, by the essay on irony. I am grateful for those who asked me to write on specific topics because they still seem to think I have something to say.

In 1990 I gave the New College Lectures at the University of New South Wales. Those lectures became *After Christendom? How the Church Is to Behave If Freedom, Justice, and a Christian Nation Are Bad Ideas.* (A second edition of *After Christendom* with a new "Preface" was published in 1999. I mention it only because I think that "Preface" addresses many of the criticisms made of the book.) I was honored to be asked by Trevor Cairney, the master of New College, to give the New College Lectures again in 2013. Chapters One, Seven, and Nine of *The Work of Theology* constituted those lectures. Paula and I are extremely grateful for the wonderful hospitality Trevor and his colleagues gave us during our time in Australia. We were grateful, moreover, that we were able to spend time with our friends Bruce and Louise Kaye. Bruce was master of New College when I gave the first set of lectures.

I am as usual in the debt of many friends for reading and criticizing drafts of these chapters. I am particularly in Greg Jones's debt for his astute suggestions about several of these chapters. I also owe him much for having the idea I should teach a seminar on time, which was supported by the Issachar Foundation and, in particular, Kurt Berends, the Director of the Issachar Foundation. The chapter on time came from the work of that seminar. As usual I am in debt to Sam Wells for his suggestions about what I needed to say more about or what I needed to say better. I am also grateful to many colleagues in Duke University and Divinity School. In particular I am indebted to David Aers, Thomas Pfau, Sarah Beckwith, Paul Griffiths, Ellen Davis, and a cast of thousands.

Current and former students continue to make what I do better. Sean Larson, who recently completed his Ph.D., and Ben Dillon, who will soon finish his Ph.D., helped me make Chapters One and Eight better. Much of what I have to say about language in this book I learned from Jonathan Tran and Peter Dula. I am the happiest of persons because I have former students who have not given up on trying to educate me. I suppose if I have any strength it is the presumption that I always still have something to learn.

I continue to enjoy the good work and support of Carole Baker. Carole will soon complete her Th.D., which means she will soon write books I will look forward to reading. She is a theologian from whom we have much to learn. For me, of course, the theologian from whom I learn bears the name of Paula Gilbert. That sentence is not an empty gesture, particularly if it is true, as I believe it to be, that a theologian is a person of prayer. I will never have Paula's gift of prayer, but I cannot help but thank God that Paula has chosen to share her life with me.

I had retired, but my retirement was interrupted by the illness and death of Allen Verhey. Because of Allen's illness I was asked to teach the core course in Christian ethics that Allen had just begun. Just as I was beginning to discover what it might mean to be retired I lost any sense that I was retired. This is not a complaint but rather an acknowledgment: retirement is going to be, at least for me, a learned art that I suspect will not come easily. What does, however, come easily is to dedicate this book to Allen Verhey. Allen's gentle graciousness, his love of his craft, and his reflections on the Christian art of dying were remarkable gifts to anyone who was fortunate enough to know him. His own life and death are but further testament to his integrity as a scholar and his commitment to being a disciple of Christ. If you ever want to know what "generous orthodoxy" means, think: Allen Verhey. He is and will be sorely missed as a Christian, a colleague, and a treasured friend.

# Introduction

## A Theologian at Work

Picasso is reported to have observed that success is dangerous. It is so, according to Picasso, because success tempts one to begin to copy oneself in the hope of sustaining the success one has had. But Picasso observes that to copy oneself is more dangerous than to copy others. The danger quite simply is that when one copies oneself the result cannot help but be sterile. I confess there are few things I fear more than sterility and boredom. I have no idea what it might mean to think of myself as a "success," though some seem intent on suggesting that adjective applies to me. I am trying very hard in this book, however, not to copy myself. Rather I am trying to force myself to think thoughts I have thought in the past, only differently. That has been hard but fun work.

Karl Barth once wrote an essay titled, "Rudolph Bultmann — An Attempt to Understand Him." The chapters that make up this book might be characterized as a series of thought experiments titled, "Stanley Hauerwas — An Attempt to Understand Him." An odd project if you think that anyone who has written as much as I have must have some idea about what he has said or at least tried to say. But I do not believe that to be necessarily the case; that is, I do not believe I know what I have said or written. I suspect I have often said less than I thought I was saying, and at times I may have said more. I do not think that to be a problem, if it is a problem, peculiar to me because I take it to be a characteristic that is true of any language user. Let me try to explain.

I need to explain, or at least try to make clear, my understanding of how we do not control the words we use because that is the fundamental presupposition that runs throughout this book. I think it was from Ludwig Wittgenstein that I first had some intimation that we often say more or less than we think we say. Richard Fleming observes, an observation I take to have Wittgensteinian roots, that it is no easy thing to "attempt to find ourselves in the complexity of the systematic order of our words, the words that we share."[1] We are never free of failing to mean what we say. Thus the necessity of saying "What I really meant to say was *x* not *y*."

That the words we use are not our words means we in fact often lose control over what we mean when we use them. Writing, which is one of the crucial sources of thought, is the struggle "to try to mean what we say using words that are not our own. We find our life fated in the language of our ancestors, in the language we inherit from them. . . . Hence to understand what words mean we must understand what those who use them mean."[2] But, of course, we must remember that those to whom we look for understanding what we say or have said may not have understood what they have said.

That we do not have control of the words we use I think is surely the case if you are determined, as I have been determined, to think in and with that tradition of speech called Christianity. I am a theologian. Theologians do not get to choose what they are to think about. Better put, theologians do not get to choose the words they use. Because they do not get to choose the words they use, they are forced to think hard about why the words they use are the ones that must be used. They must also do the equally hard work of thinking about the order that the words they use must have if the words are to do the work they are meant to do.

I hope this helps explain why I have taken the liberty in many of these essays to be unapologetically self-referential. I have done so because in this book I revisit what I have said in the past in the hope that I will better understand what I have thought. By forcing myself to think differently thoughts I

1. Richard Fleming, *First Word Philosophy: Wittgenstein-Austin-Cavell Writings on Ordinary Language Philosophy* (Lewisburg, PA: Bucknell University Press, 2004), p. 122.

2. Fleming, *First Word Philosophy*, p. 127. With his usual insight James Wetzel in an extraordinary chapter titled "Wittgenstein's Augustine," in his book *Parting Knowledge: Essays After Augustine* (Eugene, OR: Wipf & Stock, 2013) observes that Wittgenstein's loving tribute to Augustine throughout the *Investigations* simply claimed that Augustine's picture of language was not wrong but simply unnecessary. Wetzel notes that if Wittgenstein had tried to say more as he had tried in the *Tractatus* he would have usurped the power of the logos Augustine reserved for God. Wetzel then elaborates, observing that Wittgenstein, no longer master of words, prepared to confess in a voice never entirely his own the darker possibilities of conception, that is, the ones that "orphan the soul and render the body a prison-house or coffin. He is also open to the possibility of correction without self-torment" (p. 244).

thought I understood at the time, I hope to gain insight about what I should now think given what I once thought. I hope in the process what I have written will be saved from being a shameful exercise in narcissism. After all, as I just indicated, the words I use are not mine. This is, therefore, not an effort to only understand a "me"; it is also an investigation of an "us."

Accordingly I hope this book will be of use to those who have read my past work. In particular, I hope what I do can help you locate the politics that has shaped our speech habits. What we say and how we say what we say is made possible by what we do and cannot do. What we do and cannot do rightly reflects a politics nicely suggested by Richard Fleming's observation that "we would say different things if we acted differently or were made differently. Our reasons for talking about the world as we do are tied to the fact that we can and do name; we often talk about thought as we do because we do not voice all actions; we talk about language as we do because others can understand and teach us."[3]

You can, if you so desire, call this a pragmatic account of how language works.[4] I am deeply sympathetic to William James and Charles Sanders Peirce who, of course, had their own disagreements. But I am not inclined to label my work "pragmatic" because I am not inclined to labels. Labels can invite the assumption that you must have a theory — and I am not suggesting that pragmatism is a theory — before you begin to do philosophical or theological work. Stanley Fish has identified theory as "a 'method,' a recipe with premeasured ingredients which when ordered and combined according to absolutely explicit instructions will produce, all by itself, the correct result."[5] In this book I hope I make clear that I am, I think for very

---

3. Fleming, *First Word Philosophy*, p. 124. John Bowlin has elaborated this point in his extremely important essay "Aquinas and Wittgenstein on Natural Law and Moral Knowledge," in *Grammar and Grace: Reformulations of Aquinas and Wittgenstein*, ed. Jeffrey Stout and Robert MacSwain (London: SCM Press, 2004), pp. 154-74. Bowlin argues that Wittgenstein showed how some of the moral and ontological commitments constituting a linguistic bedrock are given by nature and not by convention. Accordingly it can make sense to talk about our common humanity. I am sure Bowlin is right about Wittgenstein, and Wittgenstein is right about the way our bodies are configured making a difference for what we say. I am doubtful, however, if that difference will be sufficient to settle deep differences.

4. For an account of the relation of pragmatism and language see Kevin Hector, *Theology without Metaphysics: God, Language, and the Spirit of Recognition* (Cambridge: Cambridge University Press, 2011), pp. 52-72. Jacob Goodson has written a number of good articles exploring the significance of William James's work for theology.

5. Stanley Fish, *Doing What Comes Naturally: Change, Rhetoric, and the Practice of Theory in Literary and Legal Studies* (Durham, NC: Duke University Press, 1989), p. 343.

good reasons, the great enemy of theory. It is, moreover, not easy to be an enemy of theory, as too often the denial of theory is based on a theory.

I hope to avoid being identified as someone who has a theory that denies the need for theory by exploring in the first chapter, a chapter titled "How I Think I Learned to Think Theologically," how theological reflection can be understood as an exercise in practical reason. That presumption is why "How" is in the title of the chapters that make up this book. I am more than ready to acknowledge that the "How" in some of the chapter titles of this book seems artificial and odd. I will provide a more extended account of the "How" below, but I call attention to my emphasis on the "How" to signal what I hope is the performative character of the chapters that make up this book. I am, after all, trying to say what I have to say in an interesting way in the hope that I can seduce some readers to read further. As Aristotle maintained, the conclusion of a practical syllogism is an action.

By trying to develop an account of theology as an exercise in practical reason I hope readers will find the book entertaining. For example, I hope readers will have as much fun reading my essay "How to Write a Theological Sentence" as I did writing it. I enjoyed writing that essay because in it I draw on the work of Stanley Fish, and Stanley is always entertaining. I do not want to keep you in suspense, so I will tell you that the sentence I analyze is not mine but Robert Jenson's wonderful sentence: "God is whoever raised Jesus from the dead, having before raised Israel from Egypt."

I have always tried to do theology in an entertaining manner. One consequence of that endeavor has been an attempt to defy the presumption that a strong distinction can be made between scholarly and popular work. That may seem unwise in our day when theology is not considered a worthy scholarly subject to be included in university curriculums. But I have assumed the best response to that prejudice is to show that what Christians have to say about God is very interesting. For it has been one of my self-imposed tasks to try to help us see the difference God makes for how we negotiate the world. I have done so not because I think difference is an end in itself, but because I assume that the discovery of difference is one of the conditions necessary for knowing what it might mean to say what we believe as Christians is true.

The attempt to show the difference Christian convictions can make for how the world is understood, as well as how we live in the world, has not had high priority for much of recent Christian theology. Christians, particularly in the West, have assumed they have been in control of the worlds in which they have found themselves. Accordingly they have sought to show the commonalities between themselves and those who are not Christian. That I have been trying to name the differences has earned me some rather colorful denigrating designations. Whether those descriptions are justified I hope can be tested by anyone kind enough to read *The Work of Theology*.

One of the descriptions (criticisms) of my work is that I can give no account of how tribal groups can ever come to share a language. The remarks I have made above about the words we share in common suggest that the differences between Christian and non-Christian vocabularies may not go all the way down. I certainly hope they do not go all the way down, but what commonalities there may be will have to be discovered rather than assumed.

We live at a time when Christianity is on the wane. Though that is often thought to be a particular challenge for Christians, I think it is a greater challenge for people who think of themselves as secular. The challenge before the secular is to disavow the continuing reliance on cultural and moral habits that come from Christianity and tell us why, for example, it makes sense to make promises that last a lifetime or to bring children into a world that you think is without purpose.

Of course those committed to a secular perspective can object that they do not believe we live in a world with no purpose, but I am asking how they have avoided that conclusion. My philosopher colleague at Duke, Alex Rosenberg, has written a book titled *The Atheist's Guide to Reality: Enjoying Life without Illusions*. The title does not do justice to Rosenberg's argument because, as he observes, he has no interest in putting another "nail into the intellectual coffin of theism."[6] According to Alex, that is simply a wasted effort given the fact that theism has been decisively defeated. But if theism has become hopelessly unintelligible then why should anyone continue to think it interesting to identify himself as an atheist? Atheism only makes sense against the background of some kind of theism.

For Alex atheism is not all that interesting. What Alex finds really interesting are the implications of modern science and, in particular, physics and biology for understanding our position in the universe. According to Rosenberg, those sciences have decisively shown that all that is can be explained in causal terms, which means the fact that we exist is a matter of pure chance.[7] The conscious mind is but the outworking of the chemical

6. Alex Rosenberg, *The Atheist's Guide to Reality: Enjoying Life without Illusions* (New York: Norton, 2011), p. x.

7. Rosenberg, *The Atheist's Guide to Reality*, p. 19. No one understood this better than

process of the brain. We are not creatures who can act freely, which means any idea that we possess a free will is illusory. Nor does any distinction between right and wrong make sense. From Alex's perspective it is silly to try to give reasons for why we should be moral, because there are no good reasons for being moral. Indeed we have no idea what it means to be moral. That does not mean we will cease being relatively nice people, because we have been determined through the evolutionary process to feel better when we act in a manner we associate with acting decently.

According to Alex the most significant implication of the scientific revolution is, however, "it's not story time anymore."[8] It is not story time anymore because science is not about stories — even true ones. Rather real science is a matter of blueprints, recipes, formulas, diagrams, equations, and geometrical proofs. That means when it comes to science, and finally everything comes to science and the scientific understanding of reality, stories have to give way to equations, models, laws, and theories.[9]

Alex acknowledges that he has just one problem. The physics and evolutionary process that make stories about the way things are no longer necessary also made us lovers of stories. It seems at one stage of the evolutionary process stories were useful for helping us survive. As a result, our brains are hardwired to love stories. The challenge before us, a challenge Alex has written his book to meet, is to get us over our love affair with stories. Alex recognizes, however, that he is in a difficult position because he must tell a story about the triumph of science to defeat the necessity of telling stories about our world.[10]

---

William James. Nor did anyone struggle more than James to understand how one should live given that we live in a world devoid of purpose. I have nothing but admiration for the humanity of James as a person and philosopher, as I hope is evident in *With the Grain of the Universe: The Church's Witness and Natural Theology* (Grand Rapids: Brazos Press, 2001). I suspect few noticed that a second edition of *With the Grain of the Universe* was published in 2013 with an "Afterword." I call attention to the second edition because in the "Afterword" I try to show why James is so important for the overall perspective of that book. Jacob Goodson has provided an extensive account of the importance of James for my work in his *Narrative Theology and the Hermeneutical Virtues: Humility, Patience, Prudence* (New York: Lexington Books, 2015).

8. Rosenberg, *The Atheist's Guide to Reality,* pp. 14-19.

9. Rosenberg, *The Atheist's Guide to Reality,* p. 15.

10. Rosenberg, *The Atheist's Guide to Reality,* p. 17. Rosenberg, I think, has another problem given his position, that is, how to explain why he cares so passionately that others recognize what he takes to be the truth. Robert Jenson wrote about the necessity of story as the grammatical form of Christian theology long before Rosenberg's declaration that

I call attention to Alex Rosenberg's argument not only because I admire his candor but, more important, because I think he gets the fundamental challenge right, that is, whether the world as we know it can be narrated. What we believe as Christians, I think, is quite basic and even simple. But because it is so basic we can lose any sense of the extraordinary nature of Christian beliefs and practices — beliefs so basic, for example, that we assume we can tell a story about ourselves and the world in which we find ourselves. In this book I will revisit some of what I have thought in the past in an attempt to recover at least for myself, and hopefully for anyone kind enough to read what I have written, a sense of the oddness of what we believe as Christians.

## How *The Work of Theology* Works

*The Work of Theology* is an unusual book for me. It is not a collection of random essays, but neither is it a book. At least it is not a book in which chapters are conceived to follow from one another in such a way that you can only understand the next chapter because you have just read the previous chapter. I do think, however, if you read the chapters in the order they now stand you may well find the book has an organization to it. The first four chapters, for example, tend to be more theologically and methodologically oriented than the later chapters. But that too is a generalization that is not quite right. The first chapter sets the theme for the rest of the book, that is, how theology conceived as an exercise in practical reason informs all the chapters that follow.

Chapter Seven, "How to Write a Theological Sentence," may seem to be less theological than some of the other chapters, but I hope readers will find my presentation of Jenson's great sentence will make anyone think twice about that judgment. That chapter has an "Appendix" I wrote for an event at Cardoza Law School celebrating the life and work of Stanley Fish. I thought it a pretty good piece, but I could not get anyone to publish it. So I decided to publish it on my own. I hope you like it. I certainly think it is a nice accompaniment to "How to Write a Theological Sentence."

The second chapter, "How the Holy Spirit Works," is perhaps more

---

story time is over. However, Jenson's "How the World Lost Its Story" is a decisive response to Rosenberg. See Robert Jenson, *Theology as Revisionary Metaphysics* (Eugene, OR: Wipf & Stock, 2014), pp. 50-69.

recognizable as "theology," but I hope the reader will find these two chapters interrelated in quite interesting ways. (I had not read Sarah Coakley's book *God, Sexuality, and the Self: An Essay on the Trinity* when I wrote the chapter on the Holy Spirit, but I feel the necessity to call attention to her book because I think her attempt to develop a Trinitarian theology from the perspective of the third person of the Trinity to be an extraordinarily creative proposal.)

"How to Do or Not to Do Protestant Ethics" is a chapter that had to be written for no other reason than it is meant to help readers locate themselves in the confusing world of contemporary theology and ethics. To so locate oneself may not be all that important, but it probably is important that the reader is able to locate me on that map. I suspect, however, by the time readers finish the chapter they may well wonder if it is possible for anyone in this quickly changing part of the world we call Christian to know where they are.

Those who know something of my early work will hopefully recognize how the opening chapters of *The Work of Theology* revisit questions surrounding agency, narrative, and contingency. "How to Be an Agent" returns to the work I did in *Character and the Christian Life*. The relationship between the chapter on agency and the earlier analysis of practical reason hopefully will be interesting and clarifying. I sometimes think that I am misunderstood because many who now read me have little or no sense, for example, of where my understanding of the emphasis on narrative came from.

Also running through these first essays are the themes of "contingency" and "time." We must learn to tell time, but the time we learn to tell is subject to many variations. I suspect few topics are more important in recent theology than the question of time. The great temptation is to want to stop time or, at least, get a handle on the time we are in. If only we knew what time we are in we might be able to defeat the contingencies that make our lives seem arbitrary. An ancient lady of India once maintained the earth rested on the back of a turtle. When asked by a British person what the turtle rested on, she responded, "another turtle." When asked what that turtle rested on she explained, "It is turtles all the way down." It is time all the way down. For Christians this should not be bad news because it means we have all the time in the world to be God's timeful people.

"The 'How' of Theology and Ministry" could have been put in the latter part of *The Work of Theology*, but I thought the work I do in this chapter on language not unimportant for the work I do in "How to Write a Sentence" and "How to Be Theologically Ironic." The essay on irony was occasioned by Jonathan Lear's recent work on irony. Lear's work is so rich I could not resist "having a go" at Lear's way of understanding irony. Moreover, to focus on irony meant I was able to begin to explore the social and political considerations intrinsic to the work of theology.

The chapters after the essay on irony can be read as attempts to think through social and political implications of the earlier chapters. In that respect the chapter on political theology represents a clear turn in the book. That essay, as well as the chapters on "rights" and remembering the poor, represents my attempt to provide a response to the oft-made critique of my work, that is, my stress on the church tempts me and those influenced by me to ignore the world. My worries about "inalienable rights" may only confirm for some that I do not give a damn about Christian social engagements and, in particular, the care of the poor, but I hope the approach I take in "How to Remember the Poor" will suggest otherwise.

I decided to put "How to Be Theologically Funny" near the end because I wanted to give any reader who has read through the book a present. "How to Be Theologically Funny" is meant to be fun. But like much that is funny (and Sam Wells reported to me that he did not find it all that funny; but then, he is English) it has a very serious punch line. The last essay is about me, that is, it is my attempt to think through the "how" of retirement. I am the kind of tiresome person who has to work very hard to try not to work. I suspect retirement is an art for which I have little natural talent. It is not clear to me whether that is a good or bad thing. All I have ever known is work.

That all I have ever known is work may help explain the title of this book, *The Work of Theology*. Theology is work, but it is good work. Good work is work that is so consuming you forget you are tired. Good work is work that attracts others to join you in doing the work. So the title of this book is meant to be taken literally, even while I have no idea what it would mean to take anything literally. This book has been "work" because work is first and foremost about how to do what needs to be done. It is with deep gratitude and humility that I have been given this work to do. Reading is also work, and so I am equally grateful to anyone who has deemed my work worthy of being read.

In particular I must thank Nicholas Healy for the work — sometimes tiresome, no doubt — that he invested in reading and writing about me in his book *Hauerwas: A (Very) Critical Introduction*. I have ended *The Work of Theology* with a "Postscript" that I hope is a constructive response to

Healy's criticisms of my work. Readers of the "Postscript" will discover that I think Healy's criticisms are off the mark, but he is a critic I deeply respect. I hope my response conveys that respect. Though I may not agree with Healy about how theology is to be done, I do think the cover of his book is as good as it gets.

# CHAPTER 1

# How I Think I Learned to Think Theologically

*What we aim at is truth in the concrete.*

JOHN HENRY NEWMAN

## Practicing Practical Reason

Toward the end of *Whose Justice? Which Rationality?* Alasdair MacIntyre makes a comment that I hope provides some justification for what I am going to do in this essay, that is, try to make explicit the way I have learned to think theologically. I am, of course, the declared enemy of any attempt to identify "a method" for doing theology and, in particular, any method for the way I do theology. But the denial of "method" can be understood to reflect some methodological commitments that can and should be made candid. By directing attention to MacIntyre's comment I will try to make candid why I think, to the extent there is a method for doing theology, and in particular the way I do theology, that method is best understood as an exercise in practical reason.

MacIntyre's comment came in response to the problem, a problem that is at the heart of *Whose Justice? Which Rationality?*, of how someone can act in a reasonable manner when faced by what seems to be the impossibility of deciding between antithetical accounts of what is just and/or true. This is a person, according to MacIntyre, who has not yet given their allegiance to any tradition of enquiry, hence their inability in the face of alternative traditions to know what to do. The comment to which I want to direct attention is MacIntyre's suggestion that the initial response to such a person is quite straightforward, namely, the answer "will depend upon who you are and how you understand yourself."[1]

MacIntyre observes this is not the kind of answer that those who have had even an elementary introduction to philosophy expect from a philosopher. A philosopher, it is assumed, is to give an answer that would be persuasive to anyone at any time. MacIntyre argues, however, that this standard philosophical response is based on presumptions that are false. The chief of those presumptions is that there are standards of rationality that provide adequate evaluation of rival alternatives that are equally available to all people no matter what tradition in which they happen to find themselves situated. Once this presumption is questioned it becomes clear that problems of justice and practical rationality are not the same for all people. What the problems are and how they are understood and resolved will vary not only with historical, social, and cultural contexts but also with the situation of the person who has this or that particular set of problems.

Some worry that MacIntyre's response, "it will depend on who you are and how you understand yourself," implies a vicious relativism and/or subjectivism, but such an accusation only reproduces the understanding of rationality that MacIntyre argues is mistaken. For persons in the situation he describes have the possibility of self-recognition and self-knowledge because they have learned to speak and write some language in use. Accordingly, they will have some texts through which they can test certain kinds of argumentative interventions. They will, therefore, be able to assess over time their initial responses by testing those responses with arguments in an ongoing tradition, as well as debates in that tradition of enquiry with alternative traditions.[2]

MacIntyre is acutely aware that his account of a person capable of recognizing that he or she is at home in a tradition is in marked contrast to the kind of person who thinks of himself or herself as alien to every tradition of enquiry. Persons who think they are at home nowhere assume that to be rational entails the attempt to provide neutral, impersonal, and independent standards of rational judgment. Such a view is the natural language of that strange individual associated with modernity, namely, the cosmopolitan person whose language seems to reflect a position from

1. Alasdair MacIntyre, *Whose Justice? Which Rationality?* (Notre Dame: University of Notre Dame Press, 1988), p. 391.

2. MacIntyre, *Whose Justice? Which Rationality?* p. 394.

nowhere because those who speak such a language presume such speech can be understood by anyone.

MacIntyre understands that for people who are formed by such cosmopolitan habits, nothing less than a conversion would be required if they were to acknowledge that they represent a particular tradition. Being the good Aristotelian he is, MacIntyre argues such a conversion would require these people, as people of practical reason, to recognize that they will be able to think for themselves only by thinking with others. Yet that Aristotelian point, MacIntyre argues, must be disciplined by the Augustinian insight that people of practical reason must also be ready to acknowledge that they have ignored standards internal to their mind that make possible their ability to know their deficiencies.[3]

Below I will try to show how MacIntyre's remark, "it will depend on who you are and how you understand yourself," is crucial for how I understand the work of theology as an exercise in practical reason. Theology so understood has no beginning and no end. The theologian always begins in the middle and the theologian's work is never finished. The discipline of theology so understood can be and often is quite frustrating because you often have no idea what you are doing or should be doing. But if theology is an exercise in practical reason there is no alternative. However, before I try to show what it means for theology, or at least the way I have tried to do theology, to be "practical," I need to say more about what I take to be the basic characteristics of practical reason.

## The Character of Practical Reason

In *Self, World, and Time,* the first volume of his *Ethics as Theology,* Oliver O'Donovan observes that "practical thought is the most commonplace of human rational exercises, for action is the first and elementary horizon of human existence."[4] O'Donovan argues, therefore, that morality is not about what we do but about what we think about what we are to do. He suggests, however, that we must be awakened to our agency by acquiring the concepts and descriptions that shape our understanding of the way

3. MacIntyre, *Whose Justice? Which Rationality?* p. 396.
4. Oliver O'Donovan, *Self, World, and Time,* vol. 1 of *Ethics as Theology* (Grand Rapids: Eerdmans, 2013), p. 3. O'Donovan has enriched his account of practical reason with the publication of *Finding and Seeking,* the second volume of *Ethics as Theology* (Grand Rapids: Eerdmans, 2014).

things are.[5] To be so awakened is to discover we are creatures of time, which means practical reason is an ongoing exercise in a narrative that implicates the interrelation of our agency and the world.[6]

I call attention to O'Donovan's account of practical reason not only because I think his account of practical reason is insightful, but also because I think his account helps us better understand MacIntyre's suggestion that it makes all the difference who people are, as well as how they understand themselves, for how arguments are to be developed about what is the good and true. That O'Donovan and MacIntyre both argue that it makes all the difference who we are for the exercise of practical reason is, in an interesting way, echoed by Charles Taylor's defense of practical reason as an exercise in *ad hominem* argument. Taylor's defense of *ad hominem* arguments is not meant to unleash criticisms of a person that are irrelevant to the matter at hand. Rather, by directing attention to the importance of *ad hominem* arguments Taylor is reminding us that we inhabit narratives that often are ignored but in fact make all the difference for the position a person holds.

By directing attention to *ad hominem* arguments, Taylor argues that the rise of modern skepticism is the result of despair in practical reason, fueled by naturalistic presumptions that mistakenly assume that if practical reason is to avoid arbitrary judgments it must have a ground that is unassailable. By contrast to this view, Taylor argues that an *ad hominem* understanding of practical reason is linked to our ability to affect purposes that make possible the acquisition of "potential recipes for more effective practice."[7]

Taylor acknowledges that the differences between some cultures may be too great to make *ad hominem* argument possible, but there is no reason that attempts should not be made to develop arguments in which disagreements can be located. Making *ad hominem* arguments work requires the attempt to articulate the implicit presumptions that shape the character of those making the arguments.[8] These presumptions will often take the form

---

5. O'Donovan, *Self, World, and Time,* p. 11.

6. O'Donovan argues, however, that as welcome as it is that narrative has been one of the ways a substantial place for agency has been reclaimed in ethics, this development has not sufficiently been on guard to avoid self-justifying bad faith. What is needed, according to O'Donovan, is not the narrative self as object, but the "responsible self-as-agent, emerging out of history precisely for the task that lies before it." *Self, World, and Time,* p. 37.

7. Charles Taylor, "Explanation and Practical Reason," in *The Quality of Life,* ed. Martha Nussbaum and Amartya Sen (Oxford: Oxford University Press, 1993), p. 220.

8. Jeffrey Stout's understanding of practical reason rightly emphasizes the importance of commitments that make it possible to keep "track of oneself and one's fellow partici-

of a narrative whose complexity defies easy summary. Accordingly, Taylor argues, to discover where disagreements lie will be hard and slow work.

Taylor's (and MacIntyre's) understanding of the character of practical reason owes much to Aristotle. In the *Nicomachean Ethics* Aristotle distinguishes between scientific knowledge and practical wisdom. The former deals with matters of necessity whereas practical reason is about human concerns that are open to deliberation. Accordingly practical wisdom not only entails universals, but it is also about particulars "since it is concerned with action and action is about particulars. That is why in other areas also some people who lack knowledge but have experience are better in action than others who have knowledge."[9]

Aristotle thinks it very unlikely that practical wisdom will be found in the young because they have not developed the capacity to perceive or deliberate about particulars. People of practical wisdom must have the understanding that gives them the capacity to judge last things, and judgments about ends are judgments about particulars. Such judgments Aristotle identifies as judgments of understanding, because even though they are about matters that can be otherwise they make possible the identification of universals through particulars.[10]

Therefore, the person of practical reason must have a capacity for perception of particulars that comes from being well trained. Though Aristotle sometimes sounds as if the end is a given, leaving only the question of the appropriate means to achieve the end, it is rather the case that the means are constitutive of the end. Training is required because the end and means are constitutive of one another, because for an action to be the kind of action that makes us virtuous we must not separate the end from

---

pants in terms of these normative statuses." *Democracy and Tradition* (Princeton: Princeton University Press, 2004), p. 210. Stout's account of democracy as the institutionalization of practical reason is very persuasive. If, moreover, his account of practical reason is as good as I think it is, to say his account is persuasive is a high compliment.

9. Aristotle, *Nicomachean Ethics,* trans. Terrance Irwin (Indianapolis: Hackett, 1999), 1141b15-19. O'Donovan has an interesting discussion of how Aristotle's distinction between theoretical and practical reason became assimilated to the division between the cognitive and affective powers of the soul. See his *Self, World, and Time,* pp. 22-23.

10. In his very important article, "First Principles, Final Ends, Contemporary Issues," MacIntyre argues that first principles expressed as judgments are analytic but that does not mean they are known a priori. Rather their analyticity, that is, that their predicates are essential properties of the subject, is discovered usually as the outcome of a prolonged process of empirical inquiry. This article can be found in MacIntyre's *The Tasks of Philosophy: Selected Essays* (Cambridge: Cambridge University Press, 2006), pp. 143-79.

the means. To be an agent of practical reason requires that we must be a person of virtue.[11]

Joseph Dunne, who provides one of the most careful and complete accounts we have of Aristotle's understanding of practical wisdom, suggests that for Aristotle there is an essential connection between character and practical wisdom (*phronesis*). According to Dunne, practical wisdom is a perfected form of experience because it is the virtue that makes the experience of some people not simply an accumulation of actions from the past but "a dynamic orientation to bring this systematization into play and allow it to be tested by present circumstances, to draw from it what is relevant and to see where it does not fit."[12] Practical wisdom, therefore, is a habit of attentiveness that makes past experiences a resource that allows the present, in Dunne's words, "to unconceal" its peculiar significance.

Aristotle gave an account of the work of practical reason by drawing attention to the practical syllogism, but by its very nature the conclusion of the practical syllogism does not follow strict logic. MacIntyre suggests as much by arguing that every practical syllogism is a performance by a particular person on a particular occasion. The soundness of the practical syllogism will, therefore, depend on who utters it and on what occasion. This does not mean that people must be able to formulate a practical syllogism before they act, but it does mean that they should act as someone who would have so deliberated. They must do so because they must be ready to answer the question: Why did you so act? Indeed one suspects that most moral judgments about what we do and do not do are retrospective.

Such retrospective judgments are not only possible but necessary, because even though the kind of practical rationality Aristotle describes is at odds with the modern tendency to separate the end from the means and reason from character, there are still contexts in which practical reason flourishes. We should not be surprised that there remain contexts that exemplify the work of practical reason, because such reasoning is not some esoteric achievement, but, as suggested above by O'Donovan, just to the extent we are purposive creatures we are engaged in the work of practical reason. In fact our lives are constituted by activities shaped by practices

11. Aristotle, *Nichomachean Ethics*, 1143a20-1143b5.
12. Joseph Dunne, *Back to the Rough Ground: "Phronesis" and "Techne" in Modern Philosophy and in Aristotle* (Notre Dame: University of Notre Dame Press, 1993), p. 305.

recognizable as instances of the kind of wisdom MacIntyre thinks Aristotle so acutely describes. In the words of John Henry Newman, practical reasoning is "the exercise of a living faculty in the individual intellect."[13]

For example, MacIntyre calls attention to the hockey player who in the closing seconds of a crucial game has the opportunity to pass to another player on the team who is better positioned to score the decisive goal. We think if the player has rightly perceived the situation he or she must make the needed pass. MacIntyre observes that our use of *must* to describe what the hockey player does or should do "exhibits the good of the person *qua* hockey player and member of that particular team and the action of passing, a connection such that were such a player not to pass, he or she must *either* have falsely denied that passing was for their good *qua* hockey player or would have been guilty of inconsistency or have acted as one not caring for his or her good *qua* hockey player and member of that particular team."[14]

MacIntyre comments on this example by observing that we recognize the necessity of rational action as integral to our social and political life just to the extent those aspects of our life provide the structured roles necessary for the discovery of the goods needed to make our actions intelligible. Any account of practical reason that is faithful to Aristotle, therefore, entails a politics. For it was the *polis* that provided the systematic activities of human beings "into an overall form of activity in which the achievement of each kind of good was given its due. . . . No practical rationality outside the *polis* is the Aristotelian counterpart to *extra ecclesiam nulla salus*."[15]

That practical reason entails a politics is central to Eugene Garver's important book on practical reason, *For the Sake of Argument: Practical Reasoning, Character, and the Ethics of Belief.* Garver observes that the philosophical presumptions of liberal political arrangements has resulted in severing the connection between character and reason, with the result that the definitive resolutions of mathematicians and the battle of interest and power are the only alternatives. In particular Garver calls attention to the use of "rational choice" theories of decision to legitimate and explain the behavior of modern states. Reason so understood seems suited to liberal democracies because reason so construed is formal rather than

13. John Henry Newman, *An Essay in Aid of a Grammar of Assent* (Notre Dame: University of Notre Dame Press, 1979), p. 240.

14. MacIntyre, *Whose Justice? Which Rationality?* pp. 140-41.

15. MacIntyre, *Whose Justice? Which Rationality?* p. 141.

substantive, distinguished only, as MacIntyre has suggested, by the marks of publicity, neutrality, impersonality, and universality.[16]

By contrast Garver draws on Aristotle's *Rhetoric* to argue for the essential connection between thought and character. By calling attention to rhetoric Garver develops the political presumptions of practical reason by emphasizing how language makes possible a common life. The good person must be a person of deliberation and persuasion able to avoid the temptation to engage in manipulative strategies. Rhetoric as a form of practical reason is constituted by contingency, emotion, and passionate interests but is no less rational for being such.[17]

According to Garver, friendship is crucial for the flourishing of practical wisdom. Yet it is friendship, Garver argues, that the modern state has abandoned in its quest to secure order and stability. Friendship has been abandoned in favor of trying to make justice the primary political virtue. Yet it is only through political friendship that "practical reason can aim at truth while staying committed to public argument because ethical arguments can be more powerful and more rational than arguments from reason alone."[18]

To be sure, practical reason in the concrete — and there is no other form than in the concrete — requires the acknowledgment of authority, but authority depends on the existence of an ethos that makes argument possible.[19] Such an ethos consists in narratives that constitute the memory of a community and help to establish its future. We become ethical agents through membership in such communities by being schooled in the texts and exemplars that determine the character of our lives. Narratives are, therefore, invitations for inclusion into a community. Lives embedded in such narratives make possible the ongoing testing and revision of the narratives.[20]

Garver's emphasis on the rhetorical character of practical reason sug-

---

16. Eugene Garver, *For the Sake of Argument: Practical Reasoning, Character, and the Ethics of Belief* (Chicago: University of Chicago Press, 2004), p. 13.

17. Garver, *For the Sake of Argument*, pp. 2-3.

18. Garver, *For the Sake of Argument*, p. 27.

19. O'Donovan provides an illuminating account of the communicative character of action by reminding us of the role of advice for practical reason. Accordingly the exercise of freedom depends on advice based in moral teaching that has the authority to give advice. Crucial for the exercise of authority is the resource of language for the framing of "nuanced discernment of reality." *Self, World, and Time*, p. 56.

20. Garver, *For the Sake of Argument*, pp. 78-79.

gests that reason so understood can produce an "ethical surplus" that creates alternatives that would be missed by reason alone. Garver, for example, provides a close analysis of *Brown v. Board of Education,* the Supreme Court decision that ended the segregation of schools, to illustrate how practical reason can generate more powerful conclusions than the initial premises might seem to allow.[21] Given Garver's emphasis on the internal relation between character and practical reason, I assume he might also think that the source of "ethical surplus" is to be found in the lives of those who extend the narratives that constitute a community of discourse.

In summary, practical reason deals with matters that can be other, that is, with the contingent. To reason well about matters that can be other means that how one reasons cannot be abstracted from who is doing the reasoning. So understood, there can be no strong distinction between moral and nonmoral reasoning because the descriptions that form our worlds are various and interrelated. To act rationally and well is finally tested by our ability to provide a narrative that makes sense of who we are. We often get our stories wrong, but the good news, at least the good news of the story identified as Christian, is that we are not fated by our mistakes. Not to be so fated is the result of our belief that we are creatures destined to be friends with one another and with God.

## How I Think I Think Theologically

By providing an account of practical reason I hope I have prepared the ground to explore how I think I learned to think theologically. To engage in such a project seems odd. Surely I must know how I learned to think theologically, but I am not at all sure that is the case. Therefore the first "I think" in the title of this essay is not an empty gesture, but rather indicates that I do not know without thinking how I think theologically. I think I am being honest when I confess I am not at all sure I have known how to say to myself or others what and how I have understood the work I have done as a theologian. Of course, I have some ideas about how I have understood the task of theology, but I hope there is more in what I have done theologically than is in my understanding. This last remark I hope to make intelligible by calling attention to how what I have done is best understood as an exercise in practical reason.

21. Garver, *For the Sake of Argument,* pp. 9-11, 73-75.

Some may well think that I have already said how I learned to think theologically in *Hannah's Child: A Theologian's Memoir.*[22] I should like to think that is the case. In particular I should like to think *Hannah's Child* suggests how I learned to think by being taught to read by great teachers. I think, moreover, reading is an essential exercise in practical reasoning; but that is a subject for another time. What I hope to do in this essay, however, is to complement what I did in *Hannah's Child* by making articulate what could only be suggested in the memoir.

I confess I would feel much more comfortable to have avoided the first person singular.[23] I would prefer to have tried to characterize in general how to think theologically, but to do so would avoid MacIntyre's remark about who a person is and how that person understands himself or herself if we are to address questions of the good and the true. Certainly the "I" that is the subject of *Hannah's Child* in many ways exhibits the characteristics of MacIntyre's characterization of someone who knows not where they are. Thus my oft-repeated confession in *Hannah's Child* that I did not understand what I was doing in this or that circumstance until much later. The "I" of *Hannah's Child,* I hope, is the same "I" that seeks to understand how I learned to think theologically.

But the "I" of *Hannah's Child* or the "I" of this exercise is not unique to me. Hopefully the "I" that is trying to tell the story of how I learned to think theologically will be recognized by others as not unrelated to how they too have come to think theologically. If that is the case then the story I have to tell is not just my story but a story that helps us locate where we have been, as well as what our future may be. By trying to characterize my "I," however, I hope to make concrete how I learned to think theologically in a manner that defies a theology that seems to be but one more theoretical possibility.

There is certainly a place for attempts to say in general what theology

22. Stanley Hauerwas, *Hannah's Child: A Theological Memoir* (Grand Rapids: Eerdmans, 2012). This is the paperback edition of the book with a new "Afterword" that I think will be of interest for those who are interested in practical reason.

23. Yet if William H. Poteat is right, and I think he is, the attempt to avoid the first person is an ontological mistake because what we mean by "the world" is appropriately understood only if the first-person pronoun is seen as constitutive of what we should mean by "the world." Poteat's account of the significance of the first person is complex and subtle, deserving more than this footnote. See his collected essays, *The Primacy of Persons and the Language of Culture,* ed. James Nickell and James Stines (Columbia: University of Missouri Press, 1993).

is about, but I worry that too often such characterizations of theology fail to do justice to the politics that determine the shape of theology. I certainly think that there are crucial habits associated with how Christian convictions are to be understood in relation to one another — how Christological and Trinitarian commitments are interrelated — but I think it still to be the case that the Trinitarian and Christological doctrines are not done in the abstract but are part and parcel of the attempt by Christians to think through how they should live in the world in which they find themselves.

Another way to avoid the "I" is to report on how other theologians think. Much can be learned from such an exercise, but to attend to the work of particular theologians can give the impression that theology is the speculative work of an individual rather than an office of a community. The attempt to say what theology is in and of itself, as well as what particular theologians do, can and has produced quite useful accounts of the work of theology. But those accounts cannot help but reflect the particular theological perspective of the theologian who has provided those accounts. I am sure that by trying to provide an account of how I think, I will make use of both these approaches for characterizing my work as a theologian.

It would be an act of hubris for me to claim that the way I have worked is the future of theology, but it would be an exercise in false humility to pretend I do not care that how I have tried to do theology may have implications for how theological work is done in the future. In particular I have tried to think through how theology must be done such that it presumes the end of Christendom. Many have found the results of that effort quite odd if not wrong, but I hope to suggest in this essay that there is a rationale for how I think that may be of use to others.

Taylor's defense of *ad hominem* illumines what I am trying to do by directing attention to the way I have tried to think theologically. The *ad hominem* character of argument includes all who are participants in the exchange. Too often, I fear, we assume that Taylor's point applies only to those whose minds we are trying to change. But Taylor's argument about arguments means that all sides must try to identify the narratives that have shaped how and why they assume the stance they think is so important.

That said, it is still the case that I am hesitant to direct attention to how I have tried to do theology because I so dislike the narcissistic fascination with the self that is characteristic of so many intellectuals in the modern university. Our fascination with our work no doubt has everything to do with the fact that if we did not take our work seriously then no one would take our work seriously. Theologians at least have the advantage that, though we often end up writing for other academic theologians, we are at least committed to write for people who identify themselves as Christians. This means, however, that theology as an office of the church means theologians do not get to determine what and how they think without reference to what and how theology has been done in the past. As I indicated above, when appropriately done the work of theology should reflect what has been done by other theologians.

Yet I do worry that by trying to understand how I have done theology I risk being self-absorbed in a manner that distorts the theological task. It is surely the case that the character of theology should demand that those engaged in the work of theology not take themselves overly serious. Accordingly no one should undertake the work of theology if one is devoid of a sense of humor and/or irony. Of course one of the problems with that recommendation is, ironically, that those who have no sense of humor or irony often do not know they have no sense of humor or irony. This is not an insignificant challenge if the character of theology and the theologian are inseparable.

Thus trying to think through, or at least make articulate, the way I have learned to do theology might, I hope, be useful to others. I am aware that the way I have worked is hard to imitate. In fact, to try to imitate "my style" would mean that you have not learned the lessons I hope my way of doing theology entails. Thus my infamous claim that I do not want students to think for themselves, but I want them to think like me. I do want them to think like me — only differently.

By trying to say how I think I think theologically I need to make clear that I am not trying to finally "pull it all together." I am old, but I am not about to write a "retraction" or respond to critics by "setting the record straight." Rather I want to try to show that there has been some method to the madness of my work by directing attention to how what I have done has been an exercise in practical reasoning. I am aware that the way I have learned to think theologically cannot help but frustrate many readers. There is just so much of it and there is no one essay or book to be read in order to "get it."

Moreover, since my work has been in response to assignments, the diversity of topics I have addressed is likely to make those who specialize in one or another aspect of theology weary. I am an amateur in almost every subject I address, but I am not going to apologize for attempting to respond as constructively as I am able to requests that I think about subjects that may not seem to fall under the subject matter of theology or ethics.

Seeing the connections makes all the difference, and practical reason is all about seeing the connections. That I have written much and have written broadly I should like to think reflects my conviction that theology must be the ongoing effort to construe the world as God's good work.

That I understand the work of theology in this way is one of the reasons I have grudgingly been willing to be identified as an "ethicist." Ethics at least suggests that theology is a practical science, but the very distinction between theology and ethics can reproduce the deleterious distinction between theory and practice. I certainly do not deny that theology properly understood has speculative, or I would prefer contemplative, moments, but I have tried to show that fundamental theological convictions about the Father, the Son, and the Holy Spirit are inseparable from the work they do for the formation of a people set loose in and for the world. Accordingly, if you think Christians have "beliefs" that need to be applied, I assume that something has gone wrong in your understanding of the grammar of theology.

David Starling, in a very interesting paper titled "Theology and the Future of the Church," has called attention to my injudicious claim in *After Christendom* that "the very idea of systematic theology was a result of a church with hegemonic power that belied the very substance that made it the church to begin with."[24] Starling charitably observes that I am not dismissing theology *per se,* but rather the judgment I make about systematic theology reflects my general concern that Christian theology not be treated as a timeless system of belief. Theology so understood too often elides the politics that is the condition of the possibility for thinking theologically.[25] My worry about systematic theology, therefore, reflects my judgment that Christians must learn to live in a post-Christian world.[26]

24. The quote Starling highlights is in *After Christendom* (Nashville: Abingdon, 1999), p. 19. *After Christendom* was originally published in 1991. The 1999 edition has a new "Preface." For a more extended reflection on the character of systematic theology see my "Introduction" to *Sanctify Them in the Truth: Holiness Exemplified* (Nashville: Abingdon, 1998). The first chapter of that book is also relevant, dealing as it does with questions of the relation of doctrine and ethics.

25. Starling's essay was a lecture originally given in the New College Lectures at the University of New South Wales in 2010. The lecture is titled "Not a Wisdom of This Age: Theology and the Future of the Post-Christendom Church." It has now been published in *Theology and the Future: Evangelical Assertions and Explorations,* ed. Trevor Cairney and David Starling (London: Bloomsbury, 2014), pp. 81-98.

26. O'Donovan suggests that dogmatic theology stresses the impossible universality of sin, that is, sin's significance as the defining qualification of the mis-relation between

Drawing on Paul's first letter to the Corinthians, Starling provides an account of the ecclesial presuppositions and corresponding narratives that shaped Paul's letter in a manner that can help us discern how we must learn to live and do theology in a post-Christian context. Starling, however, argues that Paul's theological commitments provided the material for the development of a kind of theological systematization that emerged in the centuries that followed Paul's missionary work. I could not agree more, but I do not think the development of theology in the early centuries of the church to be "systematic" theology. Rather I associate systematic theology with developments after the Reformation in which "doctrine" became an end in itself.[27]

That Starling draws attention to Paul's letter to the Corinthians as a source for reflecting theologically on the work of theology is very insightful. Paul's letters are occasional, but their ad hoc character is held together, as Starling notes, by Paul's understanding of what makes the church the church. Theology done as letters, or at least as reflection on letters such as the letters of Paul, has a concreteness that resists false, universalizing tendencies. I should like to think, at least in terms of form, that the way I have done theology is not unlike letters to the church.

If theology is understood as something like the writing of letters, then it should be clear that there is no place to begin or end the work of theology. Rather you always begin in the middle. The demand for "method" is often an attempt to avoid this conclusion, but there is no method that can free theology of the necessity to respond to the challenges of trying to discern what being a Christian entails in this place and at this time. There is no prolegomena for all future theology. Indeed there is no prolegomena period. It is performance all the way down. Thus my presumption that letters, sermons, and essays may well be the central genres for theological reflection.

---

humankind and God. Moral theology concentrates on the possible contingency of sin to identify the horizon to be recognized and refused in each action we undertake. *Self, World, and Time*, p. 83.

27. See, for example, Brad Gregory, *The Unintended Reformation: How a Religious Revolution Secularized Society* (Cambridge, MA: Harvard University Press, 2012), pp. 75-128. Gregory observes that doctrine prior to the Reformation was a Christian response to "life questions" such as "What should I live for and why?" or "What is meaningful in life?" After the Reformation, doctrine became a marker for authority, but since there was no consensus on which doctrines were to be considered authoritative the way was prepared for the Enlightenment attempt to make "reason alone" the standard.

I need to make clear at this point that even though I am trying in this essay to understand how I have worked theologically, I do not think the way I have done theology is the only way it can or should be done. I am sure, for example, I could not have worked the way I have worked if I had not known that Karl Barth's *Dogmatics,* James Williams McClendon's *Systematic Theology,* and Robert Jenson's *Systematic Theology* were available. A book that treats a specific topic, a book like Katherine Tanner's *Christ the Key,* is invaluable. Theology comes in many shapes and sizes, and we need most of those shapes and sizes.

In contrast to the way Barth, McClendon, Jenson, and Tanner have done theology, my work has been much more occasional. It is not by accident that most of my books are collections of essays. That character of my work I suspect drives some of my readers to distraction. Supporters and critics are often desperate to find a center that will make clear amid the chaos what I am really all "about." For example, I am often both praised and criticized for emphasizing the significance of the church as crucial for the work of theology, but I do not think that emphasis is a useful indicator of what I have been about. Some seem to think the animating center of my work revolves around the critique of liberalism, which from my perspective is clearly a side issue. Those with more friendly interpretations compliment me for reintroducing the importance of the virtues for understanding the moral life. The list could go on, but the truth is that there is no center to my work unless you count work itself the center.

Those in the field of ethics I suspect are particularly frustrated that there is no easy way to sum up what I have been about. I refuse to focus on one characteristic to determine the content of Christian ethics. For example, love is often identified as the defining concept that makes an ethic Christian. From my perspective, the attempt to put all the theological eggs in that basket usually makes fundamental theological concepts secondary. That is why I have always thought it a mistake to make love or justice the defining character of what it means to be a Christian. When love or justice is assumed to be what Christian ethics is about, Jesus often fades into the twilight.

My way of working, moreover, has got to be frustrating for those who associate theology and ethics with "having a position." I have worked very hard to avoid having a position. Of course I have positions about a host of matters. I believe that suicide is rightly understood negatively and that baseball should not be played in Florida in the summer. (Florida is for spring training.) But that is not what I mean by a "position." "Position" names the attempt by a theologian to develop a theological system that can bear his or her name. Accordingly the "position" becomes more important than what the position is allegedly about, that is, God. Theology done with the ambition to produce a position appears more like modern philosophy.

Theologians do not need to have a position because we serve a confessional community that makes our reflections on church practice possible. That means theologians may and should take a critical attitude toward the church, but to do so means they must draw on resources that the church has made available. That every Sunday the church is charged to attend to scripture means that the church cannot escape the judgment of the Holy Spirit. That is why, as I suggested above, one of the most fruitful genres for theology remains the sermon. Sermons that are faithful to scripture will defy any "position."

I have been very fortunate to have had a long life and to have had responsibilities that have given me time to think and write about what I care about. I am sure, moreover, that there have been developments in my work that at the very least suggest different emphases. The stages Sam Wells identifies in his *Transforming Fate into Destiny: The Theological Ethics of Stanley Hauerwas* I have always thought to be quite illuminating.[28] Yet I also think that the stages Wells identifies — that is, from quandary to character, from character to story, from story to community, from community to church — are exactly that, namely, "stages"; which means the latter stages only make sense in the light of the beginnings.

This means, however, that the way I work continues to presuppose that the work I did very early is crucial for understanding why I am saying what I am now saying. Yet often those who have read what I am now saying have not, for quite understandable reasons, read what I wrote at the beginning of my work. For example, the claim that "you can only act in the world you can see and you can only see what you have learned to say" is only intelligible against the background of the work I did in *Vision and Virtue,* a book that was first published in 1974. That claim, a claim that itself begs for further elaboration, is crucial if you are to understand my later declaration that "the first task of the church is not to make the world more just but to make the world the world."

I must ask the reader's patience for what can only seem a far-too-long exercise in throat-clearing. But I felt I had to clear the swamp if I was to

---

28. Samuel Wells, *Transforming Fate into Destiny: The Theological Ethics of Stanley Hauerwas* (Carlisle, UK: Paternoster, 1998).

make explicit how I have learned to do theology as a form of practical reasoning. Now I must try to say how what I have said is best understood as an exercise in practical reason.

## Back to the Beginning

When I began to write, and writing is in many ways more fundamental than thinking, I did not think what I was doing to be best understood as practical reasoning. In truth I did not think about what I was doing when I began to write — period. I do not mean I did not think I needed to have a "method" before I began. I was not that coherent. Rather I just began doing what I thought needed to be done. But given the account of practical reason I have just given, that is not a bad way to begin.

I did have something like a project. I was convinced that the current ways of thinking about ethics as a decision procedure failed to provide an appropriate account of the agent who was making the decision. Mark Ryan, in his extremely informative book *The Politics of Practical Reason: Why Theological Ethics Must Change Your Life,* suggests that early on I sensed that agency is embedded in the life of a particular community, which meant that practical inferences are licensed within communities of shared goods.[29] The strange mixture of topics in my first collection of essays, *Vision and Virtue,* a mixture that continued in subsequent books, was my way of trying to develop that understanding of agency.[30]

Ryan observes that, although my understanding of practical reason drew on Aristotle, I inflected Aristotle's account by stressing the importance of language. Thus my claim that "you can only act in the world you can see and you can only see what you have learned to say." I thought it at least a plausible suggestion that the church provides the habits of speech that

---

29. Mark Ryan, *The Politics of Practical Reason: Why Theological Ethics Must Change Your Life* (Eugene, OR: Cascade, 2011), p. 99.

30. Stanley Hauerwas, *Vision and Virtue: Essays in Christian Ethical Reflection* (Notre Dame: Fides Press, 1974). The topics addressed not only dealt with situation ethics, character, the narrative character of the self, abortion, death, and children with mental disabilities, but also had chapters on Yoder, democratic theory, and what I can only describe as an attempt at theological journalism dealing with the 1960s. *Truthfulness and Tragedy* (Notre Dame: University of Notre Dame Press, 1977) and *A Community of Character* (Notre Dame: University of Notre Dame Press, 1981) have different agendas, but I am clearly continuing to work on the same set of issues I began in *Vision and Virtue.*

shape how Christians see the world. Yet Ryan suggests that my emphasis on the church as the source of Christian language can miss what is crucial about the developing account of practical reason in my work. In contrast to the presumption that language is a tool used to achieve specific ends or is something we can change as the occasion arises, Ryan suggests I followed "Wittgenstein in believing what is needed is rigorous and disciplined attention to the constraints of grammar and its life-form-shaping rules."[31]

I call attention to Ryan's way of putting the matter because, as is so often the case, he has said what I think better than I have been able to say it. In particular he rightly says I learned from Wittgenstein that the relation of ethical deliberation to action is not external but internal, and from Aristotle I learned to name this internal relation "character."[32] Interestingly enough, this meant I was not tempted to follow Reinhold Niebuhr's assumption that you need to develop a general anthropology to get Christian ethics off the ground. As Ryan observes, to do so would betray "the connection of Christian agency with the character-shaping language that sustains it, as well as deceptively imply that we can do ethics without language."[33]

Ryan's characterization of the essential presumption about agency in my early work nicely suggests that though I was not explicitly trying to do theology as an exercise in practical reason, in fact that is what I was doing. Moreover, that was the essential move that made me a theologian. I might have preferred to stay identified as an ethicist, that is, as someone in the field of ethics who entered the field because they did not want to have to attend to fundamental theological claims about, for example, the Trinity. But given how I had learned to think that descriptions are everything, I could not avoid thinking theologically.[34] If, as I would come to say, theo-

31. Ryan, *The Politics of Practical Reason*, p. 101.
32. Ryan, *The Politics of Practical Reason*, p. 109.
33. Ryan, *The Politics of Practical Reason*, p. 101.
34. In a similar manner Oliver O'Donovan emphasizes the critical role of description for ethics. In particular he rightly objects to the characterization of practical reason as prescriptive rather than descriptive because moral reasoning, as he puts it, "has a vast stake in description. It describes particular things, describes their relations and purposes, and describes the way the world as a whole fits together. Without this descriptive exercise practical reason would not be reason at all." *Self, World, and Time*, p. 11. O'Donovan's account of time and narrative for constituting our "awakening" as agents I should like to think is commensurate with how I have tried to think about these matters. If there is any difference, a difference that I do not think amounts to a disagreement, between O'Donovan and me about these matters, I suspect it would have to do with my stress on the importance of language for how we learn to construe the world.

logical convictions are meant to construe the world, then it must surely be the case that how Christians intend the world is different from those who do not talk the way we talk. That does not mean Christians and non-Christians share nothing in common, but it does mean that what they may share in common must be discovered rather than assumed.

That theology became for me an exercise in practical reason meant the church became central for how the world was to be understood. If you can only act in the world you can say, then the "saying" has to come from a determinative community with the habits of speech necessary for the discernment of difference. Thus "the first task of the church is not to make the world more just but to make the world the world." Offensive as that claim may seem, it is but a way to make clear that the "world" cannot know it is the world unless an alternative linguistic community exists. The "world" so understood remains under God's providential care, but exactly what makes it the world is the inability to acknowledge and worship the source of all that is.

This fundamental eschatological understanding of existence entails — or better, demands — that the church make the world, which includes us, capable of being storied.[35] We are contingent creatures and we exist contingently. To say we are contingent beings is but a way to say we are creatures who did not have to exist but who do exist. The very description, "creature," is itself a story that provides a truthful account of our lives. One of the tasks of theology is to help us discern how our lives may be possessed by unacknowledged stories that make our ability to live in gratitude for the gift of our existence impossible. Worship is crucial for such discernment.

It was, of course, the work of Karl Barth and John Howard Yoder that gave me the resources necessary to emphasize the centrality of the church for discerning the challenges facing Christians in our day. The general stance of the liberal Protestant establishment, particularly in America, assumed that the church was an agent to make democracy work. In the name of being tolerant, such a view presumed that Christians must find a way to engage the ethical and political challenges using language that was not specifically Christian. From my perspective that was to give away the store.

My criticism of "liberalism" has not primarily been directed at "liberals" but rather at Christians who assume that our fundamental linguistic

---

35. For a fuller account of my understanding of the eschatological character of Christian theology and ethics, see my *Approaching the End: Eschatological Reflections on Church, Politics, and Life* (Grand Rapids: Eerdmans, 2013).

habits can be translated into the idiom of liberalism. My worry about that strategy is not only that in the process Christians lose the significance of the church as a political reality, but also that they lose the story that shapes how Christians intend the world. Thus my perhaps too-simplistic claim that liberalism names the project of modernity to create people who have no story except the story they chose when they had no story. That story reflects, as I suggested above, a view of rationality that cannot help but distort the situated character of practical reason.

I have tried to display how practical reason will by necessity reflect a determinative narrative by trying to show the connections between the gospel and everyday practices such as marriage, the birth and care of children, the commitment to the ill, being present to the dying, the demands of friendship, the disavowal of violence, the challenge of those physically and mentally disabled, the refusal to lie, and the refusal to abandon the poor. I have done so in the hope that the worship of God is seen as constitutive of a way of life that would otherwise be unintelligible if in fact the God we worship does not exist. Ryan characterizes this aspect of "my method" as the employment of narrative in a manner that bridges rather than divides our reflective lives and our practical lives by showing how practical reason is no less rational for being particular and embodied.[36]

In effect, "my method" is to show how theological language in good working order reframes what we take to be necessities by helping us see that who we are makes all the difference. For example, the justification of violence is often shaped by the assumption that in some situations there is no alternative to violence. That we must resort to violence can, therefore, be justified as a lesser of two evils. But the very existence of a people schooled by the gospel should make possible, even if it means they must suffer and die, the reality of an alternative to the assumed necessity of violence. The creation of such an alternative begins with a people who have learned to say "no." That "no" may well be the exemplification of Garver's understanding of what an ethical surplus looks like.

A theology so conceived may find that from time to time it is impossible to avoid polemics. If, as Taylor suggests, practical reason is an exercise in *ad hominem* argument, it is not surprising that the work of theology will involve polemics. The identification and location of enemies, which often entails our ability of self-recognition, is an ongoing task. The world does not want the presumption that it is intelligible without God challenged.

36. Ryan, *The Politics of Practical Reason*, p. 125.

So the Christian theologian cannot help but come into conflict with established conventions because the fundamental presuppositions that sustain the everyday are often at odds with the narrative Christians believe is true — that is, God was in Christ so that the world might be saved.

Finally, I discovered that the work of theology could not be separated from the friendships constitutive of the task itself. In particular, friendship with graduate students has been crucial for the way I have done theology. Graduate students are not only smarter than I am, but, more importantly, graduate students bring with them reading habits that constantly force me to "catch up." By being forced to catch up I've learned better how to think once Foucault, for example, has been read, a reminder that reading, as I suggested above, is a form of practical reason just to the extent the reader is able to recognize an argument or a remark that is significant because of what a friend, which may be a book, has taught them.

If I were to give any final comment on how I think I learned to think theologically, it would be that through the work of theology I have discovered friends I did not know I had. For what more could anyone ask?

# CHAPTER 2

# How the Holy Spirit Works

## Why I Allegedly Have No Account of the Holy Spirit

I am often criticized, or at least questions are raised, about what appears to be the absence of the Holy Spirit in my work. Even Sam Wells, a more sympathetic interpreter of my work than I deserve, suggests that I need to clarify some of the more doctrinal features of my position by developing an account of the role of the Holy Spirit. Wells explains that one needs "the Holy Spirit if one is to hold together the twin notions that on the one hand redemption has been achieved, while on the other hand the Church imitates and continues the work of Christ, hoping thereby to be transformed into his likeness."[1] Wells suggests that to focus on the Holy Spirit would not only help me clarify how the Holy Spirit makes Christ present in the church, but would also help me better understand how God works outside the church.

I am quite sympathetic with Wells's suggestion that I need to clarify the more doctrinal features of my work and, in particular, the doctrine of the Holy Spirit. Yet it has been one of my long-held convictions that it is unwise to isolate doctrines from the narratives that make doctrines make sense in the first place. Put differently, I think it is very important to show the work that doctrines are designed to do, that is, to be guides for telling the story that is Christianity.[2] I certainly do not mean for this

---

1. Samuel Wells, *Transforming Fate into Destiny: The Theological Ethics of Stanley Hauerwas* (Carlisle, UK: Paternoster, 1998), p. 98.

2. For an account of doctrine that I think says how I think about the role that doctrine should play in the life of the church see Gerard Loughlin, "The Basis and Authority of Scrip-

way of understanding the role of doctrine to excuse what some may think amounts to my avoidance of a proper role of doctrine in my work. In fact I think doctrines are extremely important. The very fact that doctrines are hewn from bitter controversy and tested through time is sufficient reason to make them a focus of theology.

I should like to think I am in good company with this way of understanding the role of doctrine. John Webster, for example, argues that dogmatics is a complementary but subordinate task to exegesis. According to Webster, "dogmatics seeks simply to produce a set of flexible accounts of the essential content of the gospel as it is found in Holy Scripture, with the aim of informing, guiding and correcting the Church's reading."[3] I think it is not accidental that Webster's clear statement of the task of doctrine is but one aspect of his account of holiness and, in particular, the holiness of theology. Though it may seem odd to suggest that theology, given its current character, participates in God's holiness, I think Webster is right to suggest that the work of the Holy Spirit to create a holy fellowship must include the work of theology itself.[4]

This way of understanding the role of doctrine, however, has made me a bit defensive about my alleged failure to account for the work of the Holy Spirit. I have assumed my clear commitment to a Trinitarian orthodoxy was sufficient evidence that I have not intentionally ignored the role of the Holy Spirit. It may be true, however, that my work has been so Christ-centered I may have given the impression that the Holy Spirit is an afterthought. I confess that until I read Gene Rogers's book on the Holy Spirit I was unsure how best to say what the Spirit does.

I think Rogers's work is important because he provides such an instructive response to Robert Jenson's question concerning the role of the Spirit in modern theology, that is, that you cannot help but "wonder where

---

ture," in *The Cambridge Companion to Christian Doctrine,* ed. Colin Gunton (Cambridge: Cambridge University Press, 1997), pp. 41-64. Loughlin rightly argues that all Christian doctrines "hang together" because all doctrines are about one thing — the charity of the triune God. Accordingly he argues that doctrine is best "construed as ecclesial grammar" that is dependent on that which it rules, that is, the telling of the story that is the gospel. Therefore doctrine is always secondary to the performance of the gospel. He argues that "doctrine rests upon nothing other than the church's telling of Christ's story, upon the enacted reading, the non-identical repetition, of Christ's charitable practices, heeding the command to 'follow,' to do as he does, in short, upon the ecclesial tradition of discipleship" (p. 55).

3. John Webster, *Holiness* (Grand Rapids: Eerdmans, 2003), pp. 3-4.

4. Webster, *Holiness,* pp. 25-27.

the Spirit went."[5] There are, no doubt, many reasons for the absence of appeals to the Holy Spirit in modern theology, but I suspect one of the reasons may be that any account of the work of the Spirit entails a doctrinal reading of scripture that most theologians, and I include myself in that group, are not sure how to pull off.[6] By drawing on what Rogers has done in his book *After the Spirit: A Constructive Pneumatology from Resources Outside the Modern West,* I hope to show that Rogers has provided us with a constructive and illuminating doctrinal reading of the work of the Holy Spirit in scripture.[7]

Before turning to Rogers, however, I need to clarify why I may have been hesitant to make direct appeals to the Holy Spirit in my work. I suspect there are biographical reasons for my reluctance to claim the Holy Spirit as a warrant for particular theological positions I have taken. I was once asked by a colleague from the faculty of theology at the University of Notre Dame whether I had experienced the new birth that only comes from the Holy Spirit. My colleague was a member of the Catholic charismatic movement that had begun in the 1960s at Notre Dame. My colleague, a very conservative Catholic, wanted to tell me what the Holy Spirit had recently done in her life. With the best intentions she wanted others and, at the time, me, to experience the Spirit that had become so important in her own life.

I responded, a response that was no doubt insensitive, that she had to understand that I was raised an evangelical Methodist, which meant by the time I was twelve I had enough "experience" to last me a lifetime.[8] I

---

5. Robert Jenson, "You Wonder Where the Spirit Went," *Pro Ecclesia* 2 (1993): 296-304.

6. Geoffrey Wainwright has an exemplary account of why scripture and doctrine cannot be separated for any adequate account of the Holy Spirit in his "The Holy Spirit," in Gunton, ed., *The Cambridge Companion to Christian Doctrine,* pp. 273-96. Wainwright observes that pneumatology has been a neglected doctrine in Western Christianity not only in the present but also in the Middle Ages and the Reformation. He suggests that reflection on the Holy Spirit in the Middle Ages and the Reformation was absorbed under the heading of "grace," only later to be lost entirely given Socinian and deistic accounts of the Godhead. He observes that the loss of the Spirit in Western theology, as least from an Eastern Christian point of view, may be due to the *filioque* clause in the Creed, which seems to suggest that the Spirit proceeds from the Father and the Son and not from the Father alone (p. 289).

7. Eugene Rogers, *After the Spirit: A Constructive Pneumatology from Resources outside the Modern West* (Grand Rapids: Eerdmans, 2005).

8. I would love to know how the Methodist emphasis on holiness was transmuted into the need to have an experience of the Holy Spirit. "To have an experience of the Holy Spirit" is not incompatible with an account of holiness, but neither is it an equivalent, particularly

assured her that I did not want to have an experience of salvation — even one that allegedly was the work of the Spirit. I explained that I had not only learned to distrust the staying power of such experiences, but I also thought the need "to be born again" undercut the significance of baptism. Generalized appeals to the Holy Spirit, I observed, could result in an attenuated understanding of the relation of the Holy Spirit and the church. It was a point I assumed would not be lost on a Roman Catholic.

I am aware that my worries about appeals to the Holy Spirit may seem odd given the Pentecostal revivals that have swept across the world over the last century. I have no doubt that in 1906 something quite remarkable began in a modest building on Azusa Street in Los Angeles.[9] I consider it significant that the Holy Spirit seems to have a particular relation to people who possess little. I have no reason to question the validity of the development associated with the growth of Pentecostalism. I do worry about the tendency of some to associate the gift of the Spirit with particular behaviors such as speaking in tongues, but in general I see no reason not to be grateful for this work of the Spirit.

I am not, however, a "charismatic." I have no doubt that for some, to become a Christian may involve an experience of ecstasy. Yet I do not think such an experience is necessary for someone to be a Christian. An emphasis on such experience I fear can be a way to try to catch rather than be caught by the Holy Spirit. I use the language of being "caught" by the Holy Spirit to suggest — a suggestion I think justified by the role the Spirit plays particularly in the Book of Acts — that we usually know, a knowing that normally comes retrospectively, we are being guided by the Spirit when the plans for our lives have been revealed to be little more than the outworking of our pretentious presumption that it is finally "up to us." In Acts, under the guidance of the Spirit, Paul usually has to do what he does because he has been rejected and has no other alternative but to go where the Spirit leads him.

Paul, however, seems never to have lost confidence that he was doing the work of the Holy Spirit. I am quite hesitant to make that claim about

---

when the former underwrites an individualism that is incompatible with, as Webster argues, the work of the Spirit to call into existence a commonwealth of God's people. Webster, *Holiness*, pp. 26-27.

9. Grant Wacker rightly reminds us that there were "beginnings" prior to Azusa Street, but just to the extent Azusa Street represents a kind of institutionalization of the Pentecostal movement it rightly is seen as quite significant. See Grant Wacker, *Heaven Below: Early Pentecostals and American Culture* (Cambridge, MA: Harvard University Press, 2001), pp. 1-10.

my life or my work. I am not trying to be humble. My reluctance to suggest that what I have to say may be inspired by the Holy Spirit is but an expression of the ambiguous role theologians play in the life of the church in our day. I seldom reference the work of the Holy Spirit in my work because I do not want to give the impression that the Holy Spirit is on my side. That does not mean I think the Holy Spirit does not have a side; I am just unsure I get to claim that side as my side.

I am happy to have discovered that my hesitancy to appeal to the Holy Spirit is something I share with the great John M. Perkins. The work Perkins has done in Mendenhall, Mississippi, as well as his theological understanding of that work, makes his identification of the Holy Spirit with his work more creditable than I could justify about my work. Yet in an essay on Perkins, Lowell Noble notes that Perkins rarely says much about the Holy Spirit. When asked why he seldom references the Holy Spirit, Perkins observed that he feels that too many people too casually say the Holy Spirit said this or told them to do that when there is not enough substance in their lives to justify identification with the Spirit. Secondly, Perkins said he did not want the Holy Spirit blamed for his mistakes. At what he describes as "an opportune moment," Noble pressed Perkins to articulate how the Holy Spirit worked in his life only to have Perkins "retreat" by providing "a rather lofty theological treatise on the Holy Spirit and the Trinity."[10]

Though I am not sure it is a retreat, I want to engage in the same kind of "lofty theological" considerations as Perkins by drawing on the work of Eugene Rogers. I am, after all, a follower of Barth. My response to my colleague at Notre Dame was one I should like to think was informed by Barth. I learned from Barth that God is God, which makes impossible the presumption, a presumption often justified by appeals to the work of the Holy Spirit, that God is ever ready and available to meet my self-projected needs.[11]

Moreover, as I reminded my colleague, I am a Methodist. I come out of the belly of the beast that bears the name "pietism." Accordingly I found Barth's critical attitude toward Protestant pietism liberating. I learned from Barth that I did not need to have an experience of God to be a Chris-

---

10. Lowell Noble, "The Four Ministries of the Holy Spirit," in *Mobilizing for the Common Good: The Lived Theology of John M. Perkins,* ed. Peter Slade, Charles Marsh, and Peter Goodwin Heltzel (Jackson: University of Mississippi Press, 2013), p. 203.

11. For what I can only characterize as Barth's rather "cold" account of the Holy Spirit see *Church Dogmatics* I/1 (Edinburgh: T. & T. Clark, 1960), pp. 513-60.

tian.[12] Barth, moreover, helped me see how appeals to the Holy Spirit in order to ground theological claims by those identified with pietism was the breeding ground for liberal Protestant theology.[13] Given the stress on the significance of scripture by theologians associated with pietism, to suggest that there is a connection between pietism and Protestant liberalism may seem counterintuitive. As a movement pietism is assumed to be theologically conservative. But appeals to the Holy Spirit as the source of an individual's "experience" of God structurally can underwrite the presumption that theological claims are first and foremost about us and not God.[14]

There is an odd reversal associated with the emphasis on experience as the work of the Holy Spirit that makes God's holiness to be but a mode of God's otherness and transcendence. God is so "other" that we only know who God is by experiencing the difference between God and us. The problem with that alternative is, as John Webster observes, God's difference — or distance — from us does not constitute God's holiness. Rather, as Webster puts it, "God is holy precisely as the one who in majesty and freedom and sovereign power bends down to us in mercy. God is the Holy One. But he is the Holy One 'in your midst,' as Hosea put it (Hosea 11:9)."[15] Protestant liberal theology often stressed God's transcendence as the basis for affirming God's holiness as mediated by the Spirit, but as a result God's work as the Spirit to create a new heaven and earth was lost.

There are, of course, quite sophisticated and substantive forms of Protestant liberal theology that are to be rightly respected. But too often I fear the authority given to our subjectivity in the name of the Holy Spirit by Protestant liberals resulted in an attenuated account of the gospel. I have thought this to be a particular problem in mainline Protestant churches just to the degree the members of these churches represent a social class of well-educated people who too often presume they get to make up their minds about what kind of god they choose to worship or not worship.

My concern about the use of the Holy Spirit to legitimate a particular "experience" was shaped as much by philosophical as by theological con-

---

12. Eberhard Busch provides an illuminating account of Barth's relation to the Pietist in his *Karl Barth and the Pietist* (Downers Grove: InterVarsity, 2004).

13. Rogers makes a similar point in *After the Spirit*, pp. 5-6.

14. In his great book *Protestant Theology and the Making of the Modern German University* (Oxford: Oxford University Press, 2006), Thomas Albert Howard provides an insightful account of the role of pietism for shaping as well as reflecting modern humanistic assumptions in the formation of the University of Halle (pp. 93-97).

15. Webster, *Holiness*, p. 45.

cerns. Appeals to experience, even the experience of the Holy Spirit, often seemed to suggest that the experience was prior to how the experience was linguistically expressed. These are philosophically complex matters that involve fundamental questions about our being as language users. Suffice it to say that under the influence of Wittgenstein, and in particular his arguments about private language, I could not be anything but suspicious of appeals to some experience that could not be linguistically expressed.

These are some of the worries that made me quite reticent to appeal to the Holy Spirit in my work. It was not because I do not believe in the Holy Spirit. Rather I was trying to work in a manner such that what I had to say was unintelligible if God is not the Father, Son, and Holy Spirit. I sometimes think, though it seems quite odd, we forget when we confess that we believe in the Holy Spirit that we are talking about God. Talk about God, moreover, is quite different from how, for example, we talk about the church. There is an essential connection between our affirmation of the Holy Spirit and the church, but they are not of the same status. I think it is extremely significant that in the third article of the Nicene Creed, as well as the Apostles' Creed, we confess we "believe in one holy catholic and apostolic church," as a correlative to our belief in the Holy Spirit. The grammar of the Creeds means we first and foremost believe in the Holy Spirit and because of the work of that Spirit we also believe in the existence of the church.[16]

Rowan Williams points out that the Greek of the Nicene Creed does not say that we believe in the church, but "that we believe the Church."[17] Williams suggests this means that the church which tells us to believe in the Father, Son, and Holy Spirit is not to have the same status as what we say we believe when we affirm our belief in the Father, the Son, and the Holy Spirit. But, Williams argues, because we believe that the Holy Spirit vivifies the church, we can trust the church when we are told by the church to believe in the Holy Spirit. We believe as Christians that the Holy Spirit makes us believers in the Holy Spirit through the witness of the church. The Holy Spirit is, therefore, at once the subject and the object of our

16. I owe this way of putting the matter to Stephen Pickard. See his *Seeking the Church: An Introduction to Ecclesiology* (London: SCM Press, 2012), p. 24. Claude Welch makes a similar point, observing that "Faith in the proper sense can have only God as its object, and we can really speak of faith in the church not 'in itself' but only in relation to God in Jesus Christ." *The Reality of the Church* (New York: Scribner's Sons, 1958), p. 42.

17. Rowan Williams, *Tokens of Trust: An Introduction to Christian Belief* (Louisville: Westminster John Knox, 2007), p. 105.

faith. That is why the Holy Spirit is rightly understood to be the animating principle of the central practices that make the church the church; that is, it is the Spirit that makes preaching, baptism, and Eucharist more than just another way of communication, initiation, or sharing a meal.

Williams recognizes that to be asked to believe the church may seem to ask more than most of us are willing to do, given that the church is often less than faithful. Yet it is exactly because the Spirit does not abandon the church when she is unfaithful that makes it possible to trust the church when the church tells us to believe in the Holy Spirit. We can trust the church because the church is the sort of community that it is. It is a community of active peacemaking and peacekeeping in which no one exists in isolation or grows up in isolation. That does not mean, according to Williams, that the church is a community in which our individuality is submerged in the collective. Our differences remain, but that is the way we learn of our dependency on one another as the outworking of the gift of the Holy Spirit. For it is the work of the Holy Spirit to help us recognize the unique gift of the other as crucial for a common life that makes the recognition of a common good possible.[18]

These last observations by Williams make clear why the appeal to the Holy Spirit to legitimate someone's self-understanding of *their* experience is antithetical to the work of the Holy Spirit. The work of the Holy Spirit is a communal work. The Holy Spirit works to help us find one another so that we will not suffer the fears and anxieties that fuel the violence derived from our being alone. To be so located is to discover that God invites us to share his very life found in Jesus of Nazareth. For it turns out the principal work of the Holy Spirit, as I think is clear from the role the Spirit plays in scripture, is to point to Jesus. I should like to think that is what I have tried to do in all that I have written, that is, to point to Jesus.

To point to Jesus, however, means you cannot forget that Jesus can be known only through the connections the Spirit makes possible. Thus my claim: "No Israel, no Jesus. No Church, no Jesus." This formula is meant to remind us that the God we worship as Christians is a God who wills to be present to his creation in a startling particular fashion. In his remarkable book *The Reality of the Church*, Claude Welch observes that though in the scriptures the Holy Spirit is free to remain transcendent over all forms of life, it is clear that the Holy Spirit is even more determinatively free "to bind himself to the concrete, to use precisely the fragile vessels, the

18. Williams, *Tokens of Trust,* p. 106.

workaday pots of our historical forms. God does not choose to redeem history apart from history, nor create new community apart from human community. The Spirit works in and by means of flesh and time and human togetherness."[19] Thus we affirm that the Spirit "has spoken through the prophets."

Welch imaginatively but with great care suggests that the work of the Spirit in the creation and sustaining of the church is commensurate with the relation of Christ's humanity and divinity. Just as the Holy Spirit made it possible that our humanity could become the home of the Son, by analogy the Spirit makes himself known in the church. Welch notes this does not mean we can equate the being of God in the church with God's being in Christ. We cannot say, as I am tempted to say, that the church is the extension of the Incarnation. Yet if there were no church, then Christians would not know what they say when they say "God."

I am aware that to suggest the primary role of the Holy Spirit is to point to Jesus may seem to some a far-too-limited account. I hope to show that is not the case by following how Gene Rogers helps us see how the work of the Holy Spirit can be understood if we attend to the interactions of the Spirit and Jesus found in the scriptures. Drawing on the Eastern tradition's understanding of the Holy Spirit, Rogers provides a robust account of the Spirit's work, which I think has been implicit in the way I have tried to do Christian theology. Better put, I should like to think that Rogers's account of what work the Holy Spirit does provides the theological resources I have needed for the arguments I have tried to make about the nature of the Christian moral life.

## Gene Rogers on What the Spirit Does

Rogers begins *After the Spirit* by asking, "Is There Nothing the Spirit Can Do That the Son Can't Do Better?"[20] This question, a question that serves as the title of the first chapter of his book, sets the problematic for the rest of the book. Rogers explains why he takes the question to be so important by observing that though we live in a time that has enjoyed a revival of Trinitarian theology, a revival inspired by Karl Barth, that revival has seemed to slight the role of the Holy Spirit. The question of where the

19. Welch, *The Reality of the Church*, pp. 75-76.
20. Rogers, *After the Spirit*, pp. 19-32.

Spirit has gone, a question that as noted above had been first posed by Robert Jenson, is one that Jenson and Rogers both assume to be directed at Barth.

Rogers and Jenson direct the question concerning the absence of the Spirit to Barth because if anyone should have an account of the Spirit it should be Barth. They know it seems strange to ask about the role of the Spirit in Barth's theology because Barth provides extensive discussion of the Holy Spirit. In fact, they acknowledge that Barth places great emphasis on the work of the Holy Spirit for making us capable of responding to the Father through the Son. Yet Rogers worries that Barth's Christology threatens to eclipse "the illumination of the Spirit with the material objectivity of the Son."[21] As a result, the Holy Spirit in Barth's theology appears surprisingly as an impersonal power with no gift to give as a person of the Trinity to the Father or the Son.

Rogers is acutely aware that to ask the question about the distinctive work of the Spirit risks betraying the fundamental unity that is at the heart of the church's confession that our God is three-in-one. For example, the widespread presumption that creation is the work of the Father, redemption is the work of Jesus, and sanctification or transformation is the work of the Holy Spirit fails to do justice to the unity of the Godhead. Against such a view of the Trinity, Rogers rightly insists that "because the acts of the Trinity toward the world are indivisible, the only time one could distinguish the Spirit from the Son would be when the narratives give glimpses of their *intratrinitarian* interaction."[22]

According to Rogers this Trinitarian rule means the identity of the Spirit can never be found apart from the Son, but the identity of the Spirit can be distinctly described through her interactions with Jesus made manifest in the narratives of scripture.[23] These narratives are crucial for the display of the Holy Spirit as a person. They are so, and Rogers credits the emphasis on narrative to the influence of Hans Frei, because to characterize a person means we must tell a story about them. The appeal to narrative for displaying the work of the Spirit only makes explicit,

---

21. Rogers, *After the Spirit*, p. 20.

22. Rogers, *After the Spirit*, p. 7.

23. Rogers uses the feminine pronoun for the Spirit, which seems somehow "right." I had quoted Welch previously, who had used the masculine "his" without comment. I did not call attention to Welch's use of the masculine because the crucial issue is how the use of either the masculine or the feminine pronoun rightly suggests that the Holy Spirit is, like the Father and the Son, a person.

Rogers argues, what has always been at the heart of Christian reflection on the Trinity.

For example Rogers calls attention to an observation by Gregory of Nazianzus as an exemplification of the storied character of the Spirit: "Christ is born; the Spirit is His Forerunner. He is baptized, the Spirit bears witness. He is tempted; the Spirit leads Him up. He works miracles; the Spirit accompanies them. He ascends; the Spirit takes his place."[24] Gregory of Nazianzus, according to Rogers, rightly sees that the Spirit has a history analogous to the life of Christ. Metaphysical claims are surely being made about the persons of the Trinity by Gregory and Basil, but those claims are in service to how the persons of the Trinity each manifest a narrative identity through the love they share.[25]

In particular, Rogers calls attention to the peculiar work of the Spirit in those stories that suggest that the Spirit has a penchant for the body. Rogers puts it this way: "The Spirit is a person with an affinity for material things. The Spirit characteristically befriends the body."[26] Rogers is, however, careful to emphasize that to so understand the work of the Spirit does not mean that the Spirit acts in a manner that the Father and Son cannot. The Spirit is not distinguishable from the Father and the Son because the Trinity's activity in the world is of one piece.

But the Spirit does what the Trinity does in a particular way by incorporating the particular, that is, the particular present in the gathering of the community, in baptism and Eucharist, through which those gathered are made participants in the life of the Trinity. Just as the Spirit comes to rest on the body of Jesus, so the Spirit comes to rest on us.[27] Rogers, therefore, seeks to recover the work of the Spirit as crucial for expressing how we become "participants in the divine nature" (2 Pet. 1:4), or, in the language of the East, how we are deified.[28]

Rogers thereby answers the question whether there is anything the Spirit can do that the Son cannot do better with a resounding "yes." What the Spirit does that the Son does not do is come to rest on the Son. But by coming to rest on the Son the Son is made available to us. The character of the rest the Spirit makes possible has the character of the time given in

24. Rogers, *After the Spirit,* p. 56.

25. For an anticipation of Rogers's understanding of these matters see Robert Jenson, *The Triune Identity* (Philadelphia: Fortress Press, 1982).

26. Rogers, *After the Spirit,* p. 60.

27. Rogers, *After the Spirit,* pp. 60-61.

28. Rogers, *After the Spirit,* p. 9.

the Sabbath. Sabbath time is the time of perfect activity, a time of prayer and contemplation, made possible by the gift of the Spirit.

The Spirit rests on the body of the Son and by so doing manifests the love that constitutes the relation of the Father and the Son. That relation is itself the expression of the Oneness of God. What is crucial, therefore, for rightly understanding the relation between the persons of the Trinity is the recognition that they do not need the gifts they give one another, but the gifts they give to one another constitute their unity. In support of this way of understanding the unique work of the Spirit, Rogers quotes Basil of Caesarea, who maintained:

> The Father's work is in no way imperfect, since He accomplishes all in all, nor is the Son's work deficient if it is not completed by the Spirit. The Father creates through His will alone and does not *need* the Son, yet chooses to work through the Son. Likewise the Son works as the Father's likeness, and needs no other co-operation, but he chooses to have his work completed through the Spirit.[29]

That Rogers quotes Basil is but an indication that how he reads scripture is determined by Nicea. At Nicea the subordination of the Son and the Spirit inherent in Arius's emphasis on the uniqueness and transcendence of the Father was decisively rejected.[30] The correlative view of the Arians that

---

29. Rogers, *After the Spirit*, p. 71. Rogers is, of course, quoting from St. Basil the Great, *On the Holy Spirit* (Crestwood, NY: St. Vladimir's Seminary Press, 2011). Though both sides at Nicea, and there were obviously more than two, are often criticized for logic chopping, I think Basil rightly defends paying close attention to the words we use. He observes, "[I]t is not for the slothful in piety to listen attentively to theological words and to try to search for the meaning hidden in each phrase and in each syllable; rather, this belongs to those who know the goal of our calling: it is offered to us to become like God as much as human nature allows. Likeness to God, however, cannot be had without knowledge, and knowledge comes from teaching. Speech, though, is the beginning of teaching, and the parts of speech are syllables and words. So, the investigation of syllables does not fall outside the goal of our calling" (p. 29).

30. I still find J. N. D. Kelly's account of the controversies that resulted in Nicea to be exemplary for the clarity he brings to the debates about terminology surrounding such words as *ousia* and *hypostasis*. For example, Kelly suggests that Basil's analogical use of these terms to negotiate the relation of the universal and particular meant that the essence of Godhead is "determined by its appropriate particularizing characteristic, or identifying peculiarity, just as each individual man represents the universal 'man' determined by certain characteristics which mark him off from other men." *Early Christian Doctrines* (New York: Harper & Brothers, 1960), p. 265. Kelly's way of putting these fundamental moves made by

there was a time when the Son "was not" was rightly seen by Athanasius and the Cappadocians as threatening to make the salvation wrought by Christ unintelligible. For what was at stake at Nicea was not just a question of metaphysics, though certainly metaphysical issues were unavoidable, but how the transformation of the life of Christians was to be read in the light of scripture. These are the "givens" Rogers brings to his readings of the New Testament.

Rogers offers readings of what he describes as "iconic New Testament scenes," that is, the Annunciation, Baptism, Transfiguration, and Resurrection, to display how the Spirit comes to rest on the body. He begins with the Resurrection because he takes Romans 8:11 to be a central Trinitarian text. Paul writes, "If the Spirit of the One who raised Christ Jesus from the dead dwells in your mortal bodies, you too shall rise from the dead." This text, which Jenson calls "the most remarkable Trinitarian passage in the New Testament," makes clear that the Spirit of the One who raised Jesus is the same Spirit through which we are made participants in the Trinity.[31]

Drawing on Hilary of Poitiers, Rogers argues that what Paul's affirmation in Romans 8:11 suggests is that the Spirit of the Raiser and the Spirit of the Raised are the same Spirit, which means their relation is internal because they are in essential communion with one another. It is the Spirit that manifests the union constituted by the love between the persons of the Trinity that makes possible our inclusion in such a love. Rogers quotes Hilary's claim that "though the Spirit of Christ is in us, yet His Spirit is also in us Who raised Christ from the dead, and He Who raised Christ from the dead shall quicken our mortal bodies also on account of His Spirit that dwelleth in us."[32] These are not abstract claims about how the resurrection in theory includes the human into the life of the Trinity, but a statement about how through baptism we are raised by the Spirit with Christ.

Rogers asks why Jesus, who was without sin, had to be baptized. Was it just a charade? He argues that the baptism of Jesus can only make sense as an inter-Trinitarian event in which the Spirit bears witness to the love between the Father and the Son. What the Spirit adds to the expression and reception of that love is to include "witnesses to the love between the

---

Basil I think make clear that Rogers's calling attention to the role of narrative for the display of the work of the persons of the Trinity is a constructive elaboration of the fundamental insights of Nicea.

31. Rogers, *After the Spirit,* pp. 76-77.
32. Rogers, *After the Spirit,* p. 82.

Father and the Son among the disciples and among other human beings."[33] In short, the Spirit is present at Jesus' baptism to bear witness to the reality that the love between the Father and the Son can be shared. It is a love, moreover, that is quite particular, witnessing as it does to the solidarity of the Son with human beings even unto death.[34]

It is not accidental that water plays an essential role in the work of the Spirit. There is no life without water and the Spirit is life itself. That the Spirit is life itself has tempted some in the Christian tradition to identify the animation of the world with the Spirit in a manner that makes unclear the relation of the Spirit to the Father and the Son in the Trinity. But the Spirit that hovers over the waters at creation is the same Spirit that animates the waters of Mary's womb. It is the same Spirit that alights on Jesus in the waters of the Jordan at his baptism. It is the Spirit that rules over nature even to kindling a fire in the water. The Spirit rests on all that is, making possible through sacrament and storytelling a recognition that we live in a world alive with God's purposes. The Holy Spirit comes to rest on the water and by so doing makes nature a character in the story of God's good care of the world, which includes us, determinately exemplified in the stories found in scripture.[35]

Rogers develops this theme by directing attention to the fact, a fact easily overlooked, that in the Gospel of Luke at the Transfiguration Jesus was engaged in prayer. Jesus praying to the Father is one Person of the Trinity praying to another. The suggestion that it must be the humanity of Jesus that prays is rejected by Rogers on the grounds that there is no other "person" in Jesus than the Word. Accordingly the human nature of Jesus is the human nature of the Word. That such is the case means Jesus' prayers cannot be attributed to his humanity abstracted from his divinity. Rather what we see as Jesus prays is that prayer is determinative of God's inner life. That prayer is constitutive of the Trinity means that when we pray as human beings we are caught up in the triune activity itself. Thus we ask the Spirit to "pray for us" and with that prayer we are transfigured by the Spirit by being transformed into beings that did not know how to pray but now do so.[36]

To pray is to be glorified by being made a liturgical being. All creatures

---

33. Rogers, *After the Spirit,* p. 137.
34. Rogers, *After the Spirit,* p. 141.
35. Rogers, *After the Spirit,* p. 151.
36. Rogers, *After the Spirit,* p. 174.

have been created by God to glorify God. Human beings, however, are creatures who have been given the gift to glorify God intentionally. That our chief end is to glorify God means, according to Rogers, that we are "a glorifying being, a thanks-giving being, a being that not only receives, but receives also the permission to give back and again."[37] The Spirit is the link between the earthly offering of praise and the eternal liturgy of the Trinity, making us through baptism assume the priestly role through which the world is seen as sacrament.

Rogers has, I think, quite successfully managed to avoid separating the Spirit from the Son while nonetheless maintaining their distinctive tasks toward one another and the Father by focusing on those scriptural passages in which the Son and the Spirit interact. He acknowledges, however, that Pentecost seems to make that way of proceeding problematic because Pentecost is not part of the life of Jesus. Yet Rogers argues that though the Ascension seems unrelated to Pentecost they belong together. By going to his death and going to the Father, according to Rogers, Jesus humbles himself and awaits the Spirit who will make him a gift for the renewed life of his mortal body (Rom. 8:11) and for his churchly body after his ascension.[38]

At Pentecost, just as the Spirit came to "rest" on God's becoming this human being named Jesus, so the Spirit comes to rest on those gathered in Jerusalem so that all humanity might be incorporated into God's unending act of being God. "The Spirit who comes on the Sabbath of Sabbaths is the Spirit therefore who sanctifies time and gives diverse human beings a history."[39] For Rogers, the relation of the Spirit and Jesus is finally about God's befriending of time, begun by the Spirit's impregnation of Mary. Time continues to be storied by Jesus by submitting to the guidance of the Spirit at his baptism, by the Spirit calling him to begin his ministry, by the Spirit driving him into the wilderness, by his willingly undergoing death, and finally by witnessing the Spirit give his gift to the Gentiles.[40]

I hope I have said enough to at least suggest what a rich, imaginative, and constructive account of the work of the Holy Spirit Rogers has developed. If, as I argued above, the God we worship as Christians has willed to be known through the calling of Israel and the life, death, and resurrection of Christ, Rogers has helped us see how that God makes those realities

37. Rogers, *After the Spirit,* p. 178.
38. Rogers, *After the Spirit,* p. 201.
39. Rogers, *After the Spirit,* p. 204.
40. Rogers, *After the Spirit,* p. 205. I have not done justice to Rogers's theme throughout of how the Spirit uses Jesus' "failure" to redeem Israel to take God's promise to the Gentiles.

living realities through the work of the Spirit. The name of the agency the Holy Spirit enables is "church." Put as strongly as I can, the very existence of the church is necessary for all that is to be storied. That is the fundamental presumption behind my claim that the first task of the church is not to make the world more just but to make the world the world. A strong claim to be sure, but one I hope to show is justified once the relation between the work of the Spirit and the existence of the church are understood to be inseparable.

## On Being the Church

In his book *The Reality of the Church,* Claude Welch observes how the profusion of images of the church in the New Testament reference, in quite different ways, the person and work of Christ as well as the Father and the Spirit. According to Welch this means that Christ, the Holy Spirit, and the church belong together. "There is no gospel of Jesus Christ which does not include the church, and certainly no notion of a church which does not center in Christ."[41] Welch develops this claim by suggesting that the historical particularity of the church is analogous to the historical character of Christ. Just as God humbles himself to be incarnate in Jesus Christ, so God does not scorn meeting us in the history in which we find ourselves.[42]

In his fine book *Seeking the Church: An Introduction to Ecclesiology,* Stephen Pickard makes a similar point about the mutual involvement of the Son and the Spirit for the constitution of the church.[43] Pickard, by way of commenting on Barth's understanding of the relation of Christ and the church, notes that the church's relation to Christ is analogous to the way the humanity of Christ is enfolded within his divinity. While we may not, as I suggested above, believe in the church in the same way we believe in the Father, the Son, and the Holy Spirit, Pickard rightly argues that "when we believe in the Triune God, we simultaneously bear witness to our believing that we are *of* the *ecclesia* of God, *in* the *ecclesia* of God and *for* the *ecclesia* of God. The church is no longer at a distance but participates in our believing in God."[44]

41. Welch, *The Reality of the Church,* pp. 26-27.

42. Welch, *The Reality of the Church,* p. 64.

43. Stephen Pickard, *Seeking the Church: An Introduction to Ecclesiology* (London: SCM, 2012), p. 18.

44. Pickard, *Seeking the Church,* p. 25.

Welch, as I suggested above, makes a similar move by arguing that just as the unity of God and man in Christ is constituted by the movement of God toward man and of man toward God, so there is a unity whereby the church is at once an immanent-historical community and yet the people of God. Just as Christ in his person is one, so the church is one in being both a social form of humanity and the creation of the Spirit. The church's social reality is formed by the common direction of love of God and man, but it is such "just as God works in its life, as its love for God becomes a oneness with God in his love for man, and as God gives himself through it in love. That is, like the humanity of Christ which cannot be spoken of independently of the incarnation, the church has no existence as immanent historical community independent of God calling it and sustaining it in being."[45]

Welch and Pickard are obviously making strong claims about the ontological reality of the church as the work of Spirit. They insist, however, that this emphasis in no way denies the human reality of the church. Welch, for example, maintains that the church's being subject to sociological analysis is not a fact to be deplored but celebrated. The human character of the church is not an accidental or unfortunate aspect of her being, but rather "is but a reflection of the nature of the church as a humanly concrete body of responding people."[46] In a very similar vein Pickard draws on the classical Christological heresies to suggest that by analogy the Docetic denial of Jesus' full humanity finds ecclesial expression in the attempt to deny the human form of the church.[47]

Pickard attributes this mistake to an inadequate monistic understanding of God that cannot help but result in Christology that denies Christ's full humanity. Docetism is but the correlative of a monarchist un-

---

45. Welch, *The Reality of the Church*, p. 121.

46. Welch, *The Reality of the Church*, p. 61. This was, of course, Jim Gustafson's argument developed in his book *Treasures in Earthen Vessels: The Church as a Human Community* (New York: Harper & Row, 1961). Gustafson references the second chapter of Welch's book as compatible with his argument, but it is not clear to me that Gustafson shared Welch's understanding of the relation between the Holy Spirit and the church.

47. Pickard, *Seeking the Church*, pp. 63-65. Nicholas Healy worries that much of modern ecclesiology may make this mistake. He suggests that quite sophisticated systematic and theoretical accounts of the church have been developed that focus on how to think the right things about the church, but too often those depictions of the church fail to deal with the "living, rather messy, confused and confusing body that the church actually is." *Church, World, and the Christian Life: Practical-Prophetic Ecclesiology* (Cambridge: Cambridge University Press, 2000), p. 3.

derstanding of God. These doctrinal mistakes have ecclesial implications, as too often a Christology that denies Christ's full humanity results in a disjunctive understanding of the relationship between church and world. Docetism invites a sectarian understanding of the church that legitimates a Manichean dualism between church and world. Such a dualism fails to account for creation as the Trinity's good work, with the result that the calling into existence of the church by the Holy Spirit fails to acknowledge the continuity between our sociality and the formation of our bodies into the body of Christ.[48]

Pickard argues that the opposite Christological heresy to Docetism, namely the Ebionite denial of Jesus' full divinity, also has disastrous implications for the church. Rather than making the church more than it can be as the Docetist does, the Ebionite denial of Jesus' full divinity often produces an account of the church in which the church in effect disappears into the world. Just as Manichean expression is correlative to a Docetic Christology, Pickard suggests that a Pelagian emphasis on our ability to effect our own salvation is the natural expression of the failure to acknowledge the full deity of Jesus and the Spirit. Pelagian ethic, according to Pickard, is an expression of anxiety about the status of the church — an anxiety born of the loss of the presumption that through the work of the Holy Spirit the church participates in the reality of the Godhead. As a result the church becomes dominated by the attempt to secure her status by "trying harder." From such a perspective the reform of the church is undertaken with great zeal but with the presumption that reform is "up to us" because we cannot trust the work of the Holy Spirit.[49]

Pickard and Welch are not suggesting there is a strict causal relation between the classical heresies spawned by the challenge of making sense of the Incarnation and how the Holy Spirit should be understood in relation to the church and to the world. But there is surely something right about the interconnections they suggest may exist between doctrine and ecclesial practice. It is, moreover, a two-way street. For as Yoder helps us see — a "seeing" that owes much to the work of Ernst Troeltsch — the positioning of the church in the world may have Christological implications that make what is said to be believed by Christians about Christ and the Holy Spirit unintelligible.[50] So Pickard and Welch help us see how a failure to give

48. Pickard, *Seeking the Church*, pp. 65-66.
49. Pickard, *Seeking the Church*, pp. 73-77.
50. For my suggestions about Yoder's development of Troeltsch's insight see "Fore-

an account of the distinctive yet interrelated work of Christ and the Holy Spirit in relation to the Father's mission can mislead how the church is understood, as well as the work she has been called into the world to perform.

Pickard's account of the relation of these heresies to ecclesiology cannot help but make me acutely aware that my emphasis on the necessity of the church to be the church in order to make the world the world can be read as my doing the impossible; that is, I may seem to commit two antithetical heresies at the same time. My stress on the necessity of the church to be the church in opposition to the world can sound far too Manichean, suggesting as it might that the world is evil and the church is not. Yet my emphasis on the church's responsibility to be an alternative to the world through discipleship can be understood as a Pelagian desire to force God's hand. I should like to think I have avoided those unhappy alternatives, but I do not think at this late date an appeal to the Spirit is sufficient to defeat those who would like to read me as Manichean or Pelagian.

Rather I should like to think that I have been caught by the Spirit. Under the influence of Yoder I have taken a stance about the church that I think can only make sense if the Spirit is the agent who comes to rest on the body we call the church. But in an odd way I suspect that is the way it is supposed to work, namely, that the Spirit is quite good at catching us unaware. The Spirit is, as Pentecostals remind us, no tame Spirit. Rather the Spirit is full of unanticipated surprises.

One of those surprises, for which I cannot account, is how I came to the judgment that the church must matter for how we think about the lives we should live as disciples of Jesus. This is no ideal church, but it is the church we know. It is the church that seems incapable of making up its mind to be a welfare agency at best or one of the last hedges we have against loneliness. Welfare agencies and hedges against loneliness are not bad things, but they are not the first-order business of the church. The first-order business of the church is to be a people who under the guidance of the Spirit point the world to Jesus Christ.

Stephen Pickard ends his book with reflections on the current state of the church in what were once presumed to be Christian cultures. It is

word" to John Howard Yoder, *The Priestly Kingdom: Social Ethics as Gospel* (Notre Dame: University of Notre Dame Press, 2001), pp. viii-ix. In the first volume of her systematic theology, *God, Sexuality, and the Self: An Essay 'On the Trinity'* (Cambridge: Cambridge University Press, 2013), Sarah Coakley uses Troeltsch to make some fascinating suggestions about the relationship between the "church-type" and a charismatic understanding of the work of the Holy Spirit (pp. 115-21).

no secret that the church has rapidly lost its standing in those cultures, leading, at least according to Pickard, to two equally disastrous strategies. One alternative Pickard characterizes as the "fast-asleep church," which he associates with churches that continue to rely on the general presumption that religion is a "good thing," so nothing about the church needs to change. The other strategy he characterizes as the "frenetic church," which he describes as the attempt to force new life into a dying church by meeting consumer demand. He doubts either response to the loss of the church's status will be successful. Each in its own way fails to rely on the Holy Spirit.[51]

Pickard proposes an alternative understanding he calls the slow church. We are a culture of speed, but Pickard, drawing on the example of monasticism, argues that the work of the Spirit is work for the long haul. It is the work of Holy Saturday in which patience and perseverance are made possible and required. Pickard refuses any suggestion that a slow church is a church that no longer has passion for justice and change, but the change sought is not that of solutions that do not last. Rather it is the kind of church that makes possible companionship in a world based on isolation. The Spirit rests on our bodies, making us capable of friendship.[52] I call attention to Pickard's account of what it would mean for the church to be a slow church because I am confident that he is pointing the church to where the Spirit is leading us.[53]

I am confident that the last sentence denoting confidence in where the Spirit is leading is the first time I have ever written a sentence with that grammar. I could not have written that sentence if I had not been forced

51. Pickard, *Seeking the Church*, pp. 216-17.

52. Pickard engages the work of Peter Dula, who has criticized me for needing the world to be overly dark that the church might be viewed favorably. Pickard thinks Dula rightly challenges my call for the church to be a community just to the extent that such a community can be too conformist and suppress otherness. I have no reason to deny that companionship may be a better way to describe what the church should be about than community, but what I take to be crucial is exemplification, not whether one chooses between the words "community" or "companionship."

53. For my account of what being slow might entail see Stanley Hauerwas and Jean Vanier, *Living Gently in a Violent World: The Prophetic Witness of Weakness* (Downers Grove: InterVarsity, 2008). The relation of nonviolence and what it means to be a slow church is, I hope, an obvious topic that needs exploration. For a critique of church-growth strategies by one who was caught in them see Tim Suttle, *Shrink: Faithful Ministry in a Church-Growth Culture* (Grand Rapids: Zondervan, 2014). Suttle has some quite insightful suggestions about alternatives to church-growth paradigms.

to say what I think needs to be said about the work of the Holy Spirit. I can only pray that what I have said will be made true by the Spirit.

To be possessed by the Holy Spirit is surely a frightening prospect. The temptation to domesticate the Spirit is almost irresistible. I cannot pretend to have done justice to the Holy Spirit in what I have written. I am, for example, hesitant to pray as Newman did when he asked:

> Stay with me, and then I shall begin to shine as You shine: so to shine as to be a light to others. The light, O Jesus, will be all from You. None of it will be mine. It will be You who shines through me upon others. O let me thus praise You, in the way which You love best, by shining on all those around me. Give light to them as well as to me; light them with me, through me. Teach me to show forth Your praise, Your truth, Your will. Make me preach You without preaching — not by words, but by example and by the catching force, the sympathetic influence, of what I do — by my visible resemblance to Your Saints, and the evident fullness of the love which my heart bears to You.[54]

I can only hope something I have said or written may have such a "catching force," but if it has, I pray it is not me. Indeed I pray, with the Holy Spirit, that it is the Spirit's work.

54. I am indebted to Carole Baker for the gift of this prayer.

# CHAPTER 3

# How to Do or Not to Do Protestant Ethics

## On Being a Protestant Christian Ethicist

I should like to say that I care deeply about the future of Protestant Christian ethics. I should like to say that I care deeply about the future of Protestant Christian ethics because I am after all a Protestant. Yet honesty requires me, or at least candor requires me, to confess I am not particularly concerned about the future of Protestant Christian ethics. That I must make such a confession expresses my existential situation, that is, I have never thought of myself as someone deeply committed to being a Protestant.

I was, after all, raised an American Methodist, which means no matter how much you study Wesley it is very hard to take your denominational identity seriously.[1] I have, moreover, described my ecclesial identity as being a high church Mennonite. That description has taken on a life of its own, but at the very least, as I will suggest below, it indicates that I think of myself as being on the Catholic side of the Reformation. I do so partly be-

---

1. For a more extended set of reflections on Protestantism and, in particular, Methodism see my chapter "The End of Protestantism," in my book, *Approaching the End: Eschatological Reflections on Church, Politics, and Life* (Grand Rapids: Eerdmans, 2013), pp. 87-97. My use of "End" in the title is meant to refer not only to questions of the continued existence of Protestant churches, but also to the telos of those churches.

---

This paper was written for a conference at the University of Aberdeen in October 2014. The conference title was "The Freedom of a Christian Ethicist: The Future of a Reformation Legacy."

cause, as I will suggest below, I think the way the Anabaptists understood church put them on the Catholic side of the Reformation. That is not to deny that increasingly Luther is being recovered, particularly by Finnish theologians, as a Catholic thinker.[2]

Of course that I have little at stake in the future of Protestant ethics — or even being a Protestant — is a very Protestant position. Only Protestant theologians or ethicists would think that it makes little difference whether they are or are not Protestant for the work they do. Yet my lack of passion or commitment to Protestantism, as well as the commitment to do ethics in a manner that can be identified as Protestant, risks making me a representative of that most despised position, at least despised by me, namely, the theologian as a "thinker." Yet given the loss of any clear Protestant ecclesial identity it is not apparent to me if a Protestant can avoid that fate in our time.

What it means to be a "thinker" I can illustrate by telling a story about a faculty meeting at Notre Dame during the time I was a member of the theology faculty. We were discussing yet one more time what it might mean to be an ecumenical department of theology in a Catholic context. My colleagues contributed to the discussion by indicating what difference they thought being Lutheran, Reformed, Anabaptist, Anglican, and even Jesuit might make for helping us know better what it meant to be Catholic. I was trying as hard as I could to think what special gift Methodism might bring to our endeavors. But then the thought hit me, "Hell! I am not a Methodist. I went to Yale." I think to be so identified is not peculiar to me but applies to most Christian theologians and ethicists at this time — namely, we are people determined more by where we went to graduate school than by our ecclesial identity.

My disavowal of the significance of being a Protestant for how I do ethics, however, can be an invitation to self-deception. I am, after all, going to die the death of a Protestant Christian. I know this to be the case because my wife, who is an ordained Methodist appointed to an Episcopal church, and I have bought a niche in the columbarium of the Church of the Holy

2. For a good introduction to the Finnish Luther see *Union with Christ: The New Finnish Interpretation of Luther,* ed. Carl E. Braaten and Robert W. Jenson (Grand Rapids: Eerdmans, 1998). Mannerma's chapter "Why Is Luther So Fascinating?" is a particularly helpful article about this turn in Luther interpretation. In short, Mannerma and his colleagues are suggesting that Luther's understanding of justification by faith through grace is similar to accounts of *theosis* in the East. If that is right, it also means that Wesley's understanding of sanctification can be read in a similar way.

Family in Chapel Hill, North Carolina. Holy Family is an Episcopal church even if the name is primarily associated with Roman Catholic churches. I can assure you, however, that Holy Family is a Protestant church because we call the basement the undercroft. That clearly makes us Episcopalian, that is, people who are determined to let no pretension go unused.

That I will die a Protestant does not mean that Catholicism has not had and continues to have a significant role in my life. Fourteen years at the University of Notre Dame cannot help but leave its mark on you. During those years I was drawn into a world I had not known existed prior to coming to Notre Dame. I had known from graduate school that something called Catholic theology and ethics exists, but, at least in America, Catholicism is a material faith that cannot be reduced to what Catholics may or may not think. That does not mean that what Catholic theologians and moralists think is not important, but neither is what they think that which makes Catholicism Catholic.

While teaching at Notre Dame, of course, I became acquainted with theologians about whom I had never heard. They simply were not part of the Protestant canon. For example, soon after arriving at Notre Dame I found myself on a committee for a dissertation concerned with Catholic modernism. I had never heard of Catholic modernism. Though I had taken a course with Bernard Häring during my graduate work, I was innocent of Catholic moral theology prior to Vatican II. I began to read widely in Catholic moral theology as well as the Social Encyclicals. I soon began to teach courses in Catholic moral theology because I assumed that was something even a Protestant should do given that most of our students were Catholic. That they were Catholic meant, of course, that they knew very little about Catholicism and even less about the Catholic moral tradition.

I do not want to be misunderstood. I did not teach Catholic moral theology only because the students were Catholic. I taught Catholic moral theology because it is such a rich theological tradition. In particular, that Catholics had the confessional meant they had to think concretely about moral problems in a manner that was largely unknown to Protestants. Accordingly I simply assumed when I came to Duke Divinity School that I should continue to teach Catholic moral theology along with the Social Encyclicals.[3] I did so because I thought those go-

---

3. For my "take" on the Social Encyclicals see my chapter with Jana Bennett, " 'A Recall to Christian Life': What Is Social about the Catholic Social Teachings," in my book *Working with Words: On Learning to Speak Christian* (Eugene, OR: Cascade, 2013), pp. 233-54.

ing into the Protestant ministry would benefit from such a course, but I also thought graduate students needed to know the Catholic tradition because it was more than likely that a Catholic institution is where they would end up teaching.

It did not occur to me to identify as a Protestant or Catholic ethicist. I simply thought I was doing Christian ethics. What that meant can be illustrated by an exchange during my initial interview for the position at Notre Dame. I was asked what I would like to teach. Among the courses I mentioned I said I would like to teach a course on Thomas Aquinas. In response I was asked why, as a Protestant, I wanted to teach Aquinas, because Aquinas was a Roman Catholic. I challenged that description, pointing out that Aquinas could not have known he was a Roman Catholic because the Reformation had not yet taken place. I then observed that I had no reason to think Aquinas was only of use to Roman Catholics. As a Christian ethicist I assumed Aquinas was fair game for anyone committed to doing Christian ethics in a manner that reflected what I thought to be the growing ecumenical commitments by Catholics and Protestants.[4]

Of course the more pressing question was not whether as a Protestant I could or should use Aquinas but rather how anyone like me whose way of thinking had been as deeply shaped by Barth could also be influenced by Aquinas. Barth and Aquinas not only came from different ages and contexts, but their fundamental presuppositions seemed irreconcilable. The difference is at least suggested by a question I sometimes asked graduate students taking their preliminary exams. I would ask the student to comment on the proposition that Aristotle is to Aquinas as Kant is to Barth. As I will try to suggest below, if we are living in a post-Christian world I do not think it is absurd to think that Barth and Aquinas are important allies to help us negotiate that world.

The fact that my identity as a Christian ethicist did not require me to be Protestant or Catholic does not mean, however, that I had a clear idea of what being a Christian ethicist entailed. How could I know what it means to be a Christian ethicist given the fact that Christian ethics is a

4. For my attempt to respond to George Lindbeck's question about my lack of interest in the Protestant ecumenical movement, see my chapter "Which Church? What Unity? Or an Attempt to Say What I May Think about the Future of Christian Unity," in *Approaching the End*, pp. 98-119. Also relevant is *Postliberal Theology and the Church Catholic: Conversations with George Lindbeck, David Burrell, and Stanley Hauerwas*, ed. John Wright (Grand Rapids: Baker, 2012).

relatively new discipline and lacks any generally agreed-upon "method" or clearly defined subject matter? I have tried to provide an account of the development of Christian ethics in America by focusing on figures such as Walter Rauschenbusch, Reinhold Niebuhr, H. Richard Niebuhr, Paul Ramsey, James Gustafson, and John Howard Yoder. These are substantive figures, but it is not clear that their legacy has been sufficient to sustain a discipline called Protestant Christian ethics. Thus my suggestion that Christian ethics in America has come to a dead end. It has done so because the subject of Christian ethics in America was America. Just to the extent that America became what Christian ethicists wanted, Christian ethics became unintelligible to itself.[5]

Of course the question of the future of Protestant ethics is a question inseparable from the larger question of whether Protestantism itself has a future. The decline of Protestant churches is a stark reality. Of course Protestant ethics as an academic subject may be able to continue in some form even though there are few Protestants and, in particular, Protestant ministers, left to read what Protestant ethicists write. But then it must be asked if one of the reasons for the decline of Protestantism was and is the failure of Protestant theologians to do theology in a manner that could help Protestant Christians have a reason for being Protestant.

The very description "protestant" suggests a movement of reform within the church catholic. When Protestantism became an end in itself, when Protestant churches became denominations, Protestantism became unintelligible to itself. No doubt the suggestion that Protestantism has become unintelligible to itself is a generalization that threatens oversimplification given the complex historical development we now call the "Reformation." But then almost any attempt to say what the Reformation was turns out to be hard to sustain, a fact clearly indicated by the question of whether "reformation" is an accurate or useful description of what is alleged to have happened five hundred years ago. For as odd as it may seem, it is not at all clear we know yet what happened five hundred years ago, even though what did happen resulted in some of us now being known as "Protestants."

---

5. For my account of these developments see my chapter "Christian Ethics in America (and the *Journal of Religious Ethics*): A Report on a Book I Will Not Write," in my book *A Better Hope: Resources for a Church Confronting Capitalism, Democracy, and Postmodernity* (Grand Rapids: Brazos, 2000), pp. 55-69.

## Yet the Reformation Matters

To this point I have been engaged in what Jeff Stout has called to our attention, that is, given that academics seldom have anything that is interesting to say, the academic temptation is to engage in extended exercises in interminable throat-clearing in the hope you will not notice I have given up on the wreck. I have been delaying as long as possible. I have tried to say something about the legacy of the Reformation, but I fear that would be an empty gesture by me. But given the upcoming anniversary of the Reformation it seems incumbent upon us to say something about how we understand the Reformation legacy to have informed how we do theological ethics. Of course that entails some account of what one takes the Reformation legacy to be. The problem with trying to answer that question is that there are too many "reformations" — each of which has a different legacy.

It is generally assumed that there are at least four Reformations — the Lutheran, the Reformed, the Anabaptist, and the Church of England — but those descriptions fail to do justice to the complexity that the names suggest. Those reformations were not isolated from one another, which meant they often shared more in common than they differed. It is also true that Catholicism can be thought to have gone through a reformation in response to the Reformation. That said, I am sure each of those "Reformations" has played a role in how I have learned to think about theological ethics, though it is not clear to me I would recognize what that role has been.

Moreover, any attempt to get a handle on the Reformation is complicated by recent developments that attempt to put the Reformation in a new light. Eamon Duffy's *The Stripping of the Altars: Traditional Religion in England 1400-1580* and Brad Gregory's *The Unintended Reformation: How a Religious Revolution Secularized Society* are representatives of this development.[6] Duffy and Gregory deny they are romanticizing the past by arguing that the religious character of church and society prior to the Reformation was not nearly as corrupt as Protestant historiography has implied. They do not deny that the church needed reforming, but they

---

6. Eamon Duffy, *The Stripping of the Altars: Traditional Religion in England 1400-1580* (New Haven: Yale University Press, 1992), and Brad Gregory, *The Unintended Reformation: How a Religious Revolution Secularized Society* (Cambridge, MA: Harvard University Press, 2012).

imply that reformation could have been possible without dividing Christendom.[7] It is beyond my competence to assess their arguments, though their work clearly has implications for how Christian ethics should take account of the Reformation legacy.

There is, however, one glaring, undeniable, and decisive influence of the Reformation on me that is crucial for how I have worked as a Christian ethicist. That influence bears a name — John Howard Yoder. I think it important to call attention to Yoder's influence because he represents aspects of the Reformation that are often forgotten by those who think that the primary concern of the Reformers was doctrine. Doctrine was and is extremely important, but equally significant was the question of whether the habits of Constantinian Christianity should be continued. That question has doctrinal implication by making clear that the very isolation of doctrine from ethics and politics was and is a Constantinian strategy.

I do not want to be misunderstood. The magisterial Reformers' recovery of the Christological center of the Christian faith expressed in the language of justification by faith through grace is of singular significance. Yet as Protestantism developed, the emphasis on justification became divorced from Christology and as a result justification by grace through faith became a description of the anthropological conditions necessary to have "faith." In short, the Lutheran emphasis on justification became the breeding grounds for the development of Protestant liberalism and the subsequent moralization of Christian theology. By "moralization of Christian theology" I simply mean that once justification was lost as a way to talk about the priority of God's grace, Kant's attempt to "save" Christian convictions by construing them as ethics was inevitable. *Religion within the Limits of Reason Alone* is the great text in Protestant moral theology.[8]

Kant's account of Christian ethics served to reinforce the general character of how the Christian life was depicted by Protestant theologians. For example, Kant insisted that the "sacred narrative," which is appropriately employed on behalf of ecclesiastical faith, "can have and, taken by itself, ought to have absolutely no influence on the adoption of moral maxims."[9] The adoption of such maxims must be based on reason itself. The Chris-

---

7. For a strong critique of Duffy see David Aers, "Altars of Power: Reflections on Eamon Duffy's *The Stripping of the Altars,*" *Literature and History* 3 (1994): 90-105. Duffy's reply can be found in the "Preface to the Second Edition" of *The Stripping of the Altars,* pp. xxi-xxv.

8. Immanuel Kant, *Religion within the Limits of Reason Alone,* trans. Theodore Greene (New York: Harper & Brothers, 1934).

9. Kant, *Religion within the Limits of Reason Alone,* p. 123.

tological implications are clear; that is, what is crucial is not what strikes the senses and can be known through experience by the appearance of the God-Man (on earth), but "rather the archetype, lying in our reason, that we attribute to him (since, so far as his example can be known, he is found to conform thereto), which is really the object of saving faith."[10]

Kant's philosophical transformation of Protestant theological ethics assumed as well as reinforced the ecclesial politics of the magisterial Reformers.[11] Troeltsch put the matter this way: "The Lutheran ethic is summed up in the following characteristic features: confidence in God founded on His grace, and love of one's neighbor which is exercised in the social duties of one's calling, combined with an obedient surrender to the order of Society created by the Law of Nature."[12] Whether Luther's challenge to the theological and ecclesial presumptions of the day is understood as radical or not, there is no question that the Lutheran Reformation was politically and socially conservative. That it was so, moreover, had the effect over time of making it difficult to maintain the truthful status of fundamental theological claims.

The underwriting of the status quo by the magisterial Reformers is why it is so important that those groups generally described by the not very useful name "Anabaptist" not be forgotten or ignored. Of course it is by no means clear who the Anabaptists were. Some seemed to be quite mad.[13] Some rejected the main tenets of the Christian faith while others

10. Kant, *Religion within the Limits of Reason Alone*, p. 110. Kant is equally clear about the atonement. Thus his claim that "no reasonable man" who knows he merits punishment can believe that all he needs to do is accept forgiveness (p. 107).

11. Thus Kant's claim that the "sovereignty of the good principle is attainable only through the establishment and spread of a society in accordance with, and for the sake of, the laws of virtue, a society whose task and duty it is rationally to impress these laws in all their scope upon the entire human race." *Religion within the Limits of Reason Alone*, p. 86. Kant, like most Protestant liberals, simply assumed that Germany was *the* norm for how Christians should live.

12. Ernst Troeltsch, *The Social Teachings of the Christian Church*, vol. 2, trans. Olive Wyon (New York: Macmillan, 1931), pp. 509-10. This characterization of Luther's politics has recently been challenged by Michael Laffin in his University of Aberdeen dissertation (2014) titled *Martin Luther and Political Theology: A Constructive Reappraisal of Luther's Political Thought with Special Reference to the Institutions*. Laffin argues that if one attends to Luther's sacramental and ecclesial reflections, Luther has a much more complex understanding of the role of the church in the world than the interpretation of Luther in terms of the orders of creation.

13. For a wonderful fictionalized account of the Anabaptist at the time of the Reformation see Luther Blissett, *Q: A Novel* (New York: Harcourt, 2000).

seemed not to know there were main tenets of the Christian faith. Some would baptize children but others would not. Those who would not baptize children allegedly would not do so because they thought that you could be baptized only if you knew what you were doing. The matter is, however, more complex. For many, believers' baptism was a norm because the baptized must be ready to be subject to communal discipline.

From my perspective, a perspective shaped by my Methodist commitments, the most interesting way to understand the Anabaptists is to recognize they were rediscovering the congregational practices necessary to sustain the holiness of the church. As Harold Snyder observes in his *Anabaptist History and Theology: An Introduction*, at the heart of the radical reformers' vision was the regenerating activity of the Holy Spirit that made possible the life of discipleship for all Christians. According to Snyder what set the Anabaptists apart from more radical reformers, as well as the magisterial reformers, was an ecclesiology in which believers pledged themselves to be a community of discipline in solidarity with other members of the body of Christ — a solidarity that meant at the very least they could not kill one another.[14]

One of the frustrations in calling attention to the importance of the Anabaptists for how we should understand Christian ethics is that there is no decisive figure or document to which one can appeal as defining what makes the Anabaptists Anabaptist. The temptation is to try to make the Schleitheim Confession of 1527, a confession written by Michael Sattler, who not long after drafting the Confession was executed in Zurich, the normative statement that defines what it means to be an Anabaptist. That Confession certainly deals with practices that have defined Anabaptist life, such as the refusal of infant baptism, the use of the ban, the significance of the unity enacted by the Eucharist, the separation from the world or, better put, a refusal to compromise with what is clearly antithetical to being a disciple of Jesus, the authority of those in positions of leadership, and the disavowal of the sword and of oaths.[15] All of these articles are important as markers of Anabaptist life, but to turn them into a checklist to decide who is and who is not an Anabaptist is not a very Anabaptist thing to do.[16]

14. C. Arnold Snyder, *Anabaptist History and Thought: An Introduction* (Kitchener, ON: Pandora, 1995), p. 95.

15. The Schleitheim Confession was translated by J. C. Wenger and reprinted in *The Mennonite Quarterly Review* 19, no. 4 (October 1945): 247-53.

16. Harold Bender wrote a famous pamphlet in 1943 titled "The Anabaptist Vision" in which he identified the "essence" of Anabaptist theology and life with three emphases:

Walter Klaassen observes in his classic book, *Anabaptism: Neither Catholic nor Protestant,* what is at the heart of Anabaptist ecclesiology is the conviction that truth will be discovered through a communal process in which theology and ethics are not abstracted from one another. He puts what he takes to be the heart of Anabaptist life this way: "Life in community is necessary in order not to lose hold on the truth. That the disciple will remain true is not axiomatic since the world is full of deception. The distress of persecution and the strain under which that puts a Christian becomes a convincing reason for not neglecting the close association with others of like commitment. The danger of being deceived and the reality of persecution make it imperative for one to know what is important and basic."[17]

Klaassen suggests that the Anabaptist concern for the relationship between theology and life can be seen by their understanding of the Lord's Supper. For Anabaptists the Supper was not a meal for individuals but was a corporate act signifying the oneness and unity of the church. To participate in the Eucharist was a pledge to be at peace with one's neighbor and a commitment to the life of the community. That is why Anabaptists insisted that the Lord's Supper should not take place without the practice of binding and loosing required by Matthew 18. The Supper was a feast of reconciled people.[18]

That Klaassen calls attention to the Anabaptist understanding of the Lord's Supper, an account that is no doubt in tension with the presumption that most Anabaptists were followers of Zwingli, serves as evidence for his contention that the Anabaptists are neither Protestant nor Catholic. Rather they represent a recovery of the radical implications of an eschatological Christology in which the church is understood to be an alternative politics to the world. Klaassen defends his account of the significance of the Anabaptist Reformation by quoting Menno Simons's fundamental conviction:

> The Prince of peace is Christ Jesus. His kingdom is the kingdom of peace. His Word is the word of peace. His body is the body of peace;

---

(1) discipleship, (2) the church as a brotherhood, and (3) a new ethic of love and nonresistance. His attempt at finding an "essence" to characterize Anabaptist life was criticized by younger Mennonites such as Yoder as an attempt to make the Mennonite church in America merely another denomination. For my discussion of Bender see my *In Good Company: The Church as Polis* (Notre Dame: University of Notre Dame Press, 1995), pp. 65-78.

17. Walter Klaassen, *Anabaptism: Neither Catholic nor Protestant* (Waterloo, ON: Conrad Grebel Press, 1973), p. 24.

18. Klaassen, *Anabaptism: Neither Catholic nor Protestant,* p. 45.

His children are the seed of peace; and His inheritance and reward are the inheritance and reward of peace. In short with this king and in His kingdom and reign, it is nothing but peace.[19]

Klaassen argues that this understanding of Christ and the church is why Anabaptists are neither Protestant nor Catholic, but in many ways represent the best of both traditions. Though the Anabaptists underwrote the Protestant emphasis on "faith alone" and "scripture alone," they did so without excluding the importance of works. They also insisted that scripture was to be read through "the life and doctrine of Christ and the apostles."[20] Klaassen argues, therefore, that the Anabaptists were closer to the Catholics just to the extent they maintained that the church, a very concrete and visible church, must be the interpreter of scripture.

Though the Anabaptists were obviously critical of the Catholic Church, Klaassen suggests that the very seeds of the revolt the Anabaptist represented were present in Catholicism. That is why Anabaptists, Klaassen argues, can never completely dissociate themselves from Catholicism. He observes that "it is the soil out of which we grew and we have brought with us more from that soil than we remember. We are children of the Catholic church and the sooner we acknowledge it the better for us, for it will help to rid us of our feeling of superiority."[21]

I have called attention to Klaassen's argument because I am obviously in sympathy with the main lines of his position. That position, that is, my general agreement with Klaassen's understanding of the Anabaptist reformation, was ably summed up some years ago by Gerald Schlabach who observed:

Hauerwas has discovered a dirty little secret — Anabaptists who reject historic Christendom may not actually be rejecting the vision of Christendom as a society in which all of life is integrated under the Lordship of Christ. On this reading, Christendom may in fact be a vision of shalom, and our argument with Constantinianism is not over the vision so much as the sinful effort to grasp at its fullness through violence, before its eschatological time. Hauerwas is quite consistent once you see that he does want to create a Christian society (polis, societas) — a

19. Klaassen, *Anabaptism: Neither Catholic nor Protestant*, p. 50.
20. Klaassen, *Anabaptism: Neither Catholic nor Protestant*, pp. 77-79.
21. Klaassen, *Anabaptism: Neither Catholic nor Protestant*, p. 66.

community and way of life shaped fully by Christian convictions. He rejects Constantinianism because "the world" cannot be this society and we only distract ourselves from building a truly Christian society by trying to make our nation into that society, rather than be content with living as a community in exile. So Hauerwas wants Catholics to be more Anabaptist, and Anabaptists to be more Catholic, and Protestants to be both, and the only way he can put this together in terms of his own ecclesial location is to be a "Catholic" Methodist in roughly the way that some Episcopalians are Anglo-Catholic.[22]

Schlabach has got it exactly right. That is what I want.[23] That is what I take to be a constructive way to go on "after the Reformation." Klaassen's understanding of the ecclesial process necessary for living truthfully with one another I take to be the heart of my way of doing Christian ethics. I should like to think that way of doing ethics is neither Catholic nor Protestant, but somehow is both. So as an attempt to make sense of this let me end by trying to suggest why I do not think my use of Barth, who is clearly a Reformation theologian all the way down, and Aquinas, who is not a Reformation theologian in any conceivable way, is not as strange as it may seem.

## On Karl Barth and Thomas Aquinas

As Christians who are living not only "after the Reformation," but, at least if the Anabaptists are right, "after Christendom," we need all the help we can get. In such a situation we should not be surprised that the differences that seemed so defining in the past simply no longer seem that significant.

22. Schlabach's quote can be found in the "Preface" to the second edition of my *After Christendom* (Nashville: Abingdon, 1999), pp. 9-10. Schlabach has developed this perspective in his lovely book *Unlearning Protestantism: Sustaining Christian Community in an Unstable Age* (Grand Rapids: Brazos, 2010).

23. Peter Leithart has located his understanding of what it would mean to be a "Reformational Catholic Church," with which I have deep sympathy. He suggests such a church would mean that "insofar as definitional opposition to Catholicism is constitutive of Protestant identity, to the extent that 'Protestant' entails 'of-another-Church-from-Catholic,' insofar as Protestants, whatever their theology, have acted as if they are members of a different Church from Roman Catholics and Orthodox, Jesus bids Protestantism to come and die." "The Future of Protestantism," *First Things* 245 (August/September 2014): 26. That is an altar call that I believe must shape the future of Protestantism.

At least in America, denominationalism seems clearly to be coming to an end. Few people are Methodist because they think Methodism represents a holiness movement. Some people may, given the oddity of the difference, be Freewill Baptists because they are convinced God's grace does not override a free will, but that seems an odd place to draw a line in the sand to determine what makes a Christian a Christian.

That we find ourselves in such an ambiguous situation is why I think I find it hard to identify as a Protestant ethicist. Of course, everything depends on who you think the "we" is in the preceding sentence. I assume the "we" is not only the Protestant "we," but the "we" of all Christians in the world in which we find ourselves. The help we need, moreover, is not what is so often identified as "ethics," that is, some decision procedure. Rather we need the ability to recover our distinctive way of speaking to God, and about God, and about the difference God makes for how our lives are lived.

We will need all the help we can get for such a project. Yet if we need all the help we can get then I see no reason why Barth and Aquinas, clearly two of the major theologians in the Christian tradition, cannot be used to help form the future of the church in a world Christians no longer control. I think it quite interesting, therefore, that we recently had published *Thomas Aquinas and Karl Barth: An Unofficial Catholic-Protestant Dialogue,* edited by Bruce L. McCormack and Thomas Joseph White, O.P.[24] In his "Introduction" to the book Thomas White, O.P., identifies three topics in which Barth and Thomas can be fruitfully compared: (1) how they approach theology considered as a science of divine revelation; (2) why Christology is the core organizing principle for Barth and Trinitarian monotheism is central for Thomas; and (3) how Thomists and Barthians understand the status of theology in modernity.[25]

White's elaboration of those topics suggests that, given the differences that Barth and Thomas represent, they nonetheless share in common a commitment to show the difference God makes and how that difference is manifest in the life of the church and the lives of Christians. Barth is clearly a modern thinker, but nonetheless he is a tradition-determined theologian who, like Thomas, is rearticulating truths of patristic and medieval thinkers in a post-Reformation, post-Kantian, and post-Hegelian way. In like manner, White suggests Thomas can be read in a more Barthian fashion if he is

---

24. *Thomas Aquinas and Karl Barth: An Unofficial Catholic-Protestant Dialogue,* ed. Bruce L. McCormack and Thomas Joseph White, O.P. (Grand Rapids: Eerdmans, 2013).

25. *Thomas Aquinas and Karl Barth,* p. 6.

rightly seen as a quasi-eclectic thinker who is seeking to widen the scope of theological claims to include all the strands of philosophy in his time. So interpreted, for both Thomas and Barth it is "theology all the way down."[26]

I call attention to White's suggestion of how Barth and Thomas can be read in a complementary fashion without denying their differences because at the very least his analysis, as well as almost every essay in this extraordinary book, suggests that, given where we are as Christians, Barth and Thomas are resources for helping us learn the skills necessary to sustain our speech in a world that thinks what we say is unintelligible.[27] For it turns out that if we are to learn to live as Christians, how we say what we are and articulate what we do and do not do is crucial if our lives are to be witnesses to that which has made us possible. Barth and Thomas, to be sure in quite different ways, can be read as offering us essential exercises in Christian speech.

In his book on Thomas, Denys Turner makes the observation that Thomas, as well as his teacher, Albert, had the virtue of "allowing words to speak for themselves." According to Turner you can only safely let words speak for themselves if it is the words' effect that you want to make count for students or readers rather than the impression you make on either.[28] Turner attributes Thomas's ability to let words speak for themselves to Dominic, who took the business of words so seriously he "could conceive of a community of preachers whose holiness would be won or lost in the

26. *Thomas Aquinas and Karl Barth*, pp. 14-15. I find it quite interesting that Nigel Biggar has identified his way of doing "public ethics" as "Barthian Thomism." See his *Behaving in Public: How to Do Christian Ethics* (Grand Rapids: Eerdmans, 2011), pp. 107-11. The differences between Biggar and myself are a subject for another time, but we clearly have radically different understandings of the task of the church that makes all the difference for the role Barth and Thomas play in our work. That difference is not Biggar's suspicion that, unlike Barth and Aquinas who for quite different reasons used wisdom that comes from non-Christian sources, I have no use for such wisdom. Nor would I disavow what Biggar identifies as his English commitment to learn from "concrete experience," though I am uneasy with the word "experience." No, I think the fundamental differences between us are eschatological. But as I say, that is a subject for another day.

27. There is not a bad essay in this book, but given the subject of this essay I should in particular call attention to John Bowlin's chapter titled "Barth and Aquinas on Election, Relationship, and Requirement," in *Thomas Aquinas and Karl Barth*, pp. 237-61. Bowlin argues that Barth and Thomas share a social theory of obligation, they agree about its basic features, and they use those features to say how divine action creates human obligation (p. 238). Bowlin also provides a stunning account of election as a form of friendship.

28. Denys Turner, *Thomas Aquinas: A Portrait* (New Haven: Yale University Press, 2013), p. 5.

success or failure of their pursuit of the *bon mot*."[29] Accordingly there is an inherent relationship between that community called the church and what is said that cannot be said if the church did not exist as an alternative to the speech of the world.

To so understand the significance of allowing words to speak for themselves is to refuse to force words to do more than they can. Nonviolence is a grammar of truthful speech. That grammar often is in the form of silence, particularly when the speech is directed to or about God. According to Turner, Thomas exemplified the conviction that all theology emerges from silence, just as the millions of words of theology that Thomas wrote do. Those words, the words he wrote, participate in that same silence. The many words Thomas wrote end in silence because "it is through the Son who is the Word that we enter into the silence of the Father, the Godhead itself, which is utterly beyond comprehension. For Thomas, silence is not the absence of speech. It is what the fullness of speech demonstrates — namely that, even at its best, speech falls short."[30]

Theological speech, in particular, falls short. Speech is at once the glory and humbling of theology. It is so because speech must disclose the name of that silence from which the Word comes and returns. Turner reminds us the name of that Word is God. Turner quotes Aquinas, a quote that could have been written by Barth, that "in this life we do not know what God is, even by the grace of faith. And so it is that by grace we are made one with God *quasi ei ignoto,* as to something unknown to us."[31] It turns out, therefore, Thomas, like Barth, thinks we are only able to know we are in need of grace through grace. Accordingly the famous Thomistic phrase "nature is perfected by grace" does not mean that by nature we know what we want, but rather through grace we have revealed to us the depth of our need for grace.[32]

The stress on the importance of speech for Barth and Thomas may seem quite foreign to questions concerning the future of Protestant ethics. Nor is it clear how this emphasis on speech involves the ecclesial developments I associated with the Anabaptist Reformation and the end of Christendom. However, if our ecclesial future is one that cannot use violence to

---

29. Turner, *Thomas Aquinas*, p. 17.

30. Turner, *Thomas Aquinas*, p. 42. For a profound account of church history and theology in terms of silence see Diarmaid MacCulloch, *Silence: A Christian History* (New York: Viking, 2013).

31. Turner, *Thomas Aquinas*, p. 44.

32. Turner, *Thomas Aquinas*, p. 171.

ensure our safety, nothing is more important than for the church to regain confidence in the words we have been given. For it is through learning the words we have been given that we might be a people capable of prayer.

I think it no accident that Barth identified prayer as a crucial practice to sustain the moral life.[33] Prayer reminds us that when everything is said and done this is about God. Barth even suggests that prayer goes "back" to the knowledge of God "as the basic act of human reason. Even as God summons man to pray to Him, He points to the fact that He has created him for Himself and appeals to this determination of his reason,"[34] a claim with which I think Thomas Aquinas could only agree.

I have called attention to what I think are some of the resources in Barth and Thomas to aid the church to negotiate the world "after the Reformation." But there are, of course, other strong theological alternatives. I think it is not accidental that a number of young Protestant theological ethicists have turned to Augustine. In particular I am thinking of Eric Gregory's *Politics and the Order of Love: An Augustinian Ethic of Democratic Citizenship* and Charles Mathewes's *A Theology of Public Life*.[35] Their attempt to use Augustine to develop a more positive approach to liberal political arrangements I regard as quite promising. The question remains, however, whether there will be enough of a church left to produce Christians able to approach their engagement in society in an Augustinian manner. Of course it is finally not a matter of "how many" but "how faithful."

We live "after the Reformation." It remains unclear to me, however, if we know where we are or in what time we are living by that description. "After the Reformation" is a description that assumes our history remains the history of Christianity. That assumption reproduces a Constantinian presumption. But if we are in the final stages of Protestantism it is not clear

33. Karl Barth, *Church Dogmatics* III/4 (Edinburgh: T. & T. Clark, 1961), pp. 87-115.

34. Barth, *Church Dogmatics* III/4, p. 87.

35. Eric Gregory, *Politics and the Order of Love: An Augustinian Ethic of Democratic Citizenship* (Chicago: University of Chicago Press, 2008); and Charles Mathewes, *A Theology of Public Life* (Cambridge: Cambridge University Press, 2007) and *The Republic of Grace: Augustinian Thoughts for Dark Times* (Grand Rapids: Eerdmans, 2010). I do not want to give the impression that Gregory and Mathewes have the same "take" on Augustine or agree about Augustine's importance for how we should think about Christian ethics and political engagements, but they certainly represent a "direction," a direction I would characterize as "What to Do 'After Hauerwas,'" that is shared by many. Gregory focuses our attention on Augustine's understanding of love and Mathewes emphasizes more the virtue of hope, but both draw on Augustine's ambivalence about political engagement to suggest how Christians should regard our political responsibilities.

how we should tell the story of where we have been or what we think the future holds.

Accordingly, I do not think we know what it might mean to be a Protestant ethicist now any more than I did forty years ago. In the meantime, however, I see no reason why we should not make the most of what we have got; that is, given the demise of Christendom we are finally free. It is not the task of the church to ensure a stable world. Our task is to be faithful to the Lord who has taught us to pray, asking that we be united by the Holy Spirit. To learn to pray, to learn the language of prayer, may make it possible for us to speak the truth to one another. If we Christians cannot hold one another accountable for our prideful divisions, this world has little resource for knowing peace.

CHAPTER 4

# How to Be an Agent: Why Character Matters

## Back to the Beginning

*If "God's will" means "God's voluntary action" then it is a synonym for God himself; for what is a person but his voluntary action? Finite persons, indeed, such as we are, are so imperfectly integrated that they have no full possession of themselves and are not wholly in their acts; but such qualifications seem meaningless when transferred to God, and in any case play no part in the religious fact.[1]*

I begin with this quote from the great English philosophical theologian Austin Farrer because Farrer was able to say what Christians should say about action and was capable of acting with a remarkable economy of expression. Farrer's ability to put the matter so succinctly was the hard-won result of having thought about these issues for years. He had previously explored questions surrounding action and agency in his Gifford Lectures, which were delivered in 1957 and published as *The Freedom of the Will*.[2]

Farrer's observation is important first and foremost because he suggests that how God is understood has implications for how we understand ourselves. It is easy to miss the significance of this presumption. It is easy to miss the significance of such a move because the metaphysic associated with discussions of God's existence has not been associated with action as the fundamental metaphysical term. Yet Farrer seems to be following

---

1. Austin Farrer, *Faith and Speculation* (New York: New York University Press, 1967), p. 57.
2. Austin Farrer, *The Freedom of the Will* (New York: Charles Scribner's Sons, 1958).

Aquinas by suggesting that action is the basic metaphysical notion for any account of what it means for God to be God. As David Burrell would later argue — an argument that supports Farrer's account of voluntary action and in particular Aquinas's understanding of God as pure act — a metaphysics of action is at the heart of Aquinas's understanding of God.[3]

I begin with these remarks to signal that I will explore the concept of action for the role the concept can and perhaps must play in Christian theology. By focusing on the formation of Christian character I hope to suggest how the relation of God, the self, and agency can be or, perhaps better, should be understood. This is not a new theme for me. Indeed it has been at the heart of what I have been about for what is now quite literally a lifetime. But by exploring Farrer's observation that we are finite creatures who are not in full possession of ourselves and "not wholly in our acts" I hope to force myself to think thoughts I should have considered more thoroughly than I have in the past. I have been so intent on trying to show that the virtues help us better understand what being Christian entails that I may have not paid sufficient attention to our capacity to deceive others — but most of all ourselves.[4] In particular I want to investigate how even if we are never fully in our acts we nonetheless must be sufficiently who we seem to be in order to discover in what ways we are not who we seem to be. Our agency depends on our being people of character, and character depends on the development of those habits we call the virtues, which are necessary for us to discover that we have not done what we thought we were doing.[5]

---

3. David Burrell, *Aquinas: God and Action* (London: Routledge & Kegan Paul, 1979), pp. 146-75. For an illuminating account of Farrer's reflections on natural theology see Robert MacSwain, *"Solved by Sacrifice": Austin Farrer, Fideism, and the Evidence of Faith* (Leuven: Peeters, 2013). MacSwain's account of the influence of Diogenes Allen on Farrer is not only of great scholarly interest, but is also a contribution to help us better understand the grammar of faith.

4. I should like to think that our penchant for self-deception has, however, never been far from my understanding of the moral life. See, for example, David Burrell's and my chapter, "Self-Deception and Autobiography: Reflections on Speer's *Inside the Third Reich*," in my *Truthfulness and Tragedy: Further Investigations into Christian Ethics* (Notre Dame: University of Notre Dame Press, 1977), pp. 82-100. I have always assumed that our desperate desire to make sense of our lives is at once the source of our goodness and the source of our ability to live the lie.

5. The role of habits for agency is a complex subject that deserves more attention than I have given it in this essay. For a more extended analysis see my chapter, "Habit Matters: The Bodily Character of the Virtues," in my book *Approaching the End: Eschatological Reflections on Church, Politics, and Life* (Grand Rapids: Eerdmans, 2013), pp. 158-75. In this chapter I

In order to set the context for how I am approaching the question of action, I think it will be helpful to give a brief account of my early work. In 1968 I completed my dissertation at Yale University. The dissertation, as dissertations tend to do, bore the "dramatic" title *Moral Character as a Problem for Theological Ethics*. That admittedly mundane title at least indicated that the focus of the dissertation was on how to understand that our lives acquire a history, a character, which reflects as well as enhances our agency.

The focus on character was my attempt to articulate an alternative to the emphasis in ethics on discrete decisions that at the time dominated ethical theory. Joseph Fletcher's *Situation Ethics,* a book in which a rather crude form of act-utilitarianism was defended as the expression of the love ethic of Christianity, was the center of discussions in Christian ethics.[6] I had read Aristotle. There was simply nothing in Fletcher about character and the virtues, nor did he spend any time trying to develop an account of practical reason. Fletcher was not alone in ignoring the significance of the virtues. Broader work in philosophical as well as theological work in ethics devoted little space to exploring the role of the virtues in the moral life.

Any account of the significance of character and the virtues I assumed had to attend to Aristotle's distinction between *techne* and *phronesis,* which, as Joseph Dunne would later argue, is based on Aristotle's prior distinction between making and acting.[7] I took Fletcher to be the exemplification of the kind of technical rationality that Aristotle thought would defeat the kind of agent we must be if we are to acquire the habits that make us virtuous. Aristotle was surely right to argue that any constructive understanding of the virtues would depend on an account of action in which the end and the means are inseparable.[8] There simply seemed no

---

explore what Jennifer Herdt characterizes as the "mystery of habituation," that is, how habits acquired through imitation become habits that make us virtuous.

6. Joseph Fletcher, *Situation Ethics: The New Morality* (Philadelphia: Westminster, 1966).

7. Joseph Dunne, *Back to the Rough Ground: "Phronesis" and "Techne" in Modern Philosophy and in Aristotle* (Notre Dame: University of Notre Dame Press, 1993), p. 244.

8. Aristotle's understanding of the relation of the ends and the means is complex, as he sometimes seems to suggest that the end is simply a given, but his account of the relation of the means to the end suggests that the means to achieve the end will transform how the end is understood. Crucial for me is his claim that we deliberate about what is up to us, which means persons of character will confront challenges that those without character cannot even imagine. Aristotle, *Nicomachean Ethics,* trans. Terence Irwin (Indianapolis: Hackett, 1999), 1112a-1112b. For my more extended discussion of Aristotle see Charles Pinches and

place in Fletcher's account of moral choice for the difference a person's character might make for how what we do and how we do it is crucial for the formation of our ability to be moral agents.[9]

Rather than focusing on individual virtues, I thought I needed to explore how character is best understood.[10] I assumed that character suggested the kind of person we must be to be a person of wise judgment and, therefore, capable of acquiring the virtues. In order to develop an account of character, however, I thought I needed a thicker account of agency if I was to give expression to Aristotle's essential insights. Such an account I mistakenly assumed could be had by drawing on the developing work in philosophy loosely associated with what was called "action theory." I was attracted to action theory because the subsequent account of action seemed to offer a way to avoid the unhappy alternatives of libertarian and determinist accounts of agent causality.[11]

Accordingly I defined character as "the qualification of a person's self-agency through his or her beliefs, intentions, and actions, by which a person acquires a moral history befitting his or her nature as a self-determining being."[12] That I had little sense of what needed to be said to sustain an

---

my *Christians among the Virtues: Theological Conversations with Ancient and Modern Ethics* (Notre Dame: University of Notre Dame Press, 1997), pp. 3-54.

9. Also missing from Fletcher's understanding of the moral life was the role of language. Fletcher seemed to assume that descriptions fell from the sky. Crucial for me was Joseph Kovesi's important but still sadly overlooked book *Moral Notions* (New York: Humanities Press, 1967).

10. The relation of character and the virtues is a fascinating question that depends on one's views about the unity of the virtues. The presumption that to have any virtue requires that you have *all* the virtues clearly cannot be sustained, but exactly because the different virtues are acquired across time does not mean a person of virtue may be understood to "have character." To "have character" at the very least means the person can be trusted to be who he or she seems to be, that is, the person has acquired a moral history that means what he or she does and does not do "makes sense."

11. I find it interesting that at the time Miss Anscombe's article "Thought and Action in Aristotle" was probably more important to me than *Intention* (Oxford: Basil Blackwell, 1957). I find it interesting because if I had attended to *Intention* I might have avoided the mistake of thinking an account of agency could be sustained in terms of what makes an action an action.

12. Stanley Hauerwas, *Character and the Christian Life: A Study in Theological Ethics* (Notre Dame: University of Notre Dame Press, 1994), p. 11. The original quote uses only the masculine pronoun, which I find painful to read. Because it is my prose I assumed I could give myself permission, I could exercise my agency, to change the masculine pronouns here. *Character and the Christian Life* was originally published by Trinity University Press in 1975. The University of Notre Dame edition has the new "Introduction."

account of character and the virtues is evident by the fact that I called my understanding of character a "definition." Even more problematic was my assumption that I could give a defense of "self-agency" on grounds that an account of action qua action was sufficient to sustain the claim that we are "self-determining" beings.

I tried to defend the account of agency I thought I needed to sustain the significance of character by asserting that "to be a person is to be an autonomous center of activity and the source of one's own determinations: all we know, all we will, all we do issues from that very act by which we know what we are."[13] This quote makes clear that I was not clear whether agency was somehow prior to character or whether character is the form our agency takes. I therefore tried to have it both ways by claiming that character entails the presumption that we can act in a manner that determines our lives without the loss of ourselves in those determinations.[14] Only later did I come to realize that character is not the qualification of our agency, but our character constitutes our agency.

That way of putting the matter was made possible by MacIntyre's *After Virtue*. Reading MacIntyre made clear to me the mistake I made in *Character and the Christian Life*. The mistake was to try to defend an account of agency to sustain what it means for us to take ownership of what we do on grounds that first-person avowals of action cannot be described in third-person language. I was, in short, trying to defend action qua action as a logically primitive notion.[15] I knew actions begged for narrative display, but I did not realize that action qua action cannot be made intelligible unless we acknowledge the narrative that renders the action intelligible. MacIntyre's argument, however, in *After Virtue* is that intelligible actions are more basic than the notion of action qua action. It follows, therefore, that an unintelligible action is a failed candidate to be counted as an intelligible action. To lump intelligible and unintelligible

13. Hauerwas, *Character and the Christian Life*, p. 18.
14. Hauerwas, *Character and the Christian Life*, p. 21.
15. For the best critique I know of action theory see Charles R. Pinches, *Theology and Action: After Theory in Christian Ethics* (Grand Rapids: Eerdmans, 2002), pp. 11-33. Pinches argues that action theory in its many variations was bound to fail because the attempt to extract particular actions from the rich narratives that characterize our lives cannot help but result in distortions (p. 27). Pinches also provides an extremely rich account of Aquinas on acts. Unfortunately Aquinas's account of acts is not closely studied, which often results in a failure to understand that Aquinas (as well as Anscombe) well understood that a number of descriptions may be true of an act.

actions under the general classification of action is to invite conceptual confusion.[16]

Once it is acknowledged that the basic concept is not action but intelligible action, the question then becomes: What narratives do actions presuppose? It is only through a narrative that the interrelationship between the intentional, the social, and the historical can be displayed. The agent's intentions, which may or may not be "conscious," locate what has been done or, better, determine what has been done given how the descriptions of the actions have a place in that person's history. The agent's account of how the actions "fit" in the agent's narrative must also be located for the agent's role in the history in which the agent exists; and this makes possible the placing of the action in the social context in which the action took place.[17] Thus MacIntyre's conclusion: "Narrative history of a certain kind turns out to be the basic and essential genre for the characterization of human actions."[18]

Yet it must also be the case that an intelligible action entails a narration that must remain open to re-narration. That surely is an implication of Farrer's suggestion that as finite creatures we are imperfectly integrated, which means we lack full possession of ourselves. If, as Farrer suggests, we are not fully present in our acts, how can we be sure that what we do is actually what we do? But if we are not wholly present in our acts, does that mean our very attempt to give narrative coherence to our lives may be an invitation to self-deception? The question then becomes whether we are ever capable of acting in a manner that makes possible the self-knowledge that seems necessary to be a person of character. The question can be turned around to ask: Given our lack of presence in our actions, how can we develop the character that makes it

16. Alasdair MacIntyre, *After Virtue,* 3rd ed. (Notre Dame: University of Notre Dame Press, 2007), p. 209. I think it quite interesting that in *Minding the Modern: Human Agency, Intellectual Traditions, and Responsible Knowledge* (Notre Dame: University of Notre Dame Press, 2013), Thomas Pfau calls attention to this passage in *After Virtue* in critique of Hume (pp. 297-98). Pfau quite rightly draws attention to the significance of speech for the intelligibility of actions.

17. In his extremely useful account of practical reason Mark Ryan puts the matter this way: "Agency is embedded in the life of a particular community, and practical inferences are licensed within communities of shared goods or reasons. This is the 'politics' component of the three interrelated concepts — agency, practical reason, and politics." Mark Ryan, *The Politics of Practical Reason: Why Theological Ethics Must Change Your Life* (Eugene, OR: Cascade, 2011), p. 99. Ryan's and Pinches's books are complementary.

18. MacIntyre, *After Virtue,* p. 208.

possible for us both to hold ourselves accountable and be held accountable for who we are?

One way to explore these questions is to investigate how what we think we have done can be and even must be redescribed retrospectively. We live our lives prospectively, but it is surely the case that we only come to understand what we have done and who we have become by what we have done retrospectively. Our lives are constituted by ongoing negotiations that are necessary for our ability to locate what story or stories have shaped as well as been shaped by our agency. It is, however, very difficult to even know how to address these issues without attending to something like biographical exemplification.[19]

MacIntyre, however, has relentlessly attempted to expose the fundamental philosophical presuppositions that shape the political and social practices that may constrain our ability to understand who we are now.[20] By directing attention to MacIntyre's diagnosis of the pathologies of our current practices I hope to show how his account helps us understand better why current ways of understanding agency are so limited. I will also try to enrich MacIntyre's account of agency by contrasting his understanding of how a "theoretical" person he identifies as "J" can be held responsible for doing great harm when contrasted with a life such as the life of Dietrich Bonhoeffer. By directing attention to Bonhoeffer, and in

19. Narcissism threatens but I cannot resist calling attention to my memoir, *Hannah's Child* (Grand Rapids: Eerdmans, 2012), and in particular, the "Afterword" to the second edition. There I reflect on how often in the memoir I must confess I begin engagements, such as going to a Divinity School, clearly not knowing what I was doing but becoming what I did by later coming to "own" what I had done. Of course that "owning" was not the same as my original engagement because what I had done was now understood as part of a different narrative.

20. "Who we are now" is a phrase meant as an allusion to Nicholas Boyle's great book, *Who Are We Now? Christian Humanism and the Global Market from Hegel to Heaney* (Notre Dame: University of Notre Dame Press, 1998). Boyle suggests the modern sense of who we are, an account he thinks best articulated by Heidegger, is that our power to make our future is by choosing a tradition and heritage. We create our past in the image of the future. "We have a fate because, like Nietzsche, we are a fate. Out of the contingencies of that 'fate' Existence chooses its particular destiny, the events it willingly shares with 'its collectivity, its people.'" Boyle observes that the flaw in this account is how it ignores how the historicity is a gift from others (p. 223). Later, Boyle contrasts this Heideggerian view, a view he thinks shared by political conservatives and postmodernists, with Christianity. According to Boyle, "the Christian belief that our identity becomes visible to us in an act of historical interpretation, in the words by which a past given to us is related to a future of our own making" (p. 318).

particular his poem "Who Am I?," I hope to show what a life looks like when lived in a manner that would be unintelligible if the God we worship as Christians does not exist.

## MacIntyre's Account of the Case of J

One of MacIntyre's achievements, an achievement I think not appropriately appreciated, is his ability to show how contemporary social realities can be obstacles for any attempt to understand moral concepts and arguments necessary for a recovery of the moral life found in Aristotle and Thomas Aquinas.[21] In an essay titled "Social Structures and Their Threats to Moral Agency," he explores this problem by asking us to imagine "the case of J."[22] MacIntyre says that J as a name could be shorthand for *jemand*, because he chose the letter J to suggest that J could stand for anyone. Or at least J stands for anyone who inhabits space in the world in which we find ourselves.

That world MacIntyre characterizes as constituted by socially approved roles that are so well defined that responsibilities and role-structured behavior can be assumed by anyone occupying these roles to be morally unproblematic. Those who occupy the hierarchy of approved roles must try to meet the expectations of those roles because if they do not they will face disapproval by others for being socially irresponsible. MacIntyre therefore tells us that J is a faithful citizen of such an order, having been formed by the concepts that legitimate such an order through the education he has received. He has been taught that he owed to others the discharge of his duties and responsibilities that were inherent in the roles he assumed throughout his life. J is not philosophically inclined, but if he were, MacIntyre suggests he might recognize that Plato's understanding of justice and Kant's account of duty express his assumption that by doing his duty he is doing what is necessary to be a moral agent (p. 186).

According to MacIntyre, J occupies a number of roles. He is a father, a participant in various sport clubs, a former soldier, and a man whose working career was with the railroads. He was responsible for scheduling

21. See, for example, MacIntyre's essay "Moral Philosophy and Contemporary Social Practice," in his *The Tasks of Philosophy*, vol. 1 (Cambridge: Cambridge University Press, 2006), pp. 104-24.

22. Alasdair MacIntyre, *Ethics and Politics: Selected Essays*, vol. 2 (Cambridge: Cambridge University Press, 2006), pp. 186-204. Page references will appear in the text.

passenger and freight trains as well as making adjustments to schedules when trains break down. Early in his career he was mildly interested in what the trains might carry, but he was instructed by his superiors that he was to take no interest in such matters, so he acquired the habit of disinterest about such matters. That remained the case even when the passengers were Jews on their way to concentration camps. When he was later questioned about his indifference he defended himself by claiming he was only doing his duty. He was innocent of the murder of the Jews because he had no knowledge of what was happening to the Jews, because a person in his position was not to have such knowledge. MacIntyre's primary interest in J is to explore whether J's defense of himself is adequate (p. 187).

MacIntyre thinks for most of us it would be obvious that such a defense is inadequate. We believe that J can be held responsible because he is a moral agent. As such he should have been aware of what was going on, and therefore he should be held responsible for the predictable effects of his actions. MacIntyre notes, however, that such a judgment about J presumes that on occasions one can and should put established standards in question. J's attempt to defend himself by claiming he was only fulfilling his responsibilities made him open to the challenge of why he assumed he had no reason to ask whether the established standards governing his role responsibilities were in fact the best standards (p. 189).

If J is to be held responsible, MacIntyre suggests, J must have been able to understand himself as a moral agent because the condition for such an understanding is that, in fact, you are a moral agent. The question then becomes whether there are forms of societal structures that would prevent you from understanding yourself as a moral agent. Before trying to answer that question MacIntyre explores what is required if we are to understand ourselves as moral agents. He argues that at least two conditions are necessary for such agency: (1) I must understand myself as well as present myself to others as someone with an identity other than the identity associated with the roles I occupy; and (2) I must understand myself not just as an individual but as a rational individual who has confidence in my critical judgments (p. 189).

Such an account of moral agency, MacIntyre argues, requires a particular social setting in which accountability to particular others is in place, some participation in critical enquiry possible, and acknowledgment of the individuality of others and oneself is recognized as conditions necessary for sustaining moral agency. These conditions for moral agency make possible the ability to stand back from our engagements to assess what we may wrongly think we are doing.[23] Another way to put the matter is this: truthfulness is required if we are to be rational agents who desire not to deceive or be deceived (p. 194).

Rational agency cannot stand alone, however, but must be supplemented by the virtues. The virtues needed may vary given different historical challenges, but MacIntyre argues that there is a core notion of the virtues without which no other virtues can be possessed. MacIntyre gives the traditional names of "integrity" and "constancy" to the virtues he argues we cannot live without. At least we cannot live without them if we are to be rational agents. Integrity and constancy are the virtues that set inflexible limits to our adaptability to the roles we may find ourselves occupying (p. 192).

Individuals who possess the virtues of integrity and constancy will not only occupy some determinative set of roles, but they will also know how to think about the goods associated with those roles. In particular they will discover a tension between their understanding of themselves as moral agents and their role obligations. Such a tension is a good, requiring as it must a critical attitude between socially embodied modes of practice and our presumption that we are moral agents. According to MacIntyre the tension between role requirements and the virtues of integrity and constancy will vary from social order and from different times (p. 194).

Having provided an account of rational agency, MacIntyre then asks what implications this understanding of agency should have for how J is to be morally assessed. He concludes that if J was a psychologically normal human being, which MacIntyre assumes he is, he must be held accountable for the murder of the Jews (p. 195). But it must then be asked what J needed if he was to exercise the power of moral agency. In a somewhat surprising formal conclusion, MacIntyre answers that J only needed, through the power of moral agency, to recognize he had the power of moral agency.[24]

---

23. The image of "standing back" from ourselves can be quite misleading because it seems to suggest I have a self somehow "behind" the self that makes me who I am. There is no question that a critical relation to oneself is one of the hallmarks of a person of character, but that critical relation to ourselves cannot be guaranteed by assuming that a formal relation with ourselves is always possible. The critical perspective we must have is finally a function of the basic narrative that constitutes our lives over time.

24. The formal character of MacIntyre's argument is reminiscent of his account of the good life in *After Virtue,* that is, "the good life for man is the life spent in seeking for the good life for man, and the virtues necessary for the seeking are those which will enable us to understand what more and what else the good life for man is" (p. 219).

It is MacIntyre's way to suggest that, though J did not exercise his capacity to understand his moral identity, he was to some degree distinct and independent from his social roles, which means in principle he could have exercised his responsibility (p. 195). To so exercise his responsibility would have required J to have the confidence that his judgments reflect the natural moral law. The knowledge of such a law is that our judgments about the moral character of human beings requires participation in social relationships in which one's reflective judgments emerge from systematic dialogue with others. Without such milieus of relationships the exercise of moral agency will be undermined (p. 196).

Yet MacIntyre fears that the social and political conditions he has identified as crucial to sustaining moral agency are increasingly undermined by the compartmentalization that is so characteristic of modern social orders. For MacIntyre, compartmentalization involves more than the differentiation of roles characteristic of every society. The compartmentalization characteristic of advanced industrial societies is based on the assumption that each sphere of social activity has its own role structure and is governed by its own specific norms, which are independent of other spheres. Social orders so constituted produce divided selves incapable of integrity or constancy. Integrity is impossible because the allegiance to any set of standards is assumed to be temporary. Constancy is problematic because any commitment to an unwavering directedness necessary to be constant is subject to changes of direction because the self must always be ready to adjust to different spheres (p. 200).

MacIntyre argues that selves formed by the modes of compartmentalization characteristic of modern societies can and should be held responsible for their failure to be moral agents because our agency can never be dissolved entirely in the distinctive roles we play. Moreover, when an individual shifts from one role to another the individual as an individual cannot help but appear even if it is to manage that transition from one role to another. In order not to confront the incoherence of their lives, the selves characteristic of compartmentalized social orders must develop habits of mind that enable them not to attend to what they would have to attend to if they would be capable of recognizing their own incoherence (p. 203). Yet even those so constituted have resources in the incoherence of their lives that might make possible a reclaiming of their moral agency.

Yet MacIntyre argues that there remains a profound difference between J and those determined by compartmentalization. The difference is quite simple. J has some awareness of his situation that those who inhabit compartmentalized societies do not. J's proud defense of his attention to duty that was characteristic of his role responsibilities is sufficient to hold him responsible for his failure to act to prevent murder. By contrast, those whose lives reflect the compartmentalization of our social orders are unable to defend their lives in a similar manner. At best they are co-authors of their social and moral worlds, which means they lack any resources that would enable them to comprehend their lives as being capable of taking responsibility for who they are. J, in contrast, chose not to move beyond his role-determined sense of responsibility.

MacIntyre ends his account of J and the effects of a compartmentalized social order by suggesting that a crucial question for those who would be moral agents is, "Ask about your social and cultural order what it needs you and others not to know." MacIntyre argues that lives that reflect the compartmentalized social orders we inhabit cannot acknowledge the power of such a question. In that respect J, in contrast to the compartmentalized souls, has more moral resources by the very fact that he was able to morally refuse knowledge that would make him responsible for refusing to know what he could have known. Even if J did not know what was to happen to the Jews, he is rightly to be held responsible for his role in their destruction. In fact, it is not just J who is guilty but his whole social and cultural order (p. 204).

MacIntyre's argument is subtle. One aspect of the subtle character of the argument is that he never makes explicit the character of the argument. There are no doubt good reasons for that, but for my purposes it is important to name what MacIntyre has done. What he has done is to develop what many would identify as a natural law argument, that is, he is able to judge J responsible on grounds anyone should acknowledge qua human being. Yet the question remains, at least the question remains for me, whether MacIntyre's appeal to rational agency is sufficient to produce people with characters capable of resisting the effects of the compartmentalization he so astutely describes as our fate. Put differently, I worry that the thick narrative he argues is required for sustaining agency is not developed in his account of J.

The virtues he commends, integrity and constancy, are no doubt crucial for sustaining the habits necessary for the flourishing of people of practical reason. But it is also the case that integrity and constancy beg for further specification through narrative exemplification. Such exemplification, moreover, cannot be had without the identification of communities that represent alternative traditions to the social orders determined by the presumption that the moral life is available to anyone without training.

MacIntyre's account of J and those suffering from the habits of compart-mentalized social orders powerfully describes pathologies that make it diffi-cult to sustain the practices necessary to produce people of character. But if it is also true, as Farrer suggests, that we are only "imperfectly integrated," then more must be said about what is required to sustain moral agency.

I noted above MacIntyre's observation that a narrative history of a cer-tain kind is an essential genre for the characterizations of human actions. I am sure he is right about that, but then I wonder if he has done justice to that claim in the manner he presents J. We do not get any idea of the thick narrative that has made J who he is. The conceit MacIntyre uses is not to give J a proper name. He is anyone, but MacIntyre knows his readers will think J is someone. J is Adolf Eichmann. Because he is Adolf Eichmann we assume MacIntyre is right to hold J responsible on the grounds that he is a rational moral agent. MacIntyre never has to mention that Eichmann was a good German. To use that description, that is, "Eichmann was a good Ger-man," MacIntyre would not only have had to show the moral failure of J's refusal to take responsibility for who the trains carried. He would also have had to be more specific about the failure of the culture that produced J.

I would not want these remarks to be taken as a decisive criticism of MacIntyre. I am only able to make them because of what MacIntyre has already given us. But MacIntyre is a philosopher who is determined to avoid theological claims as much as possible. I am, however, a theologian who thinks God has something to do with our being regarded as agents who can be held responsible for our character. In order to explore what such a suggestion might entail I want to contrast MacIntyre's account of J with that of another German — Dietrich Bonhoeffer.

## The Case of Bonhoeffer

The main details of Bonhoeffer's life are well known. His life has been the subject of a number of excellent biographies.[25] The most recent work by Charles Marsh, *Strange Glory: A Life of Dietrich Bonhoeffer*, is particularly important for the story I will tell.[26] One of the great virtues of Marsh's

25. Of course the most important biography remains Eberhard Bethge's *Dietrich Bon-hoeffer: A Biography*, rev. ed. (Minneapolis: Fortress, 1999).

26. Charles Marsh, *Strange Glory: A Life of Dietrich Bonhoeffer* (New York: Alfred A. Knopf, 2014).

biography is his reticence to explain how Bonhoeffer became the Bonhoeffer celebrated as the courageous opponent of Hitler's regime. It is not simply a matter of how to explain how this man from the upper classes of Germany, this man who took great pride in being German, became the man whose life was ended at the personal order of Hitler at Flossenburg Concentration Camp on April 9, 1945. The challenge is how to account for his life as a Christian.

Early in his life Bonhoeffer seems to have had an uncanny sense of himself. He was raised in the high culture of the German upper classes. He was immensely talented and intelligent. He was, for example, quite musical. There were no limits to what he might have done with his life. He could have followed his father into medicine or some other prestigious profession; but much to the surprise of his family, by the age of thirteen he adamantly declared he would become a theologian. His family was conventionally Christian, so his decision to become a theologian may not have seemed completely surprising. What was unusual, however, was his insistence that he desired to be ordained. His commitment to being ordained suggested that he thought being a theologian meant you had to be a serious Christian.

His sense of self was also manifest by his response to his education at the University of Berlin. Berlin was the home of Protestant liberalism. Adolf von Harnack was not only Bonhoeffer's teacher; he was also a friend of the Bonhoeffer family. Though Bonhoeffer admired Harnack, that admiration did not mean he had to agree with Harnack. Accordingly Bonhoeffer saw the significance of Karl Barth's work and closely identified with Barth's theological project. Barth's influence was evident in Bonhoeffer's first dissertation, *Sanctorum Communio,* a book Barth described as a theological miracle because he did not see how such a book could be written at the University of Berlin.

Bonhoeffer came from a well-to-do family. His tastes were the habits of those whose lives do not suffer from financial necessity. He relished good food and travel, and he liked to live comfortably. Yet in his first pastoral appointment to the Lutheran church in Spain he discovered the poor. He not only discovered the poor; he thought the poor could not be ignored because they represented the heart of the gospel. That conviction was manifest during his studies at Union Theological Seminary in New York City, where he felt most at home when worshiping with African Americans.

Bonhoeffer was a proud German Lutheran, but that did not stop him from becoming a pacifist. He was quite critical of the traditional Lutheran division between the orders of creation and redemption. These divisions, which were meant to secure the freedom of the church to preach the gospel, he saw as giving the state too much power. The Sermon on the Mount became central for his account of discipleship, which he developed as an alternative to what he described as "cheap grace" that characterized the practice of Protestant Christianity. From Bonhoeffer's perspective, the costliness of being forgiven had been lost ironically in Protestantism in the name of justification by grace alone.

Bonhoeffer was a worldly person, but he was deeply pious. Nowhere was that more evident than in the work he did to make the illegal seminary at Finkenwalde a reality. Always ready to learn from others, during his pastoral service in England he had seen how priests were formed in the Community of the Resurrection. His profound engagement with scripture, and in particular the Psalms, informed how he went about the formation of those at Finkenwalde who would become pastors in the Confessing Church.

Bonhoeffer was a person who seemed to have the confidence that comes naturally to those born to privilege. Yet he was also a person who had a gift for friendship.[27] He continued to write his former students from Finkenwalde who were serving on the Russian front. His friendship with Eberhard Bethge was one Bethge himself thought unlikely given Bethge's country-boy habits. But that did not deter Bonhoeffer, who claimed Bethge as a friend and included him in the Bonhoeffer family. His friendship with Bishop Bell of the Church of England was a testimony to their common love of God and the church.

Bonhoeffer's sense of self, his unwavering courageous intelligence, is perhaps nowhere more evident than in his early recognition of who Hitler was and in his opposition to the ascendance of Hitler. Bonhoeffer was politically astute, but the astute character of his judgments was shaped by his fundamental theological convictions. He saw the demonic character of the Third Reich early on because he knew that the attack on the Jews was a clear indication that the regime was idolatrous. With great courage in 1933 he delivered a radio address, an address he was not allowed to finish, that identified the threat Hitler represented to Germany. His opposition, of course, finally earned him prison and death.

Bonhoeffer was a German, but it would be hard to imagine anyone

27. For an analysis of Bonhoeffer's poem "The Friend," see my "Friendship and Freedom: Reflections on Bonhoeffer's 'The Friend,'" in my *Working with Words: On Learning to Speak Christian* (Eugene, OR: Cascade, 2011), pp. 270-86.

more unlike MacIntyre's J than Bonhoeffer. Bonhoeffer certainly accepted the duties that came with his roles in life. He was an exemplary pastor and teacher. But, as I hope my brief account of his life makes clear, he had a sense of self and agency that gave his life direction and purpose. If anyone could claim to be a "rational agent" in MacIntyre's sense, surely Bonhoeffer could be such a person. Yet while in prison he wrote a poem titled "Who Am I?," a poem that demands attention before we attribute to him an over-determined sense of agency. The poem reads:

**Who Am I?**
Who am I? They often tell me
I would step from my cell's confinement
Calmly, cheerfully, firmly,
Like a squire from his country house.

Who am I? They often tell me
I would talk to my warders
Freely and friendly and clearly,
As though it were mine to command.

Who am I? They also tell me
I would bear the days of misfortune
Equably, smilingly, proudly,
Like one accustomed to win.

Am I then really all that which other men tell of?
Or am I only what I know of myself,
Restless and longing and sick, like a bird in a cage,
Struggling for breath, as though hands were compressing my throat,
Yearning for colours, for flowers, for neighbourliness,
Trembling with anger at despotism and petty humiliation,

Tossing in expectation of great events,
Powerlessly trembling for friends at an infinite distance,
Weary and empty at praying, at thinking, at making,
Faint, and ready to say farewell to it all?

Who am I? This or the other?
Am I one person today and tomorrow another?

85

Am I both at once? A hypocrite before others,
And before myself a contemptible woebegone weakling?
Or is something within me still like a beaten army,
Fleeing in disorder from victory already achieved?

Who am I? They mock me, these lonely questions of mine.
Whoever I am, thou knowest, O God, I am thine.[28]

Given my account of Bonhoeffer's life, some may find the first three verses of Bonhoeffer's poem more a pose than an expression of who he "really was." Of course he is writing the poem in prison, which might make anyone, even Bonhoeffer, wonder about who they are. I do not think, however, that is what is happening with Bonhoeffer. Rather I think he is giving expression, an expression schooled by his daily reading of the Psalms from which he has learned to recognize that he cannot be sure, in Farrer's language, whether he is wholly in his acts. No doubt Bonhoeffer tried to put on a "brave face" for those who loved him, but it turned out the face he "put on" was who he was. At least we know that to be the case because of the way he went to his death.

In the letter to Bethge that accompanied this poem, Bonhoeffer distanced himself from those who stressed the importance of introspection for discovering "who we really are." He had little use for such inwardness because he thought the creation of an "inner domain," a space hidden from view, to be a strategy to displace God from the world by creating a sphere of the "personal," "the inner," or "the private" where God might still be found.[29] Michael Northcott, however, argues that Bonhoeffer is not critiquing all appeals to "inwardness," but reconfiguring what the "inner" entails by employing liturgical forms such as the lament psalms to exemplify the language of the heart.[30]

Northcott's insight is confirmed by the last line of the poem, which suggests that Bonhoeffer did not think, apart from God, we have the means

---

28. This translation of the poem is by John Bowden. The poem is to be found in *Who Am I? Bonhoeffer's Theology Through His Poetry*, ed. Bernd Wannenwetsch (London: T&T Clark, 2009), p. 13. The poem is accompanied by a fine exegetical article by Michael Northcott, "'Who Am I?': Human Identity and the Spiritual Disciplines in the Witness of Dietrich Bonhoeffer," pp. 11-29. The poem was originally published in Dietrich Bonhoeffer, *Letters and Papers from Prison* (New York: Simon & Schuster, 1997), pp. 347-48.

29. Bonhoeffer, *Letters and Papers from Prison*, p. 344.

30. Northcott, "'Who Am I?'" pp. 16-17.

to know the truth about ourselves. As Northcott observes, Bonhoeffer believed that we only acquire a true narrative of the self through incorporation into the body of Christ. That is why in the poem there is a balance or even a tension between the account of the self as that "which other men tell of" and "what I know of myself." "Any lack of fit between these two is not so much resolved as set in perspective by the concluding recognition 'O God, I am thine.'"[31] That recognition, that is, the recognition that we are God's even more than we are ourselves, comes through spiritual disciplines that make possible an ownership of our lives in such a manner that we are left with nothing to hide from God and even from ourselves. To have nothing to hide is the condition that most nearly makes possible the correspondence between what we do and who we are.

## Where Has This Gotten Us?

Above I stressed MacIntyre's contention that a narrative history is required for an account of human agency. That claim I take to be but an implication of the point that intelligible action is a more basic concept than action. I should like to think what I have done in this essay supports that contention. But if that is right, the problem then becomes what genre best exemplifies or expresses that crucial insight. The contrast between MacIntyre's J and my account of Bonhoeffer was meant to highlight that question, but the challenge remains to create the kind of reflection that not only formally helps us see the intrinsic relation between agents and action but practically helps us to be what we see.

Of course it is not simply a matter of reflection. If our agency is determined by our character and our character names the habits and virtues that make our lives our own, then questions of formation cannot be avoided. MacIntyre's J had been schooled in the habits that were assumed to make a "good German." Bonhoeffer had received some of the same formation, but there was a narrative as well as correlative virtues that made what it meant for Bonhoeffer to be a good German quite different from J. Of course Bonhoeffer's resistance to Hitler might be attributed to his class presumptions, but that kind of reductive account cannot make sense of the narrative arc of his life. If we are to know how to better understand the formation of people of character, I suspect attention to lives like the life of Bonhoeffer is crucial.

31. Northcott, "'Who Am I?'" p. 18.

Of course the story that is Dietrich Bonhoeffer is complex. The story of his life entails the interrelation of the story of Germany, the story of the rise of Hitler, the story of Bonhoeffer's family, and the story of how Dietrich Bonhoeffer found his way through these stories as well as other stories I have not highlighted. Bonhoeffer's "agency" is to be found in how he negotiated these complex narratives that made him Dietrich Bonhoeffer. That "agency" is surely to be found in the narrative that came to him through the church. His life makes no sense if the God we worship in Jesus Christ does not exist. Bonhoeffer was rightly suspicious of his public persona, but that suspicion is a given for Christians who must acknowledge that we are never "wholly in our acts."

Our inability to be wholly in our acts, however, is why we so desperately need to be incorporated into a community of practices that can provide the formation of our agency through a truthful narrative. Our character begins to be formed through what may appear to be insignificant actions that prove to be quite important because through them we become participants in a way of life that only makes sense if the God Christians worship exists. Charlie Pinches observes that Christians are told they must feed the hungry, share the Eucharist, stay faithful in their marriages, comfort the sick, venerate the cross, and seek the truth. Because Christians have the time to engage in such practices they learn how to use the action descriptions that hold this vocabulary of actions in place. It is through such a vocabulary that "Christians fill out their claim of Christ's Lordship and all it entails about the human world."[32]

Augustine begins Book Ten of his *Confessions* with somewhat surprising reflections about whether he now knows himself better for having written the *Confessions*. He observes that many would like to think that they know who he is through the *Confessions*, but he doubts whether they or he himself knows better who he is.[33] Yet Augustine takes comfort in the fact that he knows something of God that he does not know of himself. He knows he is opaque to himself, but if he knows himself through the shining of God's light, God's glory, the darkness of his life will be made as the noonday sun. For finally we only know ourselves as we are known by God.[34] Augustine's claim that we know only as we are known I take to be the last word Christians have to say about our ability to be who God has created us to be.

---

32. Pinches, *Theology and Action*, p. 229.
33. Augustine, *Confessions*, trans. F. J. Sheed (Indianapolis: Hackett, 1993), 10.3.
34. Augustine, *Confessions*, 10.5-6.

We are never fully in our acts, but Christians believe we have been given a way of life that draws us beyond our limits, making us more than we could have ever imagined. Indeed it has been imagined for us. Our character is forged through our conformity to Christ. This account of character subverts accounts of action qua action that presuppose autonomy. For to be Christian is to experience freedom in contingency; it is a freedom given and gained through submission to a Lord who was fully in his action on our behalf, that is, to die willingly on a cross that we might be free from the lies that threaten to consume us.

# CHAPTER 5

# How to Tell Time Theologically

## Time Theologically Considered

Christianity is a faith that roots those who would be Christian in time. But those same Christians are haunted by the knowledge that they cannot escape time. I want to explore this apparent "paradox" in an effort to make what I hope will be some useful observations about how Christians understand and "tell" time. In particular, as the first sentence above suggests, I will challenge the oft-made presumption that Christianity is a technology designed to aid those who are Christians to escape our temporality. If time is but a passage to the eternal, Christians risk turning Christianity into another community identified by adherence to a set of ideas rather than a people who believe that a revelation in history has made them possible.

"Out of all the peoples of the world I have called you, Israel, to be my promised people" is the claim that makes time unavoidable for Christians (Deut. 7:6). We are a faith that depends on the presumption that events have occurred that have changed the world. Accordingly Christians are a people who have staked their lives, quite literally their living and their dying, on their conviction that God has been present to us "in time."

In his now classic book, *Christ and Time: The Primitive Christian Conception of History*, Oscar Cullmann observes that it is "the cosmic extension of the historical line" that makes Christianity so offensive in modernity. Cullmann explains this claim by noting that "all Christian theology in its innermost essence is Biblical history," which means Christians believe that the ordinary processes of history constitute a straight line of time through which God reveals himself as the Lord of history and nature.[1] In short, Christians believe that a story, a story that invites and requires ongoing revision, can be told about all that is and is not. Few phrases are more significant than "In the beginning."

According to Cullmann, the unique character of the Christian conception of time as the scene of redemptive history has a twofold character. In the first place Christians believe that salvation is bound to a continuous time process that has a past, present, and future. Cullmann contrasts this understanding of "history" with the Greek cyclical conception of history in which salvation is always available in the "beyond." Secondly, Christians believe that this redemptive process in time is determined by one historical fact that constitutes the "midpoint" of time. That historical fact has an unrepeatable character, but as such it "marks" all other historical events. That fact is the death and resurrection of Jesus Christ. On that event all history and nature turn.[2]

Nothing is more telling about the significance of the presumption that all time is timed by Christ than the transformation of the Sabbath to be observed on the eighth day. That transformation, however, depended on Israel's observance of the Sabbath. For as Abraham Joshua Heschel has helped us see, the Sabbath is the heart of Israel's faith. According to Heschel the Jewish observance of the Sabbath is Judaism's cathedral, making clear that Judaism is a faith in time through which time is sanctified.[3] Heschel observes that for Israel the events of historic time were more significant than the cycle of nature, even though physical sustenance depended on the latter. That presumption, a presumption shaped by the Sabbath, is at the heart of the Christian conviction that the resurrection of Jesus constitutes a new time.

Yet that conviction that the resurrection of Jesus was a new creation entails the belief that the eternal can be present in time.[4] How can that be? Do not Christians believe that God is before all time yet still present fully in time in the person of Jesus and the work of the Holy Spirit? This has led many Christian theologians to rethink what they mean by "eternity." For

---

1. Oscar Cullmann, *Christ and Time: The Primitive Christian Conception of Time and History,* trans. Floyd Filson (Philadelphia: Westminster, 1949), p. 23.

2. Cullmann, *Christ and Time,* pp. 32-33.

3. Abraham Joshua Heschel, *The Sabbath* (New York: Farrar, Straus & Giroux, 1951), p. 8.

4. Heschel observes that Jewish tradition offers no definition of the concept of eternity, but rather tells how to experience eternity within time. The essence of the world to come is Sabbath, making the seventh day in time an exemplification of eternity (*The Sabbath,* p. 74).

example, John Howard Yoder argues that in biblical thought the eternal is not atemporal. Rather, according to Yoder, the eternal "is not less like time, but more like time. It is like time to a higher degree. If real events are the center of history — certainly the cross was a real event, certainly the resurrection is testified to as in some sense a real event — then the fulfillment and culmination of God's purposes must also be really historic. The God of the Bible is not timeless."[5]

Yoder's position on time and eternity is not unique. No less a theologian than Karl Barth seems to have views very similar to Yoder's understanding of time. Barth asserts that "even the eternal God does not live without time. He is supremely temporal. For His eternity is authentic temporality, and therefore the source of all time. But in His eternity, in the uncreated self-subsistent time which is one of the perfections of His divine nature, present, past, and future, yesterday, to-day, and to-morrow, are not successive, but simultaneous."[6]

This is not a casual remark by Barth. For example, he intensifies the claim that God lives in time by asserting that God's time just is eternity. But eternity is not time without beginning or end, for to so identify eternity, Barth suggests, would be to attribute to it an idealized form of creaturely existence. That would be wrong because to say eternity is to say God, and God is not an idealized form of creaturely existence, that is, our desire to live in a manner that refuses to believe we will ever die. Rather God is the ground and form of his existence, which means in his eternity he is Creator of time in which he himself is beginning, middle, and end. Therefore Barth maintains, like Yoder, that "eternity is not timelessness."[7]

According to Barth, that means the time in which we live as God's creation is "an allotted time." As creatures of time our task is to resist the temptation to make the time in which we live something other than a time we have been given. Since we are human and not God, we must learn to live in created time. Created time has a beginning, a middle, and an end, which means that there are boundaries to the time we have been allotted. To learn to live in the time we have been allotted from Barth's perspective is to learn that we are participants in a storied time that makes our lives more than simply one damn thing after another. We are embedded in his-

---

5. John Howard Yoder, *Preface to Theology: Christology and Theological Method* (Grand Rapids: Brazos, 2002), p. 276.

6. Karl Barth, *Church Dogmatics* III/2 (Edinburgh: T. & T. Clark, 1960), p. 437.

7. Barth, *Church Dogmatics* III/2, p. 558.

tories we have not chosen, but through having our lives storied by God, fate can be transformed into destiny.[8]

Another way to put these matters is to consider the significance of death for making possible the storied character of our lives. Death, it turns out, makes life valuable because if we did not die it would make no difference whether we loved this person rather than that person because our desires would have no limit. For Barth, therefore, death creates an economy that makes me who I am but would not be if I could live as if time had no limit.[9] We are, therefore, haunted by the time that makes the "storied" character of our lives possible because we often experience it as that condition that threatens what we have learned to call "my life."[10]

Christians are haunted by time because one of the forms time takes, particularly in our time, is our consciousness of our own historicity. Such consciousness Cullmann argues is personified in the figure of the modern historian who seeks neutrality toward that which she studies in an effort to tell time "objectively." Cullmann argues, however, that this claim to neutrality is constituted by a philosophical view of history that cannot help but make the claim that all history turns on the cross and resurrection of Christ problematic.[11]

Cullmann's historian is but a professionalized figure that represents the consciousness of "most people" in modernity. I am not referring only to a general distrust modern people have about claims that a human being was resurrected to sit at the right hand of God. Rather I am trying to make articulate the stance born of our sense that as people overwhelmed by the vastness of time we simply cannot fathom how all time can be determined by the crucifixion of an obscure Jewish man in an even more obscure outpost of the Roman Empire. To the extent Christians created a conscious-

---

8. This is the main theme that shapes Samuel Wells's extremely illuminating — illuminating at least for me — account of my work in his book *Transforming Fate into Destiny: The Theological Ethics of Stanley Hauerwas* (Carlisle, UK: Paternoster, 1998). In chapter 7 of his book, titled "From Space to Time" (pp. 141-63), Wells provides a very helpful account of why time is so crucial for my account of the character of the Christian life. Wells is not suggesting that I leave behind all considerations of space, because I obviously think space and time are mutually implicated, but Wells is quite right that I think that space must be "timed."

9. Barth, *Church Dogmatics* III/2, pp. 561-63.

10. The relation between time and narrative is complex. That is my way to say I am unsure how to even begin to understand whether time is metaphysically the condition for the possibility of narrative or whether time can never be known without a narrative. I simply am unsure how to go on to better understand the relation of time and narrative.

11. Cullmann, *Christ and Time*, pp. 21-22.

ness of time that can be storied, they gave birth to the possibility that the story they believe true is just one story among others.

This kind of time consciousness that has formed many in recent times is often identified with those who try to assume a cosmopolitan stance toward those who are different from themselves. Cosmopolitans are people who try to enact generalized humanism in an effort to be committed to the proposition that there is no people at any time or at any place that they cannot or, at least, should not be able to understand. Accordingly they believe it possible to rise above all time in an effort to avoid being limited by any time. They are a timeless people who have been made possible by a time when time no longer has the character of *a* time.

Of course there has been a theological way to try to negotiate this "haunting." Christian theologians have tried to re-present Christianity in philosophical modes that do not commit Christians to the view that the cross and resurrection of Jesus constitute time. The problem with that strategy, which has often been impressively executed, is that it is not clear why you need Jesus at all if Christianity is but the exemplification of ideas that are accessible to anyone without reference to Christ. When the cross is made a "symbol" of the possibility of redemptive suffering, there seems to be no reason, except perhaps as a historical "fact," why you need Jesus at all.

It is not only unclear why you need Jesus given this theological position, but it is equally unclear why you need a church. The church is necessary if Christianity is about a fact of time otherwise not available unless there are a people who have been witnesses to other people who become witnesses in their turn across time. So the church is a correlative of the Christian conviction that, at the appointed time, in Palestine a savior was born. The very existence of a people who are gathered to worship the God they believe to be the Lord of history is an indication that Christianity is a faith that cannot — nor does it desire to — escape time.

From an ecclesial point of view I think it is not accidental that John Howard Yoder and Karl Barth emphasize that the God Christians worship is "timeful." For both Yoder and Barth are the sworn enemies of that form of Constantinian Christianity in which the church, in order to make itself intelligible in advanced social orders, becomes a representative of generally agreed-upon ideals. That is why so much of contemporary Christianity is Gnosticism in disguise.

Charles Taylor has characterized the dominant understanding of time in our time as "empty." Taylor's description of time as empty is in an interesting way quite close to a Gnostic understanding of time. To characterize time as empty, to assume that time is indifferent to whatever is used to fill it, in a complex manner reproduces the Gnostic presumption that the task is to escape time.[12] Yet as I have tried to suggest, the Christian knows there is no escape. Put even more strongly, the Christian has no desire to escape time.

Taylor suggests it is Augustine whose account of time provides the most illuminating alternative to the empty time in which we now live.[13] Therefore I think it well worth our time to attend to Augustine on time, because by doing so we might better understand the claims just made and the political implications I've not yet articulated.

## Augustine on Time

Augustine's extended account of time is in Book Eleven of the *Confessions*.[14] Yet it would be a mistake not to regard the whole of the *Confessions* as a meditation on time. It is always tempting for readers of the *Confessions* to stop reading after Augustine is no longer telling the story of his life. Book Ten on memory and Book Eleven on time for some readers seem unrelated to his telling of God's refusal to let him be, but memory and time are at the heart of the story Augustine has to tell. For that is exactly what he discovers memory and time make possible, that is, a narrative of his life. In Books Ten and Eleven Augustine explores memory and time as crucial for his ability to tell how he has learned to tell time in the light of Christ.[15]

Earlier, in Book Four of the *Confessions,* Augustine reflects on the death of his close friend and observes, "time takes no holiday. It does not roll idly by, but through our senses works its own wonders in the mind. Time came and went from one day to the next; in its coming and its passing it brought me other hopes and other memories, and little by little patched me up again."[16] Augustine's reflections on his developing feelings about the death of his friend indicate early in his development that he began to

---

12. Charles Taylor, *A Secular Age* (Cambridge, MA: Harvard University Press, 2007), p. 58.

13. Taylor, *A Secular Age,* p. 56.

14. Augustine, *Confessions,* trans. F. J. Sheed, Introduction by Peter Brown (Indianapolis: Hackett, 1993), pp. 211-31.

15. Augustine, *Confessions* 10.5 (p. 176).

16. Augustine, *Confessions* 4.8 (p. 57).

understand the essential relation between time and death, as well as how tempting it is for us to use our memories as false comfort.

It is therefore not accidental that in Book Ten Augustine explores what memory entails, because he is aware that the *Confessions* are an exercise in memory. Memory for Augustine is a "huge court" containing sky, earth, and sea, but memory also contains the self he thinks himself to be. For memory "weaves into the past endless new likenesses of things either experienced by me or believed on the strength of things experienced, from these again I can picture actions and events and hopes for the future, and upon them all can meditate as if they were present."[17] That memory is capable of such mediation is a sign of its power; the power makes his narration possible. But it is through that very narration he discovers that the "mind is not large enough to contain itself."[18] How, for example, he asks, is he able to remember what he has forgotten? Moreover, by the very fact that he has remembered what he had forgotten it is no longer "forgetfulness."[19]

Augustine is well aware that his memory, like his life, is filled with scattered and seemingly unrelated images. He doubts, therefore, that he can tell the story of his life unless God makes such a telling possible. The ability to narrate his life is but a microcosm of what it means to tell time. But then he must ask: "But where in my memory do You abide, Lord, where in my memory do You abide?"[20] He answers that God abides in the one alone who is the Mediator between God and men, the man Christ Jesus, who "appeared between sinful mortals and the immortal Just One: for like men He was mortal, like God He was Just. . . . As man, He is Mediator; but as Word, He is not something in between, for He is equal to God, God with God, and together one God."[21]

That "answer" sets the agenda for Augustine's exploration of time in Book Eleven. Here he addresses those who ask: If something can be found in God that is not eternal but is still of God's will, if such a creature should exist from eternity, why then can we not say some creatures exist from eternity? These are the same kind of people, Augustine observes, who ask what God was doing before he made heaven and earth. Augustine is tempted to give the answer that God was preparing Hell to receive people who ask questions about what God was doing before the creation of heaven and

17. Augustine, *Confessions* 10.8 (p. 179).
18. Augustine, *Confessions* 10.8 (p. 180).
19. Augustine, *Confessions* 10.16 (pp. 185-86).
20. Augustine, *Confessions* 10.25 (p. 191).
21. Augustine, *Confessions* 10.43 (pp. 207-8).

earth. Rather than giving that answer, however, he claims he prefers to simply say "I don't know." He prefers that answer to avoid having the one who asks the question winning applause by being given a worthless answer.[22]

Augustine observes, however, that if before heaven and earth were made there was no time, then the question "What were You doing *then*?" makes no sense because "then" suggests temporality.[23] Therefore it cannot be that God was in time before all time, as otherwise God would not be before all time. God cannot be in time and at the same time be the Maker of all time. So God must be before all time, which means there was a time when there was no time. But then Augustine finds he must ask, "What then is time?" His response may well be the most quoted section from the *Confessions:*

> What is this time? If no one asks me, I know, if I want to explain it to a questioner, I do not know. But at any rate this much I dare affirm I know: that if nothing passed there would be no past time; if nothing were approaching there would be no future time; if nothing were, there would be no present time. But the two times, past and future, how can they *be,* since the past is no more and the future is not yet? On the other hand, if the present were always present and never flowed away into the past, it would not be time at all, but eternity. But if the present is only time, because it flows into the past, how can we say it *is?* For it is, only because it will cease to be. Thus we can affirm that time is only in that it tends towards non-being.[24]

Augustine responds to his own worries about time by calling attention to our everyday expressions about time. For example, we speak of long or short times in order to describe the past or the future. Thus a hundred years ago can sound like a long time past, but he asks in what sense can that which no longer exists be short? He concludes, therefore, we must not say that the past was long because it is not in existence. It seems only the present might be considered long for a day, but a day is constituted by twenty-four hours, making the hour just past no longer long. Accordingly there seems not to exist a time that was "long" or "short."[25] Augustine

22. Augustine, *Confessions* 11.12 (p. 218).
23. Augustine, *Confessions* 11.13 (p. 218).
24. Augustine, *Confessions* 11.14 (p. 219).
25. Augustine, *Confessions* 11.15 (pp. 219-21).

acknowledges that while time is passing it can be subject to measure, but once it is passed it cannot because once passed, time is not.

He continues his exploration of the past and future by asking where the past and future may be. For example he calls attention to his boyhood which no longer exists, but the likeness of his boyhood can be recalled in his memory. The same might be true of prophecies of things to come because we consider future actions in advance in the present, but it remains the case that the future action does not exist. The mystery of past and future, our inability to characterize their being, their ontological status, leads Augustine to the judgment that there are few things we know how to characterize well and time only seems to be one of those things in passing.[26] He observes that we speak and hear others speak and we understand one another because our words are plain, but that hides from us the obscurity of the words we use and why their meaning remains to be discovered.

He considers two other possibilities: (1) that time may be determined by the movement of the sun and/or (2) that time is measured by the movement of the body. Yet neither suggestion works because of the variety of the movement of the sun and the body. Augustine, therefore, ends by confessing he does not know what time is but he wonders how he even knows he does not know what time is. If he cannot know what he does not know, how then can he possibly think he knows how to measure time?

He can only conclude he is able to measure time because it is in God that time has being. He says, "What I measure is the impress produced in you by things as they pass and abiding in you when they have passed and it is present. I do not measure the things themselves whose passage produced the impress; it is the impress that I measure when I measure time. Thus either that is what time is, or I am not measuring time at all."[27] He concludes with his prayer:

> Thou, O Lord, my eternal Father, art my only solace; but I am divided up in time, whose order I do not know, and my thoughts and the deepest places of my soul are torn with every kind of tumult until the day when I shall be purified and melted in the fire of Thy love and wholly joined to Thee.[28]

26. Augustine, *Confessions* 11.19-20 (pp. 222-23).
27. Augustine, *Confessions* 11.22 (p. 229).
28. Augustine, *Confessions* 11.28 (p. 230).

Augustine's interrogation of time is the philosophical and theological expression that makes the form of the *Confessions* explicit. The form of the *Confessions* is prayer because Augustine is convinced that what makes possible the narration of his life is the time God has provided. Augustine may finally be unable to provide an account of time qua time, but in the process of that investigation he has made explicit what his *Confessions* show, that is, that his life as well as all that his life entails is storied by the God who is the Creator of time.

The Christians who gave us the New Testament presumed, a presumption almost beyond belief given the insignificance of the early followers of Jesus, that what they had witnessed in Christ made possible an account of time that we now call "history." They called it "providence." Augustine presumes providence is the primary "doctrine" that makes possible Christians' ability to tell time, which clearly means for him that time is not a "thing." Rather time is part of God's creation, making possible the narrative arc of our lives.

Sheldon Wolin observes that Augustine's conception of time was not only one of the most original and significant contributions Christianity made but it was one that had enormous political implications.[29] Wolin explains that extraordinary claim by suggesting that Christianity broke the classical closed circle of cyclic time by conceiving of time as a series of irreversible moments extending along a line of progressive development. Accordingly history was transformed into a drama of deliverance enacted under the shadow of apocalypse.[30]

According to Wolin, Augustine's conception of time with its emphatic distinction between church time and worldly time meant that the classical quest for an ideal polity was now rendered problematic. Eternity is now the province of the City of God, making the church more "political" than Rome itself. Thus Augustine's presumption that the church knows better than Rome how to tell the story of Rome. The church does so because those who make up the church know they have been storied by a gracious God who has made the story of time possible. No small feat.

29. Sheldon Wolin, *Politics and Vision*, expanded edition (Princeton: Princeton University Press, 2004), p. 112.
30. Wolin, *Politics and Vision*, p. 112.

## How Christians Tell Time

Even the most sympathetic reader may be wondering where all this has gotten us. How, if at all, has it helped us locate who we are as well as where we are in time?[31] I cannot, of course, answer that question for anyone, but I do believe that Christians have some response as a people rooted in time. Of course, as should be clear from the above, it is not any time in which Christians exist. Rather Christians believe they exist in the time God enacted in the Son. Accordingly Christians tell time on the basis of that enactment. They may not know what time is but they know it is Advent. Liturgical time turns out to be the fundamental way Christians have learned to tell time.

In his extraordinary book *The Vietnam War and Theologies of Memory,* Jonathan Tran argues that "time *as creation* is meant for worship." He then draws on Yoder's claim that cross and resurrection — not cause and effect — determine the direction of history to suggest that Christians do not believe that history is a closed system determined by an economy of immanence.[32] Rather history is the domain of God's time, which means that as creatures who worship God we are never "boxed in" by history. As Tran memorably states, because Christians have learned to tell time doxologically they are not allowed to do nothing but rather they believe they can do anything.[33] In particular Tran argues that the Eucharistic memory that shapes all Christian worship "makes possible the impossibility of forgiveness and that presages a politics of memory revolutionary in a world fixed on revenge/forgetting."[34]

Tran's book is unrelentingly theological, but that does not make it irrelevant for discussions of time by those who believe, as David Scott suggests in his *Omens of Adversity: Tragedy, Time, Memory, Justice,* that a new time consciousness is emerging everywhere in contemporary theo-

---

31. For the best account of how those questions may be answered, see Nicholas Boyle's *Who Are We Now? Christian Humanism and the Global Market from Hegel to Heaney* (Notre Dame: University of Notre Dame Press, 1998). Boyle provides an extremely important argument that the consumptive economies that shape our sense of time in effect rob us of time (pp. 154-55).

32. Yoder's dramatic claim is in his *The Politics of Jesus: Vicit Agnus Noster* (Grand Rapids: Eerdmans, 1995), p. 232.

33. Jonathan Tran, *The Vietnam War and Theologies of Memory* (Oxford: Wiley-Blackwell, 2010), p. 8.

34. Tran, *The Vietnam War and Theologies of Memory,* p. 208.

ry.[35] Like Taylor he draws on Walter Benjamin to suggest that something has happened to our sense of time just to the extent we are no longer sure how the future makes the past possible. Scott observes that this development has even made Augustine's account of the intractable problems of time intensely interesting again. Augustine has done so because, according to Scott, the once enduring temporalities of past-present-future that animated Marxist historical reason no longer line up in the purposive fashion that once seemed possible: "The old consoling sense of temporal concordance is gone."[36]

Thus Scott's judgment that Benjamin was right to describe our time as one that is out of joint. The time that is out of joint is nowhere better seen than in the disjunction between time and history, that is, the disjunction between our experience of time and the experience of history. Scott explores that disjunction by drawing on Giorgio Agamben's suggestion that "embodied in the conception of history that we moderns have taken for granted, and by which we have ordered our experience of past-present-future, there is an unexamined conception of time."[37]

Scott suggests that Agamben's assertion that an unexamined conception of time shapes our views of history can be thought of as a sense of the present as a "ruined time." Such an understanding of time, Scott argues, has been made central to the current fascination with the effect trauma has on memory. He observes that memory and trauma are at the center of discussions of reparatory justice, but such an understanding of justice carries little weight because the only truth today is that every human being has a right to a perspective on truth. "What now counts is each story of what is true." Since there is now no meta-truth by which to judge the injustices of the past, victims and their persecutors are to seek to be reconciled and thus reconstruct the past as one they can share. He concludes with the judgment that " 'forgiveness' is the name of a moral politics for an age characterized by being stranded in the present."[38]

Although there are differences in their accounts, Scott and Tran are on the same page as they each seek to negotiate a time paralyzed by a historical reality of a past that seemingly cannot be redeemed. How do you have time, how do you know how to go on, when what has been done is

35. David Scott, *Omens of Adversity: Tragedy, Time, Memory, Justice* (Durham, NC: Duke University Press, 2014), p. 1.

36. Scott, *Omens of Adversity*, p. 6.

37. Scott, *Omens of Adversity*, p. 12.

38. Scott, *Omens of Adversity*, p. 14.

so wrong that nothing can be done to put it right? Under such a condition time is brought to a standstill devoid of hope. Yet Tran refuses that refusal. He does so in the name of a time that, contra Scott, is made possible by forgiveness.

That time has been redeemed by the cross, resurrection, and ascension of Jesus Christ means the church can and must gather and celebrate, in what we call "liturgy," so that the Lord can remind us we have been given all the time we need to be reconciled to one another and thus to God. For Christians, therefore, to tell time is made possible by the hope that has been unleashed by the difficult task of learning to love our enemies. And we dare not forget that our most decisive enemy is ourselves.

To be a Christian is to submit to an extended exercise and training necessary to acknowledge we are creatures of time. The acknowledgment that we are timeful beings does not come easy given our proclivity to avoid the reality that we have a beginning and an end. It has been suggested that our acknowledgment that we are creatures who have lives that must be narrated is difficult, requiring as it does the recognition of our death.[39] But as a people who believe that God is fully present in the cross of Christ, the recognition of our deaths in the light of that cross serves to make possible that the time, the narrative, that shapes our lives gives us — in the face of death — a way to go on in which hope overwhelms despair.

---

39. It may be that birth is as significant a reality as our deaths. For an extended reflection on the significance of birth in Wittgenstein and Augustine see James Wetzel, *Parting Knowledge: Essays After Augustine* (Eugene, OR: Cascade, 2013). Wetzel observes, for example, that God's refusal to allow Adam and Eve to return to the Garden suggests God blocks a second fall that would be the undoing of birth. Wetzel comments on this observation, noting that "a birth, like death, is indelible, and in the realm of mixed parentage, where flesh moves with and against spirit, there is never one without the other" (p. 256).

# CHAPTER 6

# The "How" of Theology and the Ministry

## The Way We Live Now: Theology and the Ministry

I confess my first reaction to the theme "The Place of Theology in Ministry" was one of disorientation.[1] What has happened that we now need to ask what role theology may have for those in the ministry? I have always assumed that theology and the ministry were joined at the hip. You cannot have one without the other. Of course everything depends on what you understand theology to be as well as what you think ordination entails for those who bear the title of minister or priest.[2]

My disorientation can be illustrated by a story Methodists tell to suggest their confusions about the relation of theology and the ministry. I like the story very much but I am not prepared to stand behind its veracity. It may in general be true but some of the details may be not quite right. The story goes like this. An elderly Methodist minister was attending what Methodists in America call the Annual Conference. This was a man who

---

1. This was first delivered as a lecture for the summer school in 2014 at Trinity Seminary at the University of Melbourne. As always I found interactions with Australians engaging. I often observe that Australians are very much like Texans. They have not got anything to live "up to," so what you see is what you get.

2. The question of the difference between a minister and priest I simply cannot address in this essay. I assume that what ministers and priests do is on the whole quite similar even though the official understanding of what it means for them to be set apart, or even if they are understood to be set apart, may reflect sharp differences. Those differences I simply do not have the time or space to explore. My general position reflects my free church commitments combined with a Catholic understanding of the priesthood under a bishop. I try to develop as well as defend this strange brew in my book *War and the American Difference: Theological Reflections on Violence and National Identity* (Grand Rapids: Baker, 2011), pp. 135-65.

over many years had faithfully obeyed his bishop. That meant he had been moved to one church after another in the state of New York. He was not a scholar but he was a good minister. This annual conference was embroiled in a theological debate concerning whether a theologian who taught at the seminary at Boston University should be disciplined because he did not believe in original sin. The debate raged on for some time, which tried the patience of our elderly pastor. Finally, unable to listen to one more argument for or against original sin, he rose declaring that he had had it with all this theological hair-splitting. After all, he said, little depends on theological opinions because, as they all know, most of theology is bunk. What they must do, he argued, is forget theology and preach Christ and him crucified.

It is a well-known fact that Methodists are not people with a gift for irony, but this elderly minister seems to represent an extreme example of the absence of irony among Methodists. It simply did not occur to him that to preach Christ and him crucified represented a strong theological claim with profound moral and political implications. His intervention reflected the general presumption among Americans that theology is not all that important for the everyday life of a minister or the people the minister serves. The elderly gentleman's comment may even suggest that theology may be dangerous for those who are in the ministry. Thus the oft-made comment that this or that person who was going into the ministry was quite promising before going to seminary, where the courses she took made the ministerial candidate so confused she could not seek ordination.

I am not sure where to begin if the given task is to convince ministers that the ministry cannot be made intelligible without some theological rationale. I feel somewhat like the Texas football coach whose football team was behind at halftime seventy-two to nothing. The coach walked into the locker room holding a football over his head and said, "Gentlemen, we need to start at the beginning. This is a football." I am not sure we are behind seventy-two to nothing, but it is not clear to me how to even start trying to show the role theology should have for the ministry.

I quite appreciate, however, that the question of the place of theology for the ministry may well reflect the loss of an educated public that seems to have little if any knowledge of the basics of the Christian faith. My Dean, Richard Hays, tells the story of his visit to Western Australia to attend the annual meeting of the Society of Biblical Literature. He found himself on a bus sitting next to a person who asked him why he had come to Australia. He explained he had come for a conference of people who study the New Testament. After a long pause his seatmate asked, "The New

Testament? Does that have anything to do with a religion?" You need to be careful using such examples because they can invite the presumption that in the past Christians and non-Christians were more knowledgeable about what made them Christian than in fact they were. Yet it is also the case that many Christians and non-Christians currently have little idea of what makes Christianity tick.

There was a time, let us call it Christendom, when it was assumed that people, lay or ordained, did not need to know much about Christianity to be a Christian. The priest needed to know how to say mass. The laity, at least the laity of the lower classes, needed to pray, obey, and pay. After the Reformation — as well as the democratic revolution — it was assumed that priest and laity should have some theological sophistication. The result I fear has given us the worst of all possible worlds, that is, a laity who have little understanding of the Christian tradition but believe they get to make Christianity up because what it means to be a Christian is to have a personal relationship with God.

Of course that is oversimplistic, but it is a reminder that the question of the role of theology for the ministry will be a different question — and the answer will be different — in different times and places. If we are living, as I believe we are, in an awkward time between the loss of Christendom and a yet-to-be-determined future, then I think there is no question that those in the ministry will need to be theologically astute. The burden of proof is now on us as Christians, and I take that to be a good thing.

In an awkward time the temptation will be to try to attract people who do not know what the New Testament is by providing a truncated and simplistic account of the gospel. Those who use such strategies will be impatient with theologians who then criticize them for being simplistic. When you are struggling for survival the demand for theological integrity may seem to be a burden rather than an aid and support. In the world in which we find ourselves, a world in which the church has lost the ability to shape the lives of people who identify as Christian, it is hard to be critical of those in the ministry who seek to build their churches around what people think they need rather than what the gospel tells us we should want.

The disposition of those in the ministry to avoid strong theological claims can sometimes even be found to also be true of those who teach in seminaries. I once had a colleague who preached the closing sermon for the graduating seniors at Duke Divinity School. The sermon was organized around this piece of advice: "They do not care what you know. They want to know you care." Though I am a pacifist I wanted to kill her on the spot.

As a faculty we had worked hard to instill in these students a sense of the significance of theology for the work of the ministry, but just as they were graduating they were told the work they had done in seminary was not going to be all that important for the souls they were charged to care for. If what you know no longer matters, the ministry cannot help but be another "helping profession" whose task is to attract people to church because of the appealing personality of the minister and the friendliness of the congregation.

The strategies to attract "the unchurched" through the manipulative practices associated with church-growth advocates I take to be a desperate attempt to "save" Christianity.[3] From my perspective, church-growth strategies are but the gurgles of a dying Christendom. The church-growth strategy to simplify the gospel for persons like the one seated next to my Dean, ironically, is a version of the liberal Protestant theological presumption that the basic language of the faith is a description of our experience rather than being about God. The only difference between Protestant liberals and church-growth strategists is the latter tend to make a fetish of the Bible.[4]

The loss of an educated public for sustaining the work of the church has been long in coming but it is now a clear reality. I am quite aware that the language of "educated public" may sound elitist but that is a description I accept. Any organization that is morally serious will have elites. The work of theology is done by people who have the means to recognize the elites that constitute the church. The elite that is the first authority for Christians is, of course, the saints. Theologians are seldom saints, but their task is to help the church recognize the difficult and often unpleasant people who turn out to be saints. That task requires theologians to be agents of memory

3. I always find the locution "unchurched" hilarious. Implied by its use is that there are people out there who are already Christians, but they just do not come to church. So the task is to have them come to church, but if they do so it will effect no fundamental change in their lives because they are already "good enough." Think of the difference it would make if rather than the description "unchurched" was used they were called neo-pagans. Of course that would be a compliment since the pagans were often so much more interesting than the "unchurched." The "unchurched" continue to enjoy the benefits of the Christian formation of the cultures in the West in which killing was seen as problematic. It is not clear that worked the same way prior to Christianity. The pagan warrior knew he had to kill someone, so the pagan, I think, was more morally serious than the "unchurched."

4. How conservative and liberal theological alternatives may presume very similar methodological commitments I take to be one of the great insights of George Lindbeck. His book *The Nature of Doctrine: Religion and Theology in a Postliberal Age*, 2nd ed. (Louisville: Westminster John Knox, 2009) remains must reading for those in the ministry.

so we do not forget what God has done and continues to do to make us a people of time.

## Why Much of Theology Is No Help

Yet just at the time when the church needed theologians to be "agents of memory and linguistic self-consciousness," theology became a university discipline rather than a church discipline.[5] This mode of theology was given birth in Germany in the eighteenth century when universities were founded to reflect the Enlightenment understanding of knowledge. Those who formed these universities sought to free the university from what they regarded as servitude to the church. Rather than serving the church, the university would now be the agent to develop knowledge in service to the state. In his great book *Protestant Theology and the Making of the Modern German University,* Thomas Albert Howard tells the story of how theology became a university subject first and foremost as a servant to the developing state and only secondarily of use to the church.[6]

The development of theology as a scientific discipline deserving inclusion in the curriculum of the new universities such as the University of Berlin was the great achievement of Schleiermacher. To be sure, Schleiermacher distrusted the state, but according to Howard he enlisted the state "against ecclesiastical influence, as the necessary agent to further what he presumably regarded as the church's own highest interest: the unification of the scientific spirit and religion, which was best accomplished in a university setting."[7] These developments were slower in coming in the

5. "Agents of memory and linguistic self-consciousness" is John Howard Yoder's description of the charismata necessary to sustain the church. Yoder understands agents of memory to have a distinct task that should be distinguished from those charged with being linguistically self-conscious. I have conflated them for purposes of this essay because I assume a theologian will or perhaps even should be both. One way one might think about the difference of these tasks is to identify bishops as agents of memory and theologians as those tasked with being linguistically self-conscious. For Yoder's extremely useful account of these matters see his *The Priestly Kingdom: Social Ethics as Gospel* (Notre Dame: University of Notre Dame Press, 2001), pp. 30-33.

6. Thomas Albert Howard, *Protestant Theology and the Making of the Modern University* (New York: Oxford University Press, 2006), pp. 130-97.

7. Howard, *Protestant Theology and the Making of the Modern University,* p. 188. For a fuller discussion of the relation of theology to the university see my *The State of the University: Academic Knowledges and the Knowledge of God* (Oxford: Blackwell, 2007).

United States and Great Britain, but it was not long before theologians in both countries sought to imitate the way theology was done in Germany.

According to Hans Frei, theologians now sought to show that theology could meet the demands of being an "inquiry into the transcendental principles justifying all systematic method and explanation."[8] If theology could not free itself of its particularistic commitments, at best it would have to be relegated to being a practical discipline to train ministers who were, ironically, in Germany understood to be agents of the state. The effort to show that theology could meet the demands of being a university discipline resulted in theologians focusing on methodological issues concerning the conditions that must be met if you were to do theology. Theology became one prolegomena after another that explained how theology should be done if you ever got around to doing theology.

Given these developments, theologians wrote for and were read primarily by other theologians. They may have said and even believed they were doing theology for the church, but now their primary audience was not people in the ministry. This transformation of theology into a discipline shaped by particular individuals meant theology became identified with the work of a particular person. Those in the ministry who took theology seriously might continue to be Lutheran or Calvinist, but their more important identity was as a Barthian, Bultmannian, Tillichian, and so on. The kind of theology you represented was no longer shaped by your ecclesial tradition but by where you did your Ph.D.

There was another alternative to identifying your theological position with a particular theologian. You could show that you were theologically astute by becoming an advocate of a particular kind of theology. Thus you now could be a process theologian, a liberation theologian, a neo-orthodox theologian, a feminist theologian, an African American theologian, a contextual theologian, a liberal theologian, and the list goes on and on. The development of these distinct ways of doing theology could not help but frustrate ministers who thought they owed it to themselves as well as the people they served to "keep up" with what is going on in theology. To keep up seemed to require that one choose sides in a debate even though it was unclear what is at stake.

Equally debilitating was how these developments in theology could lead those in the ministry who continued to read theology to identify with

8. Hans Frei, *Types of Christian Theology,* ed. George Hunsinger and William Placher (New Haven: Yale University Press, 1992), p. 98.

what seemed to be the latest developments. This meant it was very hard for some ministers, as well as some theologians, to avoid being faddish. Too often, I fear, ministers who tried to stay theologically informed found themselves moving from a theology of the Word, to a theology of hope, to a theology of liberation, and so on. One can hardly blame ministers for finally giving up on reading contemporary theologians.

In truth, given the demands of the ministry, many who occupy that office have found they have little time to read, and when they do read what they read cannot be that intellectually demanding. How can you read a theologian whose work attempts to provide an alternative to Kant when you have never read Kant? And there is so much out there to read. Who can blame the priest or minister, whose time is already in constant demand, for being unwilling to read what is allegedly the new turn in this or that way of doing theology? It would seem better "to preach Christ and him crucified."

Finally, what must be added to this bill of particulars about the relation of modern theology and the church is what I can only describe as the fragmentation of theology into autonomous disciplines. Theology classically understood is fundamentally exegetical, but now the study of the Old and New Testament is assumed to be a historical discipline. The theologian must now wait on the historian to tell her what the Bible might say about this or that. Accordingly, theologians, other than Barth, seldom try to develop their positions using arguments from scripture. In a similar manner church history becomes a discipline that makes difficult the attempt by theologians to use theologians of the past in a constructive manner.

Perhaps even more frustrating for the pastor who desires to responsibly learn from the work of theology is the distinction between theology proper and the more practical disciplines that comprise the offerings of a seminary. For example, even though I am identified as an "ethicist," it simply makes no sense to me why "ethics" is distinguished from theology. The distinction between theology and ethics certainly makes no sense to me if, as I have argued, most of theology is an exercise in practical reason. Perhaps even more problematic is the separation of "pastoral" or "practical" theology from theology proper. I am not denying that there may be some pragmatic reasons to distinguish between theology and practical theology, but if theology is in service to the church, if theology is one of the ways Christian holiness is made a reality, I do not think practical theology can be separated from theology.[9]

9. I am in John Thomson's debt for his book *Living Holiness: Stanley Hauerwas and*

In this respect the Christian East's understanding of the theologian as a person of prayer continues to be a challenge to the dominant forms of theology developed since the Reformation. Of course theologians in the West may pray, but they do not necessarily do theology as a form of prayer. I think we quite literally do not know how that is to be done. I feel sure, however, we have much to learn from the traditions of Eastern Christianity that combine prayer and rigorous analytic and argumentative skills.

## How I Think I Have Tried to Do Theology

I have just described what I take to be some of the problems raised by questions about the place of theology in the ministry in our time. But I am a theologian. I am a theologian, moreover, who has assumed I am beholden to people who go to church as well as those who serve the people who go to church. I have tried to write for both audiences, though I have never liked or approved of the characterization of theology for the laity as "popular." To write in an accessible way is not to write to be popular. To write in a manner that can command attention of a reader is quite simply to know how to write well for a particular set of readers. Christian theologians are particularly fortunate because, unlike other academics who can write only for other academics, we have readers obligated to read what we write. They are called Christians. That theologians write for Christians makes the distinction between academic and popular writing problematic.

It may be true that to write for laity is different from writing for priests and ministers. Priests and ministers have been to seminary, which usually means they have some sense of where some of the bodies in the Christian tradition are buried. Going to seminary is a good thing on the whole, as I assume it is one of our last places the church has to catechize. For it has been my experience that many people who come to seminary may say they are there to prepare for ordination, but in fact they are trying to find out what Christianity is about and whether they want to be a Christian. I do not think this a bad thing because many do discover, in spite of the

---

the Church (London: Epworth Press, 2010) for highlighting the importance of holiness in my work. His book makes my work "pastoral" in a manner I would not be able to do on my own. For an account of holiness that frees it from pietistic misuse see John Webster, Holiness (Grand Rapids: Eerdmans, 2003).

fragmented curriculum they endure, that they do want to be a Christian and even discover they are called by God to the ministry.

Priests and ministers, moreover, spend most of their life in church. After all, they get paid to go to church. That is not meant to be a criticism. I also get paid to do theology. I get paid for what I love to do. Some may find it odd that some of us get paid for being a theologian, but that is the way the world is. At least that is the way I found the world and I see no good reason to seek to change it. At least by being paid, some forms of accountability may be possible.

I have written for Christians (and hopefully for those who are not Christian but "interested"), but most of the Christians for whom I have written are students. Moreover, many of them are people who have gone into the ministry or at least have planned to go into the ministry. Accordingly I have tried to teach them how to see how extraordinary their task as ministers is. That is why I taught the basic course in Christian ethics around the liturgy.[10] I organized the course around the liturgy because I wanted to show students, who would spend their life leading the Christian people in worship, what a radical practice that is. I was also trying to defeat the presumption that you have to choose between the unhappy alternative of being a minister or priest concerned primarily with worship and/or a social activist who strikes out against injustice.

I call attention to those for whom I have tried to write as well as the form that writing has taken to exemplify my conviction that theology is one of the ministries of the church. I think something has gone deeply wrong when it is assumed that the task of the theologian is to find a way to make the language of the faith "meaningful" by translating the language that has allegedly gone dead into a language that will be more accessible to those who do not speak Christian.[11] For I take it one of the challenges before Christians today is to have confidence that our language can and does work. That is why I have stressed that one of the essential tasks of the theologian is to teach speech; it is to teach Christians how to speak Christian.

What I try to do, and I am a theologian who is not ordained, is to help ministers and priests see the radical character of their everyday responsibilities. What could be more important than spending hours every week

---

10. The substance of the course can be found in *The Blackwell Companion to Christian Ethics*, 2nd ed., ed. Stanley Hauerwas and Samuel Wells (Oxford: Wiley-Blackwell, 2011).

11. This is the main argument of my book *Working with Words: On Learning to Speak Christian* (Eugene, OR: Cascade, 2011).

planning the liturgy and preparing the sermon? After all, there are better and worse ways to worship God. There can be reasons given for why it is better to sing this hymn in Advent or Ordinary Time. I should like to think that the way I have done theology might help how ministers or priests order their day. For example, I should hope that, given the way I have done theology, the minister of a congregation would spend a great amount of time reading the Bible. Moreover, one of the minister's tasks is to help the laity understand why they have a stake in their minister's study of the Bible.

I assume that one of the challenges facing those in the ministry is the multiple tasks you must perform. It is all well and good for me to suggest you need to spend time in study, but Ms. Smith has just had a heart attack and you must be with her. Yet at the same time you need to plan and carry out the funeral for a member of the church who has just died. There is also the meeting of the vestry to approve the budget for the coming year. What I take to be crucial about these diverse responsibilities is that you do them in such a manner that you and those you serve can discern the difference it makes that you are a priest. You are not just another social worker or a friend. Rather you come bearing the gift of Christ.

Nothing is more important for the ministry than your ability to see that all you do is centered in "Christ and him crucified." Sam Wells has observed that one of the great challenges before the ministry is to have that center. The fragmentation of the curriculum of most seminaries I fear can result in the same kind of fragmentation for those in the ministry. A minister may draw on Barth's understanding of the Word when writing sermons, even while the same minister's pastoral care is shaped by Tillich. This may seem a small matter, but I suggest to you it has deep implications for your ministry and the church you serve.

This may sound rather boring. Are priests and ministers doing what they are supposed to do by just continuing to do what they are already doing? My short answer is "Yes, if all you are doing only makes sense in the light of the Eucharist." Eucharist makes God present in a way that makes those who drink and eat the body of Christ an alternative to the world. This is slow work, but it is the way God has chosen to save the world. If rightly understood, this work is anything but boring because it cannot help but challenge a world that is organized by speed.[12]

---

12. For an account of what "slow work" looks like see my and Jean Vanier's book, *Living Gently in a Violent World: The Prophetic Witness of Weakness* (Downers Grove: IVP Books, 2008). I also highly recommend Samuel Wells, *God's Companions: Reimagining Christian*

I certainly do not mean to suggest that everything we are doing as Christians is theologically justified. Rather I am suggesting that one of the offices of theology for those in the ministry is to help make articulate the significance of what they do. Ministers should be the most political of animals because, in contrast to much of what passes as politics in our time, those in the ministry cannot help but be about the formation of a people who can know they need one another to survive. To ask those in the ministry to take seriously your political responsibilities may well entail a radical reorientation of what those in the ministry do. That is particularly true if you believe as I do that we are living at the end of Christendom.

## Recovering Our Speech

If there has been a center to my work it is exemplified by the following sentence: "In the shadows of a dying Christendom the challenge is how to recover a strong theological voice without that voice betraying the appropriate fragility of all speech — but particularly speech about God."[13] That sentence is meant to suggest there is a connection between what Iris Murdoch has described as "our having suffered the general loss of concepts" and the end of Christendom.[14] Murdoch's "our" is not specifically meant to include Christians, but we are surely not excluded because we are Christian. I suspect that one of the concepts Murdoch thinks has been lost is "God."

To suffer the general loss of concepts invites the introduction of some of the most complex issues in the philosophy of language and philosophical psychology that nonetheless are crucial for the future of the ministry.[15]

---

*Ethics* (Oxford: Blackwell, 2006). Wells's book says better than I have said what I have tried to say.

13. This is the sentence I made the centerpiece of the paper I wrote in response to the papers written to celebrate my retirement. The title of the paper is "Making Connections: By Way of a Response to Wells, Herdt, and Tran." It is published in *The Difference Christ Makes: Celebrating the Life, Work, and Friendship of Stanley Hauerwas,* ed. Charles M. Collier (Eugene, OR: Cascade, 2015), pp. 77-94.

14. Murdoch's claim is from her essay "Against Dryness," in *Existentialists and Mystics,* ed. Peter Conradi (New York: Penguin, 1999), p. 280. For an analysis of what it means to lose one's concepts see Niklas Forsberg, *Language Lost and Found: On Iris Murdoch and the Limits of Philosophical Discourse* (New York: Bloomsbury, 2013), p. 2.

15. For a good discussion of what it means to lose our concepts see Thomas Pfau, *Minding the Modern: Human Agency, Intellectual Traditions, and Responsible Knowledge* (Notre Dame: University of Notre Dame Press, 2013), pp. 28-72.

For example, the relation between a word and a concept is a question that needs exploration if Christians are to be witnesses to what we believe God has done in Christ.[16] To grasp a concept, say a concept like "human being" or "God," is not simply a matter of knowing how to group things under a concept. Rather, to use Cora Diamond's formulation of the matter, to grasp a concept is to be able to participate in life-with-concepts.[17] When a concept loses its meaning, it means the narrative in which the concept worked is no longer intelligible.

To be sure, as Hans Frei suggests, concepts are verbal skills, but as such these skills do not exist in some "mental storage house apart from the way in which they are acquired. To know the words of a specific language is to know how to use them appropriately or aptly in the specific context of a language."[18] Frei observes that communal Christian self-description demands knowing how to use words like "faith," "hope," and "love" in terms of how they were learned in worship and the formation of Christian identity. If we have lost our concepts, from Frei's perspective it means we have lost our ability to say what we mean.

In his book *Language Lost and Found: On Iris Murdoch and the Limits of Philosophical Discourse*, Niklas Forsberg develops an account of what it means to lose one's concepts that helps us better understand Diamond and Frei. Forsberg suggests that one way to make sense of Murdoch's claim about the loss of concepts is to see that no concepts are completely lost, but they may well be "slumbering," forgotten, or repressed. What Murdoch is trying to suggest, Forsberg argues, is that aspects of the concepts she wants to reawaken are in some sense already in play, but we fail to notice that they are doing some work. Our failure to see the work our concepts are doing is often the result of theoretical positions that hold us captive without our noticing that they do so. According to Forsberg, Murdoch is intent on making "clear to us that we are not in command of our language *now*, and that the fact that these regions of our language are

---

16. In his extremely important book *Theology without Metaphysics: God, Language, and the Spirit of Recognition* (Cambridge: Cambridge University Press, 2011), Kevin Hector provides an exploration of these issues. He quite rightly, I think, argues that the use of certain words does not in itself ensure that a particular object will be identified (p. 177). I am very sympathetic with his understanding of concepts as products of a series of precedents whose normative meaning may change when the trajectory of the concept invites a new use.

17. Cora Diamond, "Losing Your Concepts," *Ethics* 98, no. 2 (January 1988): 266.

18. Frei, *Types of Christian Theology*, p. 92.

lost on us means we have disabled our possibilities of self-reflection and so self-understanding."[19]

Murdoch is quite simply suggesting that our fundamental problem is we do not understand the language we use. In a similar way Richard Fleming argues "it is no easy thing to find ourselves in the complexity of the systematic order of our words, the words we share."[20] Which is but a way to say that we are never free of failing to mean what we say. That is why we rightly have the sentence in our language, "What I really meant to say. . . ." That the words we use are not our words means we in fact often lose control over what we mean when we use them. Writing, which is one of the crucial sources of thought, is the struggle "to try to mean what we say using words not our own. We find our life fated in the language of our ancestors, in the language we inherit from them. . . . Hence to understand what our words mean we must understand what those who use them mean."[21]

That we do not have control of the words we use I think is surely the case if you identify with that tradition of speech called Christianity. Theologians (or priests or ministers) do not get to choose what they are to think about. Better put, theologians do not get to choose the words they use. Because they do not get to choose the words they use they are forced to think hard about why the words they use are the ones that must be used. They must also do the equally hard work of thinking about the order that the words they use must have if the words are to do the work they are meant to do.

To be in the ministry, to be a priest, to be a theologian is to be in the business of word care. Theologians are people set aside to help us locate the conditions that will help us say what needs to be said. I have tried to suggest a recovery of the virtues is one of the conditions for helping us mean what we say. To focus on the virtues, however, requires a corresponding politics that makes the identification of the virtues as well as formation by those virtues possible. One of the reasons Christians have lost our concepts is that we have failed to understand how our speech has been distorted by our assumption that the church is or should be subordinate to liberal/democratic regimes. Accordingly the words we use often cannot do the work they should do because they have been abstracted from the politics

19. Forsberg, *Language Lost and Found,* p. 61.

20. Richard Fleming, *First Word Philosophy: Wittgenstein-Austin-Cavell Writings on Ordinary Language Philosophy* (Lewisburg, PA: Bucknell University Press, 2004), p. 122.

21. Fleming, *First Word Philosophy,* p. 127.

required for them to do the work they were meant to do. Think, for example, how the public/private distinction works to underwrite the presumption that the Christian faith is primarily about our individual subjectivities.

Put differently, Christians have lost our concepts because we have lost the story that is necessary for our concepts to do work. The loss of that story, the story of God's calling Israel and the story of Jesus that was confirmed by the work of the Holy Spirit in the creation of the church, has meant we have not been able to discern upon which stories our concepts depend. It is surely the case that Christians have the most entertaining story possible. It is a narrative about all that is, which should captivate the imagination of any of God's creatures. Yet for a complex set of reasons we have been talked out of the story by the presumption that people are no longer prepared to take the time to listen to a story with a complex but fascinating plot. At least one of the tasks of the theologian is to remind the Christian people that we are a storied people.

The account of the theologian's work I have given can lead to a serious misunderstanding. The theologian may on my account appear to be a perpetual scold or critic. She may seem to be an observer of the church, and her ministry ready to pounce on any sign of unfaithfulness. Given God's good care of God's creation I assume that even a theologian might in some circumstances be a prophetic critic of the church, but that is not our primary task. Rather our task is to join with those who are charged with the responsibility of helping God's people be a witness to the God who would have us say truthfully what we do not know. The relation between the theologian and the ministry is not one of an intellectual to a nonintellectual but rather of people who share a common task because we worship the same God.

I need to make one last point before trying to make all of this more concrete. I have strongly insisted that theology is a practical discipline in service to the church. That does not mean, however, there is not a proper place for the theologian to do work that is not easily accessible to those who, for example, have no background in philosophy. The church sets aside some to read what everyone does not need to read to be a Christian. You do not need to read Plato or Kant to be a Christian. It is not a bad idea for anyone to read Plato and Kant; it just is not necessary if you want to follow Christ. But someone in the church should be charged with the responsibility of reading Plato and Kant. They should read Plato and Kant because Plato and Kant are such serious minds who did not disdain the hard work necessary to discern what is true from what is false.

I fear in recent times many Christians, who often sound quite smart, have assumed what is essentially an anti-intellectual position. Fundamentalists and representatives of various liberation movements often share the presumption that much of the past Christian tradition must be left behind. Thus it is claimed that Augustine need no longer be read because of his views about *x* or *y*. I can only say such a stance is a death wish, particularly given the challenges before Christians in the cultures in which we now find ourselves.

## Trying to Be as Concrete as Possible

I am aware that the discussion of what it means to lose our concepts may seem far too "theoretical" even though I meant my account of concepts to show how the work of a theologian and the work of those in the ministry are complementary. So let me try to be as concrete as possible by addressing a challenge I recently received in the form of a letter. It is a quite supportive letter but it nonetheless goes for the jugular.

Dr. Hauerwas,

I am an Episcopal priest in McKinney, TX, and we met at Sewanee last summer when you came as the keynote speaker for the summer advanced degree program.

When you taught our class, after graciously answering a prepared list of questions, you asked us some questions. You were interested in what we were facing in our congregations, and subsequently what kinds of things we would want you to write about.

I was not prepared to respond at that time, but after six months, I know what I would like you to write about. Your theology is centered on the church the way it should be but isn't yet. You speak of a church that is both real and yet unattained. Since I am a leader of a particular congregation, I am looking for tools and strategies to implement a vision of the church that truly makes the world the world.

From your perspective in the academy, there have probably not been many opportunities to give flesh to your ideas about the church. But what if you wrote or edited a book that highlighted concrete examples of real churches that have in some way embodied your vision, your theology. I would read that book.

When finishing one of your books, a pastor is challenged by such a bold vision for what the church is and should be. But the very next thought is, "What in the hell am I supposed to do with that?" I would love to hear you answer that question.

I am including a book (*The Shaping of Things to Come: Innovation and Mission for the 21st-Century* by Michael Frost and Alan Hirsch) by two church planters who took your ideas and built actual churches. They never use your name, but your theology is obviously the foundation for their ecclesiastical perspective. I have also arrogantly included the paper I wrote comparing this book to your work.

Your work has been a blessing to me as a Christian and a priest. I hope you enjoy your retirement.

In Christ,
The Rev. Michael Hoffman

The book Rev. Hoffman sent by Frost and Hirsch, who happen to be church planters from Australia, argues that we need a revolutionary way to understand the church.[22] They contrast an evolutionary perspective on the church with a revolutionary perspective that they call the "Missional Church." A missional church is one that seeks to create communities in a post-Christian world that are united by common purpose and identity rather than doctrinal, liturgical, and hierarchical distinctions. A missional church will be one that has moved away from the church as an institution and toward a church that is driven by a calling.

They are, therefore, quite critical of what they call a model of the church as "attractional." By attractional churches they mean those churches that usually have as the main focus an evangelical charismatic preacher teamed with programs to reach the unchurched. As an alternative they want the church to be "incarnational." Incarnational churches will be composed of Christians who seek to be an alternative community within the world. Incarnational Christians will be united by the conviction that God has called them to "partner" in the work of the Kingdom. A church so constituted will be a church more agile and flexible than the established churches. You may well find the missional church in shoe shops in San Francisco, surfing communities in New Zealand, and pubs in London. Such churches will not need to meet on Sunday nor will they have a full-time salaried minister. They will engage God on their own terms.

---

22. I am relying on Rev. Hoffman's account of the book, which seems to me after a quick perusal quite accurate. I do so partly because I quite simply find such books painful to read.

In his paper titled "Hauerwas and the Church to Come," Rev. Hoffman acknowledges that while I might agree with Frost and Hirsch about the end of Christendom I probably would not share their view that an incarnational church is one that must contextualize its language, worship, symbols, rituals, and communal life in order to be sensitive to and impactful in a particular cultural context. Rev. Hoffman has certainly got it right that I have little sympathy with Frost and Hirsch's call to contextualize our language and worship, but even more, I would find it hard to agree with anyone who uses a word such as "impactful."

To be sure, I have no reason to resist liturgical developments like the "passing of the grass" that Vincent Donovan describes in his wonderful book *Christianity Rediscovered*.[23] Donovan could be flexible because he had the weight of tradition behind him, making it possible for him to discern how the passing of the grass was a powerful form of reconciliation necessary for the Masai to come to the Eucharist united and in peace with one another. But that seems to me what is lacking in Frost and Hirsch. They sound far too ready to make Christianity up.

Toward the end of his paper Rev. Hoffman calls attention to Dr. Theodora Lucy Hawksley's dissertation written at the University of Durham titled *The Ecclesiology of Stanley Hauerwas: Resident Aliens and the Concrete Church*.[24] Rev. Hoffman reports that Dr. Hawksley finds my ecclesiology compelling but argues that I describe a very idealized church that has little to do with the actual church. According to Hoffman, my church "is theoretical, not concrete." Hoffman observes that reading Hawksley reminded him that I have spent my life in the university talking about the church, so it is not surprising that my ecclesiology does not feel concrete. For example, I claim that the church should produce people who have a problem with war, but that is not actually happening. I believe the church needs to be distinct, but that is not actually happening. I believe the church should be able to produce people of virtue, but Christians are no more virtuous than nonbelievers. So where is my church?

What I think Rev. Hoffman is asking me to provide is examples. I have tried to do that from time to time. See, for example, my story of Broadway Christian Parish in the chapter titled "The Ministry of a Congregation: Rethinking Christian Ethics in a Church-Centered Seminary" in my

---

23. Vincent Donovan, *Christianity Rediscovered* (Maryknoll, NY: Orbis, 1982).

24. Theodora Lucy Hawksley, *The Ecclesiology of Stanley Hauerwas: Resident Aliens and the Concrete Church* (Durham, UK: University of Durham Press, 2007).

book *Christian Existence Today: Essays on Church, World, and Living in Between.*[25] The books I referred to earlier, that is, Thomson's book *Living Holiness: Stanley Hauerwas and the Church* and Wells's *God's Companions*, I think provide the kind of theological ethnography of the kinds of exemplification we need. But that is not what I really have to say or want to say to Rev. Hoffman.

What I really have to say to Rev. Hoffman is, "What are you waiting for?" If you think the Christian people should have a problem with war you need to think about how to preach that. If you think the church needs to be distinct, what does that mean for how you budget? If you think the church needs to offer people more determinative moral formation, what does that mean for youth groups? Rather than despair in the face of the challenges facing the church, those very challenges should instill in us an enthusiasm for what good work God has given us to do at this time.

Recently I gave a sermon for the graduates at the Seminary of the Southwest in Austin, Texas, and Nashotah House in Wisconsin.[26] At the Seminary of the Southwest I told the graduates that, after a lifetime in ministry, when asked why they did it, all they would have to say is that they faithfully went about their priestly duties because "it is true." What we Christians have to say about the world is true. At Nashotah House I directed their attention to what a wonderful thing it is for them to be priests because it has given them something to do. What they have been given to do is not given just for their lives to be busy so they will not have to reckon with the emptiness that so often accompanies those who cannot remain still. No, they have been given meaningful work, that is, to lead the Christian people Sunday after Sunday in the worship of God.

Finally that is what the theologian owes the church. What we owe the church is the reminder that when all is said and done this is about God. If we forget that, then it surely means it is all smoke and mirrors, signifying nothing. But it is not smoke and mirrors because how else can we explain that when all is said and done we exist only to be witnesses to Christ and him crucified and resurrected from the dead? If we have lost our concepts we have done so because we are living lives that make sense even if Jesus was not raised from the dead. But he was raised. It is the happy obligation

25. Stanley Hauerwas, *Christian Existence Today: Essays on Church, World, and Living in Between* (Grand Rapids: Brazos, 2001), pp. 111-32.

26. These sermons can be found in my *Without Apology: Sermons for Christ's Church* (New York: Seabury, 2013), pp. 122-38.

of the theologian to never let us forget that Jesus' resurrection makes all the difference for why we have a church and, consequently, the ministry of those called to serve that church.

# CHAPTER 7

# How to Write a Theological Sentence

## Writing Theology

I want to write about how to write theology. I want to write about how to write theology because I think we have not thought hard enough about why it is hard to write theologically. By "we" I mean those of us self-identified as theologians. Many of us so identified may have written some theology, though I suspect we have often confused writing about theology with writing theology. I have the sense that few of us have thought about the conditions necessary to write a theological sentence that has the potential to make readers stop and rethink what they thought they think.

As the last sentence suggests, I want us to think about what constitutes a theological sentence that both reflects thought and is capable of producing thought. Theological writing is usually done in essays or books, but I hope to show that if we concentrate on sentences we may well learn something we might otherwise miss. Of course, sentences work in relation to other sentences, but by focusing on particularly well-wrought sentences I think we will be able to see how the grammatical form of a sentence is shaped by a politics.

To focus on particular sentences is not my idea. Though I have in the past thought about the importance of well-wrought sentences, it was only by reading Stanley Fish's book *How to Write a Sentence and How to Read One* that I thought it might be interesting to use his account of what makes a good sentence to think about what makes a good *theological* sentence. As we shall see, his account of sentences involves strong theological claims. His book even ends with the climactic sentence, a sentence inspired by a sentence written by Gertrude Stein, that "sentences can save us. Who could ask for anything more?"[1] By suggesting that "sentences can save us" Fish does not mean that a sentence must have theological content if it is to save, but neither does his claim about the salvation offered by sentences exclude those sentences with theological content.

Before I introduce the case Fish makes for the significance of the well-written sentence, I feel the need to make some highly contentious general comments about where we are today when we try to do theology. My comments are designed to suggest that theological writing, and in particular the writing of a significant theological sentence, depends upon and reflects how Christians find themselves in the world. In particular I will argue that a theological sentence that does its proper work does so just to the extent it makes the familiar strange.

Much of modern theology, however, has been the attempt to show that the familiar is just that, i.e., familiar. That project has seemed necessary because of the widespread assumptions in our culture that strong theological convictions bear the burden of proof. One sign of this assumption is confirmed by observing theology is barely credible as an academic discipline in university curriculums. As a result, one way theologians have tried to secure academic credibility is by writing about what theologians past and present may or may not have said about God rather than writing about God.

Of course theologians throughout Christian history have rightly thought it never easy to write about God. But the reservation to write about God among current theologians seems to me to be of a different order than the past emphasis on our inability to know God unless God makes himself known to us. Today we tend to avoid writing about God because we are unsure that the God about whom we might write makes any difference in our lives and, consequently, in the sentences we use to write about our lives. We live lives that would make sense if the God we worship did not exist, so we should not be surprised that our theological writing reflects our lives.

Rather than bemoaning theology's loss of status, I am one of those theologians who think the loss of theological credibility can be quite beneficial for the writing of theology today. Theologians now have nothing to lose, so we can do our work with the freedom that comes to those who have nothing to lose. We can write without apology. At the very least that means we do not have to try to make what we believe acceptable to those

---

1. Stanley Fish, *How to Write a Sentence and How to Read One* (New York: HarperCollins, 2011), p. 160. Hereafter page references will appear in the text.

who have decided that what we believe cannot be true. I should like to think how we write as theologians would reflect our confidence in the One who makes that writing possible. That is one of the reasons, moreover, that the scriptures remain paradigmatic for how we are to write. Where, after all, could one find more great sentences than in the scriptures?

That said, I often think how strange what I say about what we are about as Christians must sound to my colleagues in the university, as well as non-Christian friends. For example, I recently criticized a church leader for responding to a question about how Christians understand the status of other religious traditions for saying the following sentence: "We believe that Jesus is our way to God, but we believe that there are other ways to God." I observed that it never seems to have occurred to the speaker that Jesus is our way to God only because, as Augustine maintained, he took on our humanity without abandoning his godhead. He therefore became our path to God by being our Mediator. Augustine maintains:

> There is hope to attain a journey's end when there is a path which stretches between the traveler and his goal. But if there is no path, or if a man does not know which way to go, there is little use in knowing the destination. As it is, there is one road, and one only, well secured against all possibility of going astray; and this road is provided by one who is himself both God and man. As God, he is the goal; as man, he is the way.[2]

The response by the religious leader who assumes that Jesus is just one way to God is, of course, one that is required by the grammatical regimes of a liberal culture that demands tolerance.[3] I hope this example helps us see that our ability to form well-wrought theological sentences depends on a particular (and peculiar) politics. The ability to write well theologically relies on a church to exist that makes such writing possible. Thus my often-made claim that *the first task of the church is not to make the world more just but to make the world the world* turns out to have implications for how theology is written. Yet that perspective may underwrite the general presumption that theology is a discipline that cannot meet the intellectual demands necessary to be included in the disciplines of the university.

2. Augustine, *The City of God,* trans. Henry Bettenson (New York: Penguin, 1972), 11.2. I am indebted to David Aers for reminding me of this passage.

3. Stanley Hauerwas, *Working with Words: On Learning to Speak Christian* (Eugene, OR: Cascade, 2011), pp. 88-89.

Of course one can always say that theology is, like many subjects in the university, a very specialized subject requiring many years of training for anyone even to begin to understand what might lead someone to think it important to say a sentence such as "Jesus is the Son of God." Just as one must learn the language of physics, so must one learn the language that is intrinsic to the discipline of theology. I have some sympathy with such a response, but I think when everything is said and done such attempts to make theology invulnerable to criticism do not do justice to the theological task. They do not do so because theology does not have a specialized subject matter.

The problematic status of theology reflects the decline of Christian practice in advanced societies and the accompanying unease that is now a characteristic of those who continue to count themselves Christian. I should say it is an unease seldom made articulate, and if made articulate it usually invites a quick denial. Nonetheless, I suspect many who count themselves Christian are not at all sure we would be Christian without the effects identified as "Christianity." In other words, we worry that what attracts us to identify as Christians is not God, but the world that Christianity made. That world may be waning, but it is nonetheless sufficiently intact to still be appealing to many.

The worry I am trying to identify is close to Kierkegaard's question concerning how it is possible to be a Christian in Christendom, but it is not quite the same.[4] He took as his task to challenge the complacency of Christians who assumed that being Christian was not that different from being a Dane. The unease I am identifying is not that kind of complacency but rather is closer to a sense of bad faith just to the extent that we are less confident than Kierkegaard's Danes that even if we identify ourselves as Christians we can trust that identification.

One very attractive strategy in response to our lack of confidence and trust in our declarations to be Christians is to "get to the essentials." For example, if we can convince ourselves or others that what is really impor-

---

4. Kierkegaard's attack on Christendom is a theme in many of his works, but for a concentrated statement see his *The Point of View for My Work as an Author: A Report to History*, trans. Walter Lowrie (New York: Harper Torchbooks, 1962), pp. 22-31. C. Stephen Evans says that Kierkegaard's fundamental message is that the church must beware of the seductive power of "Christendom." "The Church must always recognize that to be a Christian is to be in tension with 'the world,' and that a genuine commitment is required to become a Christian." *Kierkegaard on Faith and the Self: Collected Essays* (Waco, TX: Baylor University Press, 2006), p. 329.

tant is to believe that God exists then we can make up our mind about the "other stuff." If you believe in God, then whether or not God called Israel to be the promised people can remain up for grabs. Many theologians have legitimated this strategy by suggesting that Christianity has an unchanging core of beliefs and behaviors that are essential, but you get to make up your mind about the other stuff. Stuff like whether Jesus was raised from the dead or Mary was impregnated by the Holy Spirit.

The "core" is often thought to be a set of moral commitments concerning justice and love. That is why modern theology has been determined by a concern for ethics, because ethics is thought to be what Christianity is all about. This is a particularly besetting temptation for those like me who represent a field called "Christian ethics." Too often I fear "Christian ethics" is simply the name for a way of doing Christian theology without taking theology all that seriously.

I think the attempt to reduce Christianity to "the essentials" results in expressions of the faith, a kind of writing, that cannot help but underwrite the sentimentalities of our culture. Thus the widespread presumption expressed in inelegant sentences such as "God is love" or "I believe that Jesus is Lord, but that is just my personal opinion." Such sentences could only be produced when the simple complexity of the narrative that makes us Christians has been left behind. What we need to say theologically is that the truth is in the details and it is the details that produce sentences that matter.[5]

I am not suggesting that there is a strict causal relation between the accommodated character of recent Christianity and the absence of strongly written sentences in theology. I do think, however, that strong writing in theology, and I suspect with writing in general, is more likely when those who do the writing are "edgy." By "edgy" I mean they discover they cannot reproduce the grammar that sustains and legitimates the assumptions that the way things are is the way they should or must be.

I am not suggesting that the kind of strong writing I am advocating is not possible by those who find that for good or ill we are "stuck" in the most accommodated forms of Christianity. That is obviously not the case, as we have clear examples of wonderfully wrought sentences by theolo-

5. Some may retort that "God is love" is in scripture. Indeed it can be found in 1 John 4. But how this phrase operates within the context of the sentence and passage does not justify its use in our time to underwrite shallow sentimentality and liberal accounts of tolerance. In the context of 1 John 4 this phrase is part of a dependent clause. In order to understand it properly one must maintain its dependence.

gians and writers who represent what is usually identified as "mainstream Christianity." But it is hard to repress people who refuse to accept that the way things are is the way that things have to be.

Robert Jenson, for example, has written a sentence I think is exemplary for what a theological sentence should be. He begins the section titled "The Triune Identity" in volume 1 of his *Systematic Theology* with this remarkable sentence: "God is whoever raised Jesus from the dead, having before raised Israel from Egypt."[6] I will say why I think this sentence to be exemplary below, but before doing so I now need to introduce Stanley Fish's account of what makes a good sentence in his book *How to Write a Sentence.* Fish writes in order to help readers write good sentences by attending to the craft of sentence construction. For that reason alone the book is well worth attention. But it turns out, as Fish acknowledges, *How to Write a Sentence* is a book that entails theological suggestions that I will draw out in order to show why I take a sentence like Jensen's to be exemplary.

## Stanley Fish on How to Write a Sentence

Stanley Fish loves sentences. In particular he loves sentences like this one from the novel *Enderby Outside,* by Anthony Burgess: "And the words slide into the slots ordained by syntax, and glitter as with atmospheric dust with these impurities which we call meaning" (p. 2). Commenting on this sentence, Fish observes that words are just discrete items but Burgess rightly describes them as "ordained." That he does so makes clear that a sentence is constituted by what Fish calls an inexorable logic of syntax, a ligature of relationships that makes a statement about the world that we can contemplate, admire, or reject.

So understood, good sentences are not restricted to literary works but, according to Fish, can be found everywhere. For example Fish calls attention to a wonderful sentence in the movie, a movie that is also one of my favorites, *The Magnificent Seven* (1960). In that movie, upon being asked why he plunders peasants, the leader of a bandit gang responds, "If God didn't want them sheared, he would not have made them sheep" (pp. 4-5). Fish observes that this sentence has the form of proverbial wisdom in

---

6. Robert Jenson, *Systematic Theology,* vol. 1: *The Triune God* (New York: Oxford University Press, 1997), p. 63. Hereafter page references will appear in the text.

which the parallelism of the clauses, "didn't want" and "would not have," provides a sense of inevitability.

Fish argues that the pleasure derived from such sentences has little to do with their content. We delight in the structure of such sentences because they provide lessons and practices that organize the world into manageable units that can be inhabited and manipulated (p. 7). Fish argues that writing well can be learned by analyzing and imitating how good sentences do their work, thus the formula: "Sentence craft equals sentence comprehension equals sentence appreciation" (p. 11).

According to Fish, a sentence is an organization of items in the world as well as a structure of logical relationships (p. 16). Sentences are the form language takes to organize the world into manageable units that can be inhabited. What we know of the world comes through words. When we write a sentence a world is created that is *not* the world, but "the world as it appears within a dimension of assessment." Therefore when Fish uses the word "organization" he means it in the strong sense that "the skill to produce a sentence — the skill of linking events, actions, and objects in a strict logic — is also the skill of creating a world" (pp. 29-40).

Influenced by J. L. Austin (and Wittgenstein although he is not mentioned), Fish argues that language is not a handmaid to perception. Language is perception giving shape to what otherwise would be dead or unnoticed.[7] Any idea that we can distance ourselves from language is false. We can only use it in one way or another. It is, therefore, incumbent on those who would write to know the repertoire available that makes possible what we can and cannot do with the language that inhabits us.

Fish has little use for the attempt to classify sentences by textbook divisions such as parts of speech, kinds of clauses, or by identifying grammatical errors. Instead he insists that sentences are best understood as "logical forms that link actor, action, and the object of action in a way that makes available simple and complicated predications" (p. 134). He even argues in the early chapters of his book, an argument he will later disavow, that if you want to learn to write a good sentence it is better to

7. In an earlier work — I no longer remember which one — I seem to remember that Fish uses the response of an umpire to a batter questioning the umpire's call, saying, "Son, it ain't nothin' until I call it." Epistemological issues are obviously in play by the use of such examples. Fish, I think, wisely does not try to address them in this book. I suspect he does not think the idealism/realism alternative to be that helpful just to the extent that the alternative too often presumes the world is one thing and language another thing.

pay no attention to content and attend to the structure of logical relations that can be catalogued.

He thinks it useful to distinguish between styles of sentences even though there can be no end to such classifications. He identifies three, however, which he thinks serve well as examples: the subordinating style, the additive style, and the satiric. The subordinating style ranks orders, puts things in sequences, and in general gives us the sense of control over the world in which everything is in its proper place. Jane Austen's sentence from *Pride and Prejudice* is exemplary of the subordinating style: "It is a truth universally acknowledged, that a single man in possession of a good fortune must be in want of a wife" (p. 46).

By contrast the additive style gives the impression of haphazard speech in which words tumble out of the mouth with no intent that everything can be put just so. Fish names Gertrude Stein and Ernest Hemingway as masters of this style in which the author is self-effaced. A primary example is this sentence from *A Farewell to Arms:* "In the bed of the river there were pebbles and boulders, dry and white in the sun, and the water was clear and swiftly moving and blue in the channels" (p. 73). In particular, Fish calls attention to the lack of relationship between the pebbles and boulders and the water, which suggests how the very form of the sentence mirrors its content (p. 74).

The satiric style cannot be characterized without attending to the content of the sentence, which means satire is a thematic rather than a formal designation. Fish draws on J. L. Austin's *How to Do Things with Words* to illustrate what satire entails. Austin asks his readers not to be impatient with the slow development of his argument by observing: "And we must at all costs avoid over-simplifications, which one might be tempted to call the occupational disease of philosophers if it were not their occupation" (p. 90). Fish notes that Austin's style is flat but serious with the spotlight on philosophers until we realize with the use of "occupation" Austin signals that his generalization about philosophers means he is probably oversimplifying about philosophers. The joke, however, is on us just to the extent we enjoyed the generalization about philosophers (p. 91).

Fish also has chapters on first and last sentences that are filled with his analysis of wonderful examples. I suspect that the argument for the significance of sentences depends on the examples he marshals. Such a judgment is confirmed, I think, by the last chapter of the book, tellingly titled "Sentences That Are about Themselves (Aren't They All)." He begins the chapter by confessing that as he drew close to completing his book he became aware that the book stages a dramatic contest between what he calls the instrumental view of language — that is, language as a disposable vehicle of the subject it serves — and a view of language as a formal system that refuses to efface itself before the demands of content (p. 135). In the final chapter he brings these two views of language together by calling attention to sentences whose content is their form.

I think it is quite interesting that in order to show how a sentence at once says what is true but distances itself from its content his examples become explicitly theological. They do so because, as he observes, the idea that truth is at once plainly accessible and wholly hidden is central to religious thought (p. 141). For example he calls attention to a sentence from John Donne's *Devotion* that reads:

> My God, my God, thou art a direct God, may I not say a literal God, a God that wouldst be understood literally and according to the plain sense of all thou sayest, but thou art also (Lord, I intend it to thy glory, and let no profane misinterpreter abuse it to thy diminution), thou art a figurative, a metaphysical God too, a God in whose words there is such a height of figures, such voyages, such peregrinations to fetch remote and precious metaphors, such extensions, such spreadings, such curtains of allegories, such third heavens of hyperboles, so harmonious elocutions, so retired and so reserved expressions, so commanding persuasions, so persuading commandments, such sinews even in milk, and such things in thy words, as all profane authors seem of the seed of the serpent that creeps, thou are the dove that flies. (p. 142)

Fish observes this is a sentence about itself or, better put, it is a sentence about its inability to characterize its addressee. This leads Fish to make explicit a theological point that has been implicit from the beginning, that is, only God means what he says so that what he says can be taken literally. God's "literalism," the fact that God's intentions need no bridge to be actualized, means God's speech — God's sentences — need no translation. In contrast we mortals live at a distance from one another as well as ourselves and that is why we have to write sentences. Fish argues that is why Donne does not end his sentence with a proclamation of God's "plain sense," but rather uses mortal language to suggest truths it cannot express (p. 143).

Fish notes that the power of language to gesture toward a reality its forms cannot present is not limited to sentences about God but is also a characteristic of those who "profess the religion of art" (p. 145).[8] In particular Fish calls attention to the work of Ford Madox Ford, who begins his novel, *The Good Soldier,* with the famous first line: "This is the saddest story I have ever heard." The irony of that sentence is that Ford's narrator, John Dowell, proves to be incapable of understanding the story he tells. Dowell, however, becomes everyman just to the extent, and here Fish appeals to Anthony Powell's *A Dance to the Music of Time,* that time makes sentences at once possible, necessary, and incomplete.

For it is true that only mortal beings write and need to write sentences. We do so because we are mortal beings for whom death is a gift, a "gift of design and choice, of gain and loss, of hope and desperation, of failure and redemption, all modes of being that are available only to creatures who, like sentences (and novels) have a beginning, a middle, and an end. It is the inevitability of death that provides life with a narrative arc" (p. 154). Sentences are our way of making sense of our lives as creatures who can only grasp eternity by negative inference, that is, by imagining in time the negation of time (pp. 154-55).

Fish concludes his reflections on the temporality of sentences and the eternity that would make them superfluous by calling attention to Bunyan's description in *Pilgrim's Progress* of Christian's response to being told he must flee from the wrath to come: "Now he had not run far from his own door, but his wife and children perceiving it, began crying after him to return, but the man put his fingers in his ears, and ran on, crying, Life! Life! Eternal life" (p. 156). Fish notes this sentence names the reward it cannot bestow, making us recognize the price we mortal sentence makers are asked to pay as time-bound death-determined creatures.

In a brief "Epilogue" Fish expresses the hope that the discussion he has initiated with *How to Write a Sentence* will be continued. At the very least he is well aware that others will have sentences to celebrate other than those to which he has called attention. To appreciate sentences and to craft sentences is not, according to Fish, a trivial pursuit. It is through the exploration of our linguistic resources that our lives are made. Recalling Gertrude Stein's remark that nothing is more exciting than diagramming sentences, Fish comments:

8. Fish's use of the phrase "the religion of art" suggests a view very similar to Charles Taylor's account of the role of art as "the locus of a manifestation which brings us into the presence of something which is otherwise inaccessible." *Sources of the Self: The Making of Modern Identity* (Cambridge, MA: Harvard University Press, 1989), p. 419.

The reason diagramming sentences is completing is because the completing is being performed by the sentences themselves; they do it; all we have to do is attend. And if we attend faithfully, surrendering to the unfolding logic of predication, not only the completing, but the excitement of its having been done, will be ours by proxy. The reward for the effacing of ourselves before the altar of sentences will be that "incidentally" (what a great word) — without looking for it — we will possess a better self than the self we would have possessed had we not put ourselves in service. Sentences can save us. Who could ask for anything more? (p. 160)

## Writing Theology

*How to Write a Sentence* is not a book with theological implications. It is a theological book. Fish does not call attention to the theological character of the book, but he is well aware of the theological commitments constitutive of the book's argument. For example, in an interview about the book he returns to Stein's remark about the "everlasting feeling" she gets from diagramming a sentence. He does so to call attention to Stein's view that if you start thinking about language in a self-regarding way you will not get anywhere because your ego, your ambitions, your projects will get in the way. But if you submit, an interesting word for Fish to use, by reading and rereading a great sentence a better self is more likely to emerge.

Commenting on Stein's views, Fish observes that she is making an explicit religious argument. It is so because the submission of a small self to a larger power so that the small self gives up its own providence is the message of many religions but in particular Christianity. Fish concludes that "sentences can send us in direction of something greater than they and therefore greater than us so sentences in a way perform their best office when they turn us in the direction of life, life, eternal life."[9]

In *Three Rival Versions of Moral Enquiry: Encyclopaedia, Genealogy, and Tradition,* Alasdair MacIntyre calls attention to Nietzsche's remark, "I fear we are not getting rid of God because we still believe in grammar."[10]

9. "The Fate of Ideas in the Modern Age: A Conversation with Stanley Fish," *Thinking in Public*, January 10, 2011.

10. Alasdair MacIntyre, *Three Rival Versions of Moral Enquiry: Encyclopaedia, Genealogy, and Tradition* (Notre Dame: University of Notre Dame Press, 1990), p. 67.

MacIntyre calls attention to Nietzsche's comment to suggest that Nietzsche saw clearly what the critics of Christianity associated with the ninth edition of the *Encyclopaedia Britannica* did not see, that is, that their conception of rationality and language was itself theological. *How to Write a Sentence* can be read as an extended commentary on MacIntyre's observation about Nietzsche's remark. In a similar fashion Fish's argument concerning the logical form of a sentence can be seen as an elaboration of Wittgenstein's remark in the *Philosophical Investigations* that "[g]rammar tells what kind of object anything is. (Theology as grammar.)"[11]

I have no idea if Wittgenstein was responding to Nietzsche. I suspect he was not. I only call attention to their remarks to suggest the significance of Fish's understanding of the significance of sentences. Of course it is by no means clear that the God of which we cannot be rid because of our belief in grammar is the Christian God. Nor is it clear that the "effacing of the self" Fish celebrates as one result of surrendering to the logic of sentences can or should be thought to be equivalent to the kind of self-forgetfulness Christians associate with the worship of God.[12] But if *How to Write a Sentence* is a subtle form of natural theology I have no reason in principle to object to it.

Rather my concern about Fish's case for the significance of sentences, particularly in reference to theological sentences, is that he seems to think that the sentences he loves, the sentences he uses to exemplify what he takes to be great sentences, can and will be recognized as significant sentences by anyone. At least they will be recognized by anyone who has read Fish's book. I have no reason to doubt that this may sometimes be the case, but I worry that Fish's assumption that such recognition is possible fails to account for the social and political realities necessary for such recognition. I have the same worry about what makes possible the writing of such sentences.

One may well respond, as I suggested above, that gifted people are capable of writing and reading good sentences irrespective of the circum-

---

11. Ludwig Wittgenstein, *Philosophical Investigations,* trans. G. E. M. Anscombe (New York: Macmillan, 1953), p. 373.

12. Fish makes no reference to Iris Murdoch in *How to Write a Sentence,* but his account of the effect sentences can have seems quite close to Murdoch's understanding of how good art, that is, art that can provide us with "a pure delight in the independent existence of what is excellent," can for a period free us from our self-involvement and fantasies so we are enabled to see the world as it is. See for example her *The Sovereignty of Good* (New York: Schocken, 1971), p. 85.

stances of their lives. I am sure that is true. Yet Fish rightly emphasizes that both the writing and the reading of a good sentence with appreciation is a craft that comes through training. What I worry about is whether he has explored sufficiently the conditions of possibility that make such a craft possible. His analysis of the sentences he uses as examples is at once so exact and so effortless you can miss the fact that his analysis of what makes a sentence a great sentence is the result of a lifetime of training. Yet he does not expose, at least he does not expose it in this book, the conditions that made it possible for him to write *How to Write a Sentence.*

In truth I am not clear about what I am asking. I think what I feel is missing in *How to Write a Sentence,* although it may be present in other of Fish's works, is the kind of account with which I began this essay. By characterizing the current position of theology and how that position is a reflection of Christian existence today I was trying to suggest that good sentences and our ability to read them do not drop from the sky. Rather they are the result of a lifetime of training necessary to produce a soul capable of seeing through the sentimentalities we use to hide our mortality from ourselves.

I believe, for example, that Robert Jenson's sentence, "God is whoever raised Jesus from the dead, having before raised Israel from Egypt," took a lifetime to write. I do not have the gift of exposition Stanley Fish displays, but I need to at least try to show why I think Jenson's sentence is such an exemplary theological sentence. The crucial word is "whoever." With that word Jenson resists the commonplace assumption that when people say "God" they know what they are saying. I suggested above that the problem with much of modern theology is too often we confirm the familiar. "God" is a familiar name. Jenson's use of "whoever" is grammatically necessary to make the familiar strange. "Whoever" calls into question the readers' presumption that they know who God is prior to how God makes himself known.

Jenson's "whoever," therefore, is best understood against the background of Karl Barth's rejection of liberal theology. "Whoever" is a further elaboration of Barth's great sentence, "God is God," a sentence designed to avoid the presumption, so well identified by Feuerbach, that theological claims about God are our way of talking about ourselves.[13] Jenson, like Barth, thinks Feuerbach represents the decisive challenge to theology be-

---

13. For Barth's later reflections on the sentence "God is God," see his *The Humanity of God* (Richmond, VA: John Knox, 1963), pp. 42-43.

cause Feuerbach rightly saw that "in our communal life we discover and live by goods that are in fact valued among us, yet none of us finds fully available to him or herself: in consequent longing and resentment, we project the fullness of these goods on the screen of eternity, where such fullness may be conceived, and we then find our comfort and hope in what we there behold, that is, in our own communal values writ large" (pp. 52-53).

Jenson's response to Feuerbach, his "whoever," moreover entails a politics. Jenson observes that if Feuerbach is right, that there is no antecedent one God, then neither can there be one antecedent community of humankind. Feuerbach's dream of a universal humanity that shares an eternal vision of the significance of humanity turns out to be parasitic on the faith he exposes as fraudulent. As a result, Jenson observes, the kind of unbelief characteristic of our culture has had to abandon the high humanism of a universal community, knowing now only classes, genders, races, and cultures (p. 53).

If it is suspected that I am making more of Jenson's "whoever" than can be justified, I can appeal to Jenson's own understanding of the theological task. Theology for Jenson is thinking what to say in order to be saying the gospel (p. 32). Theology, according to Jenson, is best understood as a "sort of *grammar*. The church, we must say, is the community that speaks Christianese, and theology formulates the syntax and semantics of this language" (p. 18). "Whoever," therefore, is the grammar appropriate to the God who has a history. Just as Fish suggested, time is at the heart of what it means for us to be creatures determined by sentences.

According to Jenson the gospel not only must itself have a history, but the gospel itself is "an impeller and enabler" of history (p. 15). Therefore the Christian understanding of God emerges and reinterprets whatever antecedent religious or theological manifestations it encounters as a missionary community. "Whoever" indicates that the church is necessarily a missionary movement because the God who can be known only as the God who raised Jesus from the dead having before raised Israel from Egypt is known through witnesses. This remains true even in cultures that consider themselves "Christian." Indeed it is those cultures that the "whoever" is particularly challenging just to the extent that grammar calls into question the general presumption that they know who God is.

The parallel between Jesus being raised from the dead and Israel being raised from Egypt is the other striking characteristic of Jenson's sentence. "Raised Jesus from the dead" is the grammatical remark that necessitates the doctrine of the Trinity. The phrase "Father, Son, and Holy Spirit" is a compressed story gesturing to the total narrative of scripture in which God's name is specified. "Raised Jesus from the dead" is the phrase that invites the opportunity to show how the quite different but interconnected aspects of scripture climax with this man's triumph over sin-induced death. There can be no shortcuts to begin the ongoing task of comprehending what we say when we say "God" if Jesus has been raised from the dead.

That the reference to Jesus' resurrection is mentioned prior to Israel's being raised from Egypt is one of the reasons Jenson's sentence is so striking. The reader expects a chronological order. Why does Jesus' resurrection come before Israel's exodus from Egypt? Using Fish's classifications, Jenson's sentence at once seems to be an example of the subordinate and additive style. There is a clear sequence of events, but their ordering seems haphazard. The latter judgment, however, must be qualified by Jenson's use of the surprising word "raised" to describe Israel's exodus from Egypt.

By the use of "raised," Jenson gestures at once to the necessity that Christians recognize that God's promise to Israel remains good and why the Old Testament must be read Christologically. I think Jenson's commitment to hold both these claims in tension in the same sentence reflects the peculiar moment in which Christians find themselves. I doubt such a sentence would have or could have been written prior to the Holocaust. I need to be very careful about such a claim because it may seem that I am presuming to be able to read Jenson's mind. I have no idea if Jenson may or may not have been thinking about the Holocaust when he wrote the sentence I find so compelling. What I am sure about, however, is a Christian reading of the Old Testament as suggested by Jenson's use of "raised" is necessary if Christians are to even begin to understand our relation to Judaism.

According to Fish sentences are logical forms that link actor, action, and the object of action to make available predictions that would otherwise not be made. I take Jenson's sentence to be exemplary of such logic. It is a sentence that promises that the God who raised Jesus from the dead is a God that demands recognition by being worshiped. This is not a dead God. This is not a God who created the world and retreated to a realm "up there." This is the God who raised Jesus from the dead, which means this God continues to redeem. "God is whoever raised Jesus from the dead, having before raised Israel from Egypt" is a sentence that could only be written in a world in which Christians must learn again how to live, as Jews have lived for centuries, that is, out of control.

The logic of Jenson's sentence does what Fish suggests a sentence, and in particular sentences about God, must do, that is, witness to the inability to do justice to its subject. We must write about that which cannot be captured by sentences. But we can tell the story of how God's dealing with us makes possible sentences whose form and content are inseparable. After all, the question is not: does God exist, but do we?

## How I Learned and Continue to Learn to Write a Theological Sentence

"The question is not: does God exist, but do we?" is a sentence I wrote. I think it a good sentence. It is a sentence that expresses what I take to be the metaphysical implications of the observations Fish makes about our need for sentences in contrast to God's eternity. I try to produce similar sentences, which often earns me remarks such as, "That was a good lecture, but what I really liked were your asides." Usually the comment is meant as a compliment. It would be ungracious not to receive it in that spirit. But I worry that the remark might suggest there is no relation between the aside and the lecture. That may at times be true, but if it is true then it means I have not been doing my job. For whatever talent I have for the "one-liner," the remark or aside must be made possible by the content of the lecture.

In order to elaborate on this last point I am going to risk being self-indulgent by directing attention to some of the sentences I have written. I do so because as their author I should be able to make articulate the relation between how I was learning to think and the sentences that I came to write. It remains the case, however, that I am and continue to be surprised by some of the sentences I have written. I sometimes feel as if someone other than myself wrote them.

I have thought, however, that sentences were important if the general perspective I represent was to be persuasive. For example, I think the power of Reinhold Niebuhr's work owes much to his ability to craft the well-formed sentence: "Man's capacity for justice makes democracy possible; but man's inclination to injustice makes democracy necessary" is obviously a brilliant sentence that at once reflects Niebuhr's anthropology and his subsequent political theory.[14] It is a sentence, moreover, that

14. Reinhold Niebuhr, *The Children of Light and the Children of Darkness* (New York: Scribner's, 1944), p. xi. I have often thought Niebuhr's ability to write made his position compelling because it was assumed by his readers that the insightful sentences confirmed his overall position. Consider, for example, this lovely sentence from *Moral Man and Immoral Society* (New York: Scribner's, 1960): "Religion is always a citadel of hope, which is built

I suspect created thought to the extent that Niebuhr had to go on to say more exactly what a "capacity for justice" entailed. Though I have a quite critical relation to Niebuhr, I owe him much for what he taught me about the importance of writing a good sentence.

No one sentence captures the way I have learned to think theologically, but the following sentences, sentences widely scorned, indicate central themes. "The first task of the church is not to make the world more just; the first task of the church is to make the world the world." That sentence reflects the influence of John Howard Yoder and, in particular, his understanding of the eschatological character of the gospel. The sentence is, of course, meant to be offensive. Surely in this time when Christianity seems to many a faith with doubtful metaphysical commitments it becomes important to emphasize the ethical idealism many Christians embody. Yet that is what I seem to be denying.

I do mean for the sentence to challenge the assumption that Christians are the same as everyone else except for some reason they think it useful to go to church. Accordingly it is very important that readers be attentive to the phrase "first task." The sentence does not imply that Christians have no interest in justice, but it does mean that Christians have no idea what justice may entail unless we first know what it means to be "the world." In fact, the world cannot know it is the world unless there is an alternative to the world. Inherent, therefore, in the grammar of this sentence is a strong epistemological assertion with a definite politics. "The world" cannot know it is the world unless there exists a people who are not the world.

This understanding of the relation of church to world is captured in the sentence, "You can only act in the world you can see, and you can only come to see what you can say." This sentence is a modification of Iris Murdoch's remark that ethically what we do depends on the descriptions that make the world the world. Accordingly the first response is never "What should I do?" Rather the first response is to ask "What is going on?" Description precedes decision. Accordingly the language we use to make the world the world is more significant than any decisions we make in or about the world.

These sentences are designed to be interrelated. As they stand their grammar is meant to entail substantive commitments. Those commitments

---

on the edge of despair" (p. 62). You want that sentence to be true, but that would require you to accept Niebuhr's presumption that there is something called "religion." No sentence makes clearer Niebuhr's indebtedness to Protestant liberalism, though the grammar of the sentence seems to imply a critique of that tradition.

are implied by sentences such as, "If you need a theory of truth to have confidence that Jesus was raised from the dead, worship that theory, not Jesus." That sentence is designed to show how the grammar of each of these sentences is nonfoundational. What makes the world the world is its refusal to acknowledge that Jesus was raised from the dead. So the world turns out to be that which takes the time of God's patience not to live in the light of the resurrection.

To live in the light of the resurrection is to refuse to use the powers that crucified Jesus in the name of achieving justice. Thus the sentence, "Christians are called to be nonviolent not because we believe nonviolence is a strategy to make war less likely, but because in a world of war, as faithful followers of Christ, we cannot imagine being anything else than nonviolent; it is a nonviolence, moreover, that may make the world more violent because the world will use violence rather than have the order it calls peace exposed as violence." That sentence, like all the sentences I have used to this point, is designed to make clear that Christological commitments are what make these sentences not only possible but hopefully intelligible. They also are designed to challenge sentimental accounts of Christianity and, in particular, accounts of Christian nonviolence found in such slogans as "Give peace a chance."

One of my favorite sentences that does the kind of work I just described is a sentence I used to begin a sermon for a wedding in which 1 Corinthians 13 had been chosen as the text for the day. I began with the sentence, "Christians are obligated to love one another — even if they are married." That sentence is designed not only to challenge romantic conceptions of love that are associated with the love between two married people, but also to suggest that the love that should characterize the relation between Christians is the love that we share through being incorporated into God's very life.

I have hopefully supplied enough examples to suggest how certain kinds of sentences seemed to write themselves given how I was being taught to think by John Howard Yoder. I am tempted to call attention to some of the sentences in *Hannah's Child: A Theologian's Memoir* to suggest they work in a similar fashion; sentences like "I did not intend to be 'Stanley Hauerwas'" or "Most people do not have to become theologians to become a Christian but I probably did." Perhaps these reflections are better left for a separate essay in which the genres of theology are explored. So I end with a prayer that I hope captures some of the lessons Fish has to offer.

Gracious God, humble us through the violence of
Your love so we are able to know and confess
our sins. We want our sins to be interesting, but,
God forgive us, they are so ordinary: envy,
hatred, meanness, pride, self-centeredness, laziness,
boredom, lying, lust, stinginess, and so on.
You have saved us from "and so on" to be a royal
people able to witness to the world that
the powers that make us such ordinary sinners
have been defeated. So capture our attention
with the beauty of your life that
the ugliness of sin may be seen as just that —
ugly.
God, how wonderful
it is to be captivated by you.
Amen

## Fish at Work

I was raised a bricklayer. When bricklayers go to work they say they are
going or have gone to "the job." Though he is not a bricklayer Stanley Fish
goes to work because he has a job to do. His job is to read texts and parse
arguments. Few are better at that job than Stanley Fish. That may not be
quite true. The rabbis may be Stanley's superiors but then they had a tradition of examples to teach them how to do their work. Stanley has not
been without examples, but on the whole he has had to find his way on
his own. Milton studies and the law, however, have been crucial resources
to help him help us to expose or appreciate the grammar of this sentence,
that paragraph, or this book.

To attend to Fish at work usually means you are taught to see what you
would not have seen without his help. Stanley has a passion for the truth.
Though in his book on academic freedom he favorably quotes Kant, I think
Stanley cannot stand cant or Kant. At least he cannot stand how the latter
is used to underwrite a liberalism that "does not exist." Indeed one of the
things I so enjoy when reading Stanley is his ability to call into question the
sentimentalities that shape so much of our current intellectual life. For example, in his book on academic freedom he challenges the oft-made claim
by historians and other academic pretenders that debates about history are

about how to interpret the facts, not about what the facts are. No, Stanley rightly argues, it is first and foremost about what the facts are.

I admire Stanley's passion and the work he does when he goes to the job. Yet I want to use this occasion to ask how he got his job. Put differently, I want to ask: How can Fish account for the conditions that make his work possible? "Can" may be the wrong word to use to ask him what makes his work possible. A better word may be "should," because should suggests that Stanley owes us an account of why what he does needs to be done. Still another way to put the question is, "For whom does Stanley work?" or "Who does he serve?" Stanley famously argues, an argument with which I have some sympathy, that theory has no consequences. Yet there has to be some payoff somewhere to account for the passion that is Fish.

These are not questions that come from nowhere. They come from me because I am not a free mind. I am a Christian theologian. I do not think about what I want to think about. I do not even know what it would be if I thought I had permission to think about what I want to think about. I think about what my tradition and the people this tradition has formed tell me to think about. That does not mean I do not think critically about the tradition, because the tradition demands that you think critically about what the tradition is about. I may, moreover, explore some aspects of that tradition that may not be high on the agenda of those who currently identify with the tradition, but I do so because I think that exploration important for what I have been asked to think about. What I am asking Stanley is: Given he is not, as I am, under orders, how does he know what work he is to do and where the job is that makes the work possible?

Stanley may well think it unfair for me to ask him to locate or compare his work in comparison to the work of theology. He has, after all, argued that the courts have rightly afforded an exception to matters pertaining to faith and the church because such faith is not subject to secular adjudication. Faith is not open to secular reason because no matter how much you may learn about religion and/or church history (and I take "religion" to be a doubtful theological concept), it remains the case that " 'religious experience' is not a matter of empirical information or textbook knowledge." Rather to hold religious convictions is a matter of faith. By suggesting it is a matter of faith I take Stanley to indicate not that faith is without reason, but rather that faith entails a self-involving character that may be incompatible with the work of the university.

Given Stanley's respect for theological convictions it nonetheless must be asked if his understanding of the special nature of religious faith means theology may not be an appropriate subject in the curriculums of the university. I not only do not want to avoid indoctrination, my task is to indoctrinate those I teach. Can someone so committed be a creditable academic? In what follows I will only be able to ask that question indirectly, but I did not want to leave it unasked. Of course one of the problems raised by asking the question is the false abstraction implicit in the question, that is, the assumption that something called "the university" exists.

I observed at the beginning that Stanley is a master of text analysis, but he cannot function without texts that come from somewhere. Which raises the question "Why those texts?" Why Milton? Why legal texts? Stanley has often said that one argument underlies everything he has done. I think that argument is the one Stanley appeals to when he references Thomas Kuhn's claim that "there is no standard higher than the assent of the relevant community." I am not asking Stanley to claim membership in a community of communities because such a community does not exist except as eschatological hope. Rather I am asking "Why Milton?" once you no longer have people in the world whose lives have been determined by practices that make a Milton a Milton.

I do not believe these are questions that Stanley will find unwelcome. In an earlier essay titled "How to Write a Theological Sentence" I observe that Stanley is well aware that *How to Write a Sentence* is a book of theology. He observes, for example, that only mortal beings write and need to write sentences. We do so because we are mortal beings for whom death is a gift, a "gift of design and choice, of gain and loss, of hope and desperation, of failure and redemption, all modes of being that are available only to creatures who, like sentences (and novels) have a beginning, a middle, and an end. It is the inevitability of death that provides life with a narrative arc." Sentences are our way of making sense of our lives as creatures who can only grasp eternity by negative inference, that is, by imagining in time the negation of time.

The theological implications such remarks have are clear in an interview Stanley gave in response to the publication of his book. In the interview Stanley makes reference to Gertrude Stein's remark, a remark to which he pays particular attention in his book, about the "everlasting feeling" she gets from diagramming sentences. Stanley focuses on this remark in order to call attention to Stein's view that if you start thinking about language in a self-regarding way you will not get anywhere because your ego, the ambition you project, will get in the way. But if you submit, an interesting word for Fish to direct attention to and use, by reading and rereading a great sentence a better self is more likely to emerge.

Commenting on Stein's views Fish observes that she is making an explicit religious argument. It is so because the submission of a small self to a larger power so that the small self gives up its own providence is the message, Stanley observes, that is characteristic of many religions — but is particularly true of Christianity. Fish concludes that "sentences can send us in direction of something greater than they and therefore greater than us so sentences in a way perform their best office when they turn us in the direction of life, life, eternal life." The last phrase being part of what Stanley identifies as the greatest sentence in the English language, that is, Christian's cry in Bunyan's *Pilgrim's Progress,* to resist the cry of his wife and children so he might flee the wrath to come.

In *Three Rival Versions of Moral Enquiry: Encyclopaedia, Genealogy, and Tradition,* MacIntyre calls attention to Nietzsche's remark, "I fear we are not getting rid of God because we still believe in grammar." MacIntyre calls attention to Nietzsche's comment to suggest that Nietzsche saw clearly what critics of Christianity associated with the ninth edition of the *Encyclopaedia Britannica* did not see, that is, that their conception of rationality and language was itself theological. *How to Write a Sentence* can be read as an extended commentary on MacIntyre's observation about Nietzsche's remark. In a similar fashion Fish's argument concerning the logical form of a sentence can be seen as an elaboration of Wittgenstein's remark in the *Philosophical Investigations* that "[g]rammar tells what kind of object anything is. (Theology as grammar)" (p. 373).

I have no idea if Wittgenstein was responding to Nietzsche. I suspect he was not. I only call attention to these remarks about grammar to suggest the significance of Fish's understanding of the significance of sentences. Of course it is by no means clear that the god of which we cannot be rid because of our belief in grammar is the Christian God. Nor is it clear that the "effacing of the self" Fish celebrates as one result of surrendering to the logic of sentences can or should be thought to be equivalent to the kind of self-forgetfulness Christians associate with the worship of God. But if *How to Write a Sentence* is a subtle form of natural theology I would not be surprised.

My question rather is whether Fish's case for the significance of sentences, particularly in reference to sentences with theological content, shows that the sentences he loves, the sentences he uses to exemplify what he takes to be great sentences, can and will be recognized as significant sentences by anyone. At least some may be recognized as significant by those who might read Stanley's book because they think he is a literary critic rather than a theologian. I have no reason to doubt that some readers may see what Stanley is up to in *How to Write a Sentence,* but I worry that Fish's assumption that such recognition is possible fails to account for the social and political realities necessary for such recognition. Of course few have taught us more about reception of texts than Stanley, so I do not think I am asking a question he has not thought about. I am, however, not only asking about what is necessary to receive the text theologically, but I also want to know what makes it possible to write the sentences Stanley so rightly loves.

One may well respond, a response Stanley may find congenial, that gifted people are capable of writing and reading good sentences irrespective of the circumstances of their lives. I am sure that is true. Yet Fish rightly emphasizes that both the writing and reading of a good sentence with appreciation is a craft that comes through training. What I worry about is whether he has explored sufficiently the conditions of the possibility that makes such training possible. His analysis of the sentences he uses as examples are at once so exact and so effortless you can miss the fact that his analysis of what makes a sentence a great sentence is the result of a lifetime of training of Stanley Fish by Stanley Fish. Yet he does not expose, at least he does not expose it in this book, the conditions that made it possible to write *How to Write a Sentence.*

Stanley, however, has made it very clear that he is first and foremost a professional. In *Professional Correctness: Literary Studies and Political Change* he describes a professional as "a specialist, defined and limited by traditions of his craft, and it is a condition of his labors, at least as they are exerted in the United States, that he remain distanced from any effort to work changes in the structure of society." The university provides a place for people so trained to do their specialized and limited work. Stanley, accordingly, argues for and provides a strong defense of the apolitical character of the university as well as his particular field of literary criticism.

To be a literary critic is a distinctive enterprise, which simply means that the literary critic must be someone who has been trained to be who she is and do what she does and not be or do something else. Fish observes that at one time some pursued a literary life because it was a way to secure a place at court, but that day is now well gone. Now literary activity is a discipline in the academy where proficiency is measured by academic standards and rewarded by gatekeepers of academic guilds. The name for

this is professionalism, an academicizing of a life, which is a form of organization that confers membership through special training in the interest
of producing persons who are able to recognize one another as performing
"moves" in the same "game." In response to the question of why he does the
work he does as a literary critic, Stanley responds with his usual candor,
"I like the way I feel when I am doing it."

He writes:

> I like being brought up short by an effect I have experienced but do
> not yet understand analytically. I like trying to describe in flatly prosaic
> words the achievement of words that are anything but flat and prosaic.
> I like savoring the physical "taste" of language at the same time that I
> work to lay bare its physics. And when those pleasures have been (tem-
> porarily) exhausted, I like linking one moment in a poem to others and
> then to moments in other works, works by the same author or by his
> predecessors or contemporaries or successors. It doesn't finally matter
> which, so long as I can *keep going,* reaping the cognitive and tactile
> harvest of an activity as self-reflexive as I become when I engage in it.

In a previous essay titled "The Pathos of the University: The Case of
Stanley Fish," I asked why Stanley should be paid so that he can receive
so much pleasure from the study of Milton. In the process I challenged
his claim that just as virtue is its own reward he needed no justification
for the work he does as a literary critic. I am not without sympathy with
his attempt to maintain the autonomy of the university as a way to resist
oppressive demands of political and moral relevancy, but the question still
remains why anyone has a stake in Stanley Fish being Stanley Fish.

I am happy to say in his recent book, *Versions of Academic Freedom:
From Professionalism to Revolution,* Stanley responds to J. Peter Byrne's
question that if academic practices have no relation to larger concerns of
life, why should people provide resources to carry them on. Stanley resists
any suggestion that higher education is valuable because of benefits nonac-
ademics might see in it. He continues to maintain that higher education is
valuable (if it is) because "of the particular pleasures it offers to those who
are drawn to it," but he worries that his "deflationary argument" against
justifying the work of academic professionals on nonacademic grounds
may give the impression that academic work is reduced to "a set of routines
performed in obedience to norms backed up by nothing more than they
happen to be in place."

That cannot be the case, because Fish argues — an argument he has made in the past but one that has been overlooked — that the academy is the place where knowledge is advanced and truth about physical, conceptual, and social reality is pursued. The job of the university is the advancement of knowledge and the search for truth. These are not goals extrinsic to the university, but rather they are constitutive of the work of the university. Accordingly the university does not need any justification other than its own existence. There remains, however, the challenge that given that there are truths to be pursued and known through activities outside the university why those truths should not be the business of the university.

Stanley's answer is fascinating. He appeals to the tenth book of Aristotle's *Nicomachean Ethics,* a book dear to my heart, where Aristotle distinguishes between the active and contemplative life. He does so in order to suggest that his defense of professionalism is akin to Aristotle's understanding of the superiority of the contemplative life as an activity that can be loved for its own sake. Stanley argues that such a view of contemplation is a perfect account of the academy. The academy is where contemplation is pursued with no end beyond itself and where "practical activities" are admitted only as the objects of that contemplation.

The only problem with Stanley's suggestion that the work of the university can be understood as a form of Aristotelian contemplation is that it is by no means clear how to understand Aristotle's account of contemplation. For example, it is not at all clear how his emphasis on the virtues and the role that practical wisdom plays in the formation of the person of virtue is compatible with or necessary for his understanding of contemplation. Indeed it has been suggested that Aristotle's emphasis on contemplation, that is, reflection on that which cannot be other than it is, was a desperate attempt to secure some place for friendship in a world that is politically a moral chaos. Aristotle may well have thought by leading a contemplative life some may attain the stability of character sufficient to sustain the trust that makes friendship between virtuous people possible.

I do not know if Stanley's appeal to Aristotle on contemplation was meant to elicit these kinds of considerations about what makes friendship possible, but I think they help me say why I so value Stanley and the work he has done. For I should like to think that we are friends, and through what he has taught me about how to read I have learned in some small way to desire the most cherished but most complex friendship available, that is, the friendship with God.

# CHAPTER 8

# How to Be Theologically Ironic

## Why Irony?

Why irony? Theologians may use irony from time to time, but irony is seldom thought to be a central theological concept. Yet I hope to show that irony is a stance that is essential for the work of theology particularly in our day. I will try to explain below why I use the language of "stance" to describe the work irony can and should do for the task of theology. But I first need to set the stage for what I am trying to do by calling attention to irony as a theological trope.

To focus on irony is one way to explore the larger question of what genres are more appropriate or helpful for the tasks of theology. Though I have often tried to think through this question I have never been able to come to clarity about what genres are best suited for theology in our day. I am sure that theology rightly assumes different forms in different historical contexts. The audience for theology obviously makes a difference for the style and form of theology. It may well be that this is one of those questions that is best left unanswered because it may well make theologians far too self-satisfied if they think they know the answer.

I have tried, moreover, to experiment by writing in genres not usually associated with what is considered serious theology. I have done so because I have assumed, in spite of the suggestion in the sentence above, that we cannot presume in our day to know for whom it is we write. Unfortunately, given that theology is now done by people in universities, theology is primarily written for other theologians.

By experimenting with different genres I have tried to create an audience or, I would prefer, readers who are not academics.[1] I have accordingly tried to avoid specialized vocabularies. Too often specialized vocabularies are used to intimidate anyone who is not an academic theologian. There is a place for theologians to write primarily for other theologians, but if theology is genuinely a church discipline I do not see how it can be so restricted. So I have tried often to write in an entertaining manner. I do not pretend I have been successful in that undertaking, but I continue to think it an important task.

Of course it may be objected that irony is a figure of speech — not a genre. Prayer, confession, sermons, essays, apologetics, memoirs, letters are genre categories, and irony does not seem to have the same status as those categories. Satire and polemics seem to be classifications that mark off different modes of expression in which irony may occur. I must confess I am not particularly concerned about the problem of whether irony is properly understood to be a genre category because I am not sure we know what genre itself entails. And because it is not at all clear to me that we know what genre itself entails, it is not my intention to argue one way or another about how irony should be classified as a genre or a figure of speech.[2]

However, in what follows I hope to show that irony is a necessary stance in life that must find theological expression if theology is one of the gifts we have been given as Christians to enable us to live lives of truth. The relation between irony and truth is crucial for understanding why theology entails linguistic training necessary for us to be truthful in a world often dominated by mendacity. In particular I will argue that irony is theologically necessary if we are to recover what it means to be a Christian in Christendom. But just as important, I will suggest that if Christians are to negotiate a time that styles itself as ironic, we must be people confident of the truthfulness of our convictions — a confidence that ironically cannot help but call into question the presumption that in the absence of truth all we have is irony.

---

1. Because I was asked to do so I have even published a collection of prayers in a book titled *Prayers Plainly Spoken* (Downers Grove: InterVarsity, 1999). A friend recently observed that my prayers have a very different tone, a tentativeness or hesitancy, than the lectures I give in the course meant to introduce students to Christian ethics. I think that is a very astute observation, to which I can only respond that if you are to understand me, it is the prayers that make the lectures possible.

2. A more interesting question is the relation between humor and irony, but that is a subject for another essay. See chapter 12, "How to Be Theologically Funny."

By exploring the work irony can, does, or should do I hope to come to a better understanding of some of the work I have done as a theologian. I have never had a "theory" about irony or the role irony should have in theology. But then I have not had a theory about theology other than it is probably not a good thing to have theories that determine what we do as theologians. Yet it has become increasingly clear to me that I have not only often used irony in my work, but I have an ironic relation to the way I have tried to do theology. I hope to make these obscure remarks clear by the exploration I provide.

One of the reasons theologians have not attended to the role irony may play in theology is that, ironically, it is very hard to give an account of irony; that is to say, it is by no means clear we know how to characterize what makes irony irony. Put differently, it seems no definition of irony is possible because any definition fails to account for the diverse forms irony seems to take. That is no deep problem if you believe as I do that it is a mistake to assume definitions determine the meaning of a word.

In general, the presumption that irony indicates the incongruity between the literal and implied meaning of a speech act is accurate, but that understanding of irony is but the tip of the iceberg. Irony may also be associated with the incongruity that often pertains between actual results and normal expectations, but again I will try to show that what has been assumed to be ironic in different times and places cannot be so easily pinned down. It seems best, therefore, to attend to exemplifications of irony rather than attempt an abstract account of what makes irony ironical.

In a brilliant article titled "E Unibus Pluram: Television and U.S. Fiction," David Foster Wallace provides one of the most compelling accounts I know of irony and, in particular, the ironic character of our times. He does so by calling attention to the ironic character of television. In particular he argues that those who criticize as pointless the culture television produces fail to recognize that television is immune to such a charge because television is based on the assumption that it lacks any connection with the world outside it.[3] Wallace suggests that the ironic character of the medium of television is nowhere better exemplified than in the fact that the "products

---

3. Thomas Hibbs argues, however, that the popular culture represented by television is profoundly nihilistic because it represents the process "in which the highest values devalue themselves, human aspiration shrinks, and the great questions and elevating quests of previous ages no longer have any resonance in the human soul." *Shows about Nothing: Nihilism in Popular Culture from "The Exorcist" to "Seinfeld"* (Dallas: Spence Publishing, 1999), p. 6.

presented as helping you express individuality can afford to be advertised on television only because they sell to huge hordes."[4]

Wallace observes both that television fears irony's ability to expose and yet television needs irony to sustain itself. Television needs irony because the tension between what is said and what is seen is irony's territory. The capacity of television to undercut what is said by what is seen testifies to the ironic power of television to absorb the world. That way of putting the matter may not be strong enough because it is not only that television has the power to absorb the world, but rather it has the power to constitute the world, and this is what makes it the medium of irony for the determination of our lives. There is no "outside" to television because the world we see is a world seen through television.

Wallace, for example, calls attention to the relation between loneliness and television. Lonely people watch more television. This means the more time one watches television the less time one inhabits a "real" human world, the result being that the less time spent in a real human world the harder one finds it not to feel alienated from real humans. Thus we begin to think our relationships with TV personalities are an alternative to relationships with people who actually exist.[5] Watching television becomes addictive, but then television offers itself as relief from the problems it creates.[6]

Wallace uses a passage from Don DeLillo's *White Noise* to exemplify the case he is trying to make. DeLillo writes about a barn that is a tourist attraction because it is the most photographed barn in America. You know it is the most photographed barn in America because the signs proclaiming that it is the most photographed barn in America line the road you must take to get to the barn. The result is that people come to take pictures of the barn because it is the most photographed barn in America. Like the effect of television, those who take pictures of the barn do so because it is the most photographed barn. This produces the ironic effect that we who are reading DeLillo's novel are watching those who are watching the people taking pictures of the barn because it is the most photographed barn in

4. David Foster Wallace, "E Unibus Pluram: Television and U.S. Fiction," *Review of Contemporary Fiction* 13, no. 2 (Summer 1993): 161.

5. Wallace, "E Unibus Pluram," p. 163. For a profound meditation on loneliness as a theological challenge and resource see Anette Ejsing, *The Power of One: Theological Reflections on Loneliness* (Eugene, OR: Cascade, 2011). There are many different kinds of loneliness, the most destructive being when we are alone with someone. I suspect television specializes in such loneliness.

6. Wallace, "E Unibus Pluram," p. 163.

America. Wallace recognizes that by reporting on this complex interaction he has become part of the farce from which there is no escape.

Accordingly Wallace argues that irony and fear of ridicule are distinctive features of our culture because "the pretty hand of television has us by the throat." That is why even though irony and ridicule are entertaining and effective they are also agents of despair. They are so because the central tension in America between individualism and the need for communal belonging is resolved by television's ability to at once invite us to transcend the crowd by becoming one with the crowd, a crowd that is able to see through the crowd.

Irony, which in the past has been used to expose hypocrisy, Wallace argues, now tyrannizes us. It does so because irony is at once powerful and unsatisfying because it is impossible to pin down. It has become, in Wallace's language, a "sort of existential poker-face." In non-ironic prose Wallace sums up his case:

> All U.S. irony is based on an implicit "I don't really mean what I say." So what *does* irony as a cultural norm mean to say? That it is impossible to mean what you say? That maybe it's too bad it's impossible, but wake up and smell the coffee already? Most likely, I think, today's irony ends up saying: "How very *banal to ask what I mean.*" Anyone with the heretical gall to ask an ironist what he actually stands for ends up looking like a hysteric or a prig. And herein lies the oppressiveness of institutionalized irony, the too successful rebel: the ability to interdict the *question* without attending to its *content* is tyranny. It is the new junta, using the very tool that exposed its enemy to insulate itself.[7]

If Wallace is right about the tyrannical character of irony in our time, then it seems odd that I want to develop a case for the theological significance of irony. To do so seems to accept the moral psychology I have long criticized, that is, the presumption that our lives should be characterized by an ironic perspective that ensures I must act in such a way that I am able to distance myself from what I say or do. Thus the presumption that we must be able to "stand back" from any commitments we make or have made if we are to be free autonomous agents. Our freedom is understood as the autonomy that results from our having lives for which there is nothing worth dying because we are unsure if our lives are ours. Lives so consti-

7. Wallace, "E Unibus Pluram," pp. 183-84.

tuted make the acquisition of the virtues, other than the virtue of cynicism, problematic.

These are powerful objections, but I hope to show that irony has a role, as I suggested at the beginning, to help us live lives of truth. To do so I will critically engage the great defender of irony, Richard Rorty, who at once reflects as well as critically engages the world Wallace describes. Rorty did so by developing an account of the necessity of irony as a way to negotiate a world in which we no longer can or should have confidence in the language we use to make sense of our lives. The way Rorty understands and defends irony is significant because how he gets the role of language wrong is essential for the case I want to make for theological irony. The criticisms I develop of Rorty, moreover, are a preparation for the introduction of Jonathan Lear's significant account of irony, upon which I will build.

In the process I hope to make articulate connections to the account of practical reason, as well as the exploration of how to write a theological sentence, in the preceding chapters. With Lear I believe that irony is a form of practical reason for the constitution of the self. Practical reason is constituted by language that not only gives us the concepts through which we understand what we do and do not do, but in fact determines what we have or have not done. Irony turns out to be, therefore, in Lear's terms, a capacity that makes possible the use of the language we have learned as Christians. That language, moreover, must be used without apology yet also with the humility commensurate with the recognition that as Christians we are never quite what we say we are. This is particularly true for theologians who are always in the position of having to say more than we are.

I began by observing that irony is seldom identified as a theological genre. I am sure when I made that claim many reading this immediately thought that cannot be right, because they knew that there was an elephant in the room named Søren Kierkegaard.[8] The account of the theological use of irony I will develop, moreover, owes much to Kierkegaard — or at least I hope it does. Like him, but without his genius or courage, I have tried to help us recover what it means to be Christian in a world in which many call themselves Christian but, as Kierkegaard observes, "live in categories

---

8. Reinhold Niebuhr is a name that many associate with irony because of his book, *The Irony of American History* (New York: Charles Scribner's Sons, 1952). I am not going to engage Niebuhr in this essay, however, because I hope to discuss his work in a subsequent essay titled "How to (Not) Be Theologically Political."

quite foreign to Christianity."[9] Irony was one of Kierkegaard's weapons for that task.

I know enough about Kierkegaard, however, not to pretend that I am capable of giving an account of his complex and changing understanding of irony. Nor do I pretend he would agree with my attempt to use what I take to be some of his ironic interventions in what follows. I think his use of the pseudonyms as well as the development of the method of indirect communication are exemplifications of irony. They are both attempts to make possible "the communication of Christianity, where the situation is qualified by Christendom, there is no direct or straight-forward relationship, inasmuch as a vain conceit has first to be disposed of."[10] Direct communication is insufficient because it leaves the one receiving what is to be communicated undisturbed. Kierkegaard used indirect communication in an attempt to use the truth to deceive a person into the truth. Such a tactic is required if the conceits and illusions that possess those who assume that their lives are not determined by conceit or illusion are to be challenged.

That is particularly the case because Kierkegaard, in a manner that sounds very similar to Wallace's account of the tyranny of television irony, suggests that the entire population of Copenhagen "became ironical — and just so much the more ironical in proportion as the people were more ignorant and uneducated."[11] The irony of a population becoming ironic, Kierkegaard argued, implied a specific intellectual culture. It is one that is "absolutely unsocial," which is an irony given that an irony of the majority cannot be ironic. It is ironic that the crowd can think of itself as ironic because, as Kierkegaard observes, irony has one person as its limit. From his perspective, the irony of the rabble is but the confusion of vulgarity with the ironic. Kierkegaard acknowledges his use of indirect communication was necessary to get "the interminable public of ironical adepts to take aim at me, so that I should become the target of the irony of all men. Alas for me, the 'Magister of Irony.' "[12]

Kierkegaard's reflections on his point of view as an author make clear that his understanding and use of irony are extremely complex. Consider, for example, this extraordinary passage:

9. Søren Kierkegaard, *The Point of View for My Work as an Author: A Report to History,* trans. Walter Lowrie (New York: Harper Torchbooks, 1962), p. 22.

10. Kierkegaard, *Point of View,* p. 38.

11. Kierkegaard, *Point of View,* p. 54.

12. Kierkegaard, *Point of View,* p. 57. Kierkegaard's "title" refers to his dissertation, *The Concept of Irony.*

When some day my lover comes, he will easily perceive that at the time I was regarded as ironical the irony was by no means to be found where "the highly esteemed public" thought. It was to be found — and this goes without saying, for my lover cannot be so foolish as to assume that a public can understand irony, which is just as impossible as to be an individual *en masse* — he will perceive that the irony lay precisely in the fact that within this aesthetic author, under this worldly appearance, was concealed a religious author, who just at that time was consuming quite as much religiousness as commonly suffices for the provisions of an entire household. Moreover, my lover will perceive that irony appeared again in relation to the next period, and is to be discovered precisely in the fact which "the highly esteemed public" regarded as lunacy. In an ironical generation (the great aggregation of fools) there remains nothing else for the ironical man to do but to invert the relationship and himself become the target for the irony of all men.[13]

I think it is extremely important to note that Kierkegaard did not think irony applicable only as a weapon against the crowd. It was also a weapon directed at Kierkegaard himself. Like his fellow Danish brothers and sisters, he had the task of becoming a Christian when he is a "Christian of a sort."[14] In order to help others, he argues, it is necessary to understand more than they understand, though first and foremost you must understand what they understand. It does no good to try to help another in order to be admired. That is why all true effort to help another begins as well as ends with self-humiliation. Therefore to help another requires that we be servants, which will entail that we possess infinite drafts of patience.[15] In short, Kierkegaard knows that his own life must be lived ironically if he is to be a Christian.

As he says toward the end of *The Point of View for My Work as an Author*, he is "that individual" who took as his task "of translating completely into terms of reflection what Christianity is, what it means to become a Christian."[16] In a similar fashion I will try to suggest how the work I have done as a theologian is not unrelated to trying to become a Christian. I am, of course, no Kierkegaard, but his sense of the difference between who he

13. Kierkegaard, *Point of View*, pp. 62-63.
14. Kierkegaard, *Point of View*, p. 43.
15. Kierkegaard, *Point of View*, pp. 27-28.
16. Kierkegaard, *Point of View*, pp. 102-3.

is and what he writes I suspect is true for almost any theologian who tries to do theology in a world created by television.

I have only tried to say enough about Kierkegaard that his influence might be recognized in what follows. In particular Lear's account of irony has strong roots in Kierkegaard, so we are hardly leaving Kierkegaard behind. But first I need to engage Rorty, for no one has more forcefully laid down the gauntlet against the possibility of Christian speech than Rorty. Rorty must, therefore, be engaged because in Rorty's hands irony becomes a learned form of negativity that turns irony into a weapon that cannot help but destroy the possibility of Christian speech.

## It Is Turtles All the Way Down

In *Contingency, Irony, and Solidarity,* Richard Rorty writes to commend irony as a way of life. According to Rorty, the "ironist" is a person who fulfills three conditions. The "ironist" is first someone who has continuing doubts about the possibility that the final vocabulary she is using is "final." Rorty understands such a vocabulary to be necessary to justify our actions and our lives, to praise friends and criticize enemies, to express our hopes and fears, and to tell the story of our lives. The "ironist" may well recognize that she uses a vocabulary as if it were a final vocabulary, but she has been impressed by vocabularies in people or books she has encountered that others use as final. Secondly, an "ironist" acknowledges that arguments shaped by her current vocabulary cannot still her doubts about the validity of her vocabulary. In short, no knockdown arguments can assure the "ironist" that her vocabulary is true. Finally, even if Rorty's "ironist" has a philosophical perspective or skills, she will come to recognize that her vocabulary cannot be shown to be closer to reality than other final vocabularies.[17]

Rorty's "ironist" recognizes that almost anything can be made to look good or bad by being redescribed. Accordingly his "ironist" must resist all attempts to propose criteria that might allow some choice between final vocabularies. The "ironist" is a person who rightly does not take herself too seriously because she recognizes that how she understands who she is is not only without justification but will also be subject to change. The

---

17. Richard Rorty, *Contingency, Irony, and Solidarity* (Cambridge: Cambridge University Press, 1989), p. 73.

great enemies of the "ironist" — or at least those who provide a stark alternative to the "ironist" — are people of common sense. People of common sense assume the final vocabulary they use is unproblematic. If pressed, people of common sense can try to justify their vocabulary by recourse to metaphysics, that is, to show the "essence" of *x* or *y* concept, but Rorty argues that appeals to metaphysics turn out to be nothing more than the substitution of one set of descriptions for another.[18]

Rorty's "ironist" is not without social and political convictions. In particular, Rorty thinks his "ironist" will by necessity be a liberal. Liberalism is the natural expression of the ironical way of life because the central ideal of a liberal society, with respect to words as opposed to deeds and persuasion as opposed to force, is that anything goes. The belief that anything goes is not because liberals believe that truth is the result of an open encounter, but rather because the liberal is content to call true whatever the upshot of the encounters fostered by liberal arrangements produce. Put differently, the natural relation between irony and liberalism is the recognition that how we live as well as how our social and political arrangements are ordered requires no "foundation."[19] The "ironist" accordingly prefers social organizations that give everyone a chance at self-creation. That means the "ironist" identifies with the institutions associated with bourgeois societies because they assume those institutions provide the protections necessary to let those who are less able work out their private salvation.[20]

Rorty's account of the "ironist" way of life draws on his philosophical defense of the contingency of language, self, and community. He contends that "our language and our culture are as much a contingency, as much a result of thousands of small mutations finding niches (and millions of others finding no niches), as are the orchids and the anthropoids."[21] We are evolutionary accidents, but that does not lessen how marvelous such accidental results have turned out to be. Our language, like evolution, is characterized by purposeless change in which new forms kill off the old. Therefore with Nietzsche we say "God is dead," but that is only to say there

18. Rorty, *Contingency, Irony, and Solidarity,* pp. 73-74.

19. Rorty, *Contingency, Irony, and Solidarity,* pp. 51-52.

20. Rorty, *Contingency, Irony, and Solidarity,* pp. 84-85.

21. Rorty, *Contingency, Irony, and Solidarity,* p. 16. When Rorty was eight he developed an interest in wild orchids, which he describes as a "socially useless flower." See the autobiographical essay "Trotsky and the Wild Orchids" in his book, *Philosophy and Social Hope* (London: Penguin, 1999), pp. 3-20.

are no higher purposes.[22] For Rorty, just as it was for the woman from India who maintained it is turtles all the way down, it is chance all the way down.

Rorty is more than ready to accept the implications of what it means to acknowledge the contingent character of our lives and language. For example, he does not claim that what he advocates is true. Rather he suggests (argues would be too strong a word) that we should drop the idea of truth as the description for the discovery that there is something "out there in the world." That does not mean that the use of the word "truth" must be completely abandoned. Rather it means we should cease thinking of truth as a "deep matter" that philosophers worry about. We are better off if we think phrases such as "the nature of truth" are unprofitable topics that are as irrelevant to our lives as questions about the existence of God.[23] As a matter of consistency, therefore, Rorty refuses to offer arguments against the vocabularies he seeks to replace. Instead, the best he can do is to make the "ironist" way of life attractive.

Rorty is well known for his view that religion is a conversation-stopper.[24] Jeff Stout, who has a deep admiration for Rorty, has criticized Rorty's views about religion as inconsistent with Rorty's best insights.[25] In particular Stout observes that there is no reason to make religious people cease employing their vocabularies in public discussions even if their mode of defending the words they use is not persuasive to those with other vocabularies. Stout's point is well taken, but Rorty's challenge to theological speech is deeper than questions about the permissibility of Christian participation in public discussions.

If Rorty's account of what it means to be an "ironist" is right, then it must surely be the case that Christians can make no sense of the words we use. Put as dramatically as I can, if Rorty is right about the ironist's relation to her own speech, then it is hard to understand why anyone would be prepared to die for what they say. Yet Christians have paid dearly, even willing to die, rather than abandon how they have learned to speak. In short, if

22. Rorty, *Contingency, Irony, and Solidarity,* pp. 19-20.

23. Rorty, *Contingency, Irony, and Solidarity,* p. 8.

24. Rorty, *Philosophy and Social Hope,* pp. 168-74. For an extremely useful engagement with Rorty's work that makes clear that theologians can have a constructive conversation with Rorty, see *Rorty and the Religious: Christian Engagements with a Secular Philosopher,* ed. Jacob Goodson and Brad Stone, with a "Foreword" by Stanley Hauerwas and an "Afterword" by Charles Marsh (Eugene, OR: Cascade, 2012).

25. Jeffrey Stout, *Democracy and Tradition* (Princeton: Princeton University Press, 2004), pp. 85-91.

Rorty's account of irony is right then Christians can make no sense of the martyrs.[26] The vocabulary that makes martyrs, however, is a vocabulary whose concepts are the result of contingencies. "Out of all the people of the world I have called you Israel to be my promised people" is, next to creation itself, the exemplification of what did not have to be.

It is quite interesting to contrast the Christian understanding of contingency with Rorty's account of the contingent. Rorty supplies no response to the question, "Contingent to what?" As a result his account of contingency is sheer assertion. There is no reason, other than his appeals to Darwin, why we should not think that all that exists does so by necessity. Rorty seems to assume contingency is but another name for the arbitrary, but he gives no justification for why that should be the case. He provides, moreover, no account of how languages grow and develop to do the work of practical reason through which developments in how we speak open us to claims about the way things are.

Interestingly enough, Christians have not claimed our vocabularies — and the plural is important — are finished. How could they be finished given that our languages, like all that exists, are contingent because they are created? The language we learn to speak in order to be Christians, as Herbert McCabe argues, entails the sharing of our lives, which makes possible not only our ability to see something new but to have a new way of seeing. How we speak as Christians requires an acknowledgment of the contingent character of our speech and lives; thus Christians must remain open to how what we say requires recognition that our language grows. That means, according to McCabe, that "every language is in the end provisional, or at least can be seen by hindsight to have been provisional."[27]

Ironically, from McCabe's perspective, Rorty has a far-too-simple account of language. Of course all language is contingent, but the crucial question is whether the speakers have the ability to recognize the limits and possibilities of how they have learned to speak. Such recognition is made possible if it is remembered that language, contrary to Rorty's examples, is not only determined by reference to objects but also is a system of communication that makes possible moral communities. To share a language is to share concepts for the formation of a common life.[28] The

26. See, for example, Peter Leithart's "Witness unto Death," *First Things* 229 (January 2013): 45-50.

27. Herbert McCabe, *What Ethics Is All About* (Washington, DC: Corpus Press, 1969), p. 90.

28. McCabe, *What Ethics Is All About*, p. 73.

recognition of our contingency and the contingency of our language is but an invitation to discover how little we know what we say.

Alasdair MacIntyre, in a manner not unlike McCabe's account of language, criticizes Rorty's account of irony for abandoning a commitment to truthfulness, which he argues is constitutive of what we owe others by the very fact that our language enables us to communicate. MacIntyre suggests that Rorty's account of irony is an "offence" against such truthfulness just to the extent Rorty's "ironist" cannot be held accountable to others. Accordingly MacIntyre argues Rorty's "ironist" cannot acknowledge that the vocabulary she uses to make intelligible and justify her actions, beliefs, and life within a network of relationships of giving and receiving is not her vocabulary but ours. When, therefore, "I am called to account as a practical reasoner in this shared evaluative language, what I am invited to consider is whether what is said about me is or is not true and justified in light of our shared standard of truth and justification."[29]

Rorty's ironic detachment, therefore, suggests a withdrawal from our common language and the shared judgments that language makes possible. But it is only through relationships that language makes possible not only our knowledge of others but also knowledge of ourselves. Accordingly MacIntyre argues that the most troubling aspect of Rorty's account of ironic detachment is not merely the pretense it requires; rather it is that the "ironist" is required to question dependence on her community. But even more troubling is that the ironist cannot trust her understanding of others, or even herself. MacIntyre observes that Rorty might respond by arguing he was not calling into question the kind of commitments that MacIntyre calls attention to, but rather he was only suggesting that we need an ironic attitude toward our final vocabulary. Yet MacIntyre observes that such a response continues to presume it is possible to separate ourselves from our attitudes toward our vocabulary through which our commitments and solidarities are articulated and justified.[30]

I have directed attention to Rorty's account of the "ironist" because I take his position to be not only pervasive, but also quite persuasive. Moreover I think Rorty is right to see the significance of language for the role irony should play in our lives. Yet Lear rightly judges Rorty's account of irony to be "thin." In stronger terms, Lear argues from Kierkegaard's

---

29. Alasdair MacIntyre, *Dependent Rational Animals: Why Human Beings Need the Virtues* (Chicago: Open Court Press, 1999), p. 152.

30. MacIntyre, *Dependent Rational Animals*, pp. 152-53.

perspective that Rorty's account of irony is not even irony because different final vocabularies are treated as objects of disinterested choice. Lear, therefore, concludes that in a Kierkegaardian vein Rorty's irony is really a manifestation of a weariness that does not and cannot recognize itself as such.[31]

## Becoming Human

Jonathan Lear begins his account of irony with Kierkegaard's observation that "to become human does not come that easily." Lear observes that Kierkegaard's remark might be interpreted as suggesting that becoming human requires that we inhabit a practical identity constituted by our awareness of various positive and negative incentives that make arduous the task of fending off temptations that threaten the task of being human. Lear, however, argues that this is not the difficulty Kierkegaard has in mind. To show what Kierkegaard means by the difficulty of becoming human, Lear directs attention to this entry in Kierkegaard's *Journal:*

> In what did Socrates' irony really lie? In expressions and turns of speech, etc.? No, such trivialities, even his virtuosity in talking ironically, such things do not make a Socrates. No, his whole existence is and was irony; whereas the entire contemporary population of farm hands and business men and so on, all those thousands, were perfectly sure of being human and knowing what it means to be a human being, Socrates was beneath them (ironically) and occupied himself with the problem — what does it mean to be a human being? He thereby expressed that actually the *Trieben* [drives] of those thousands was a hallucination, tomfoolery, a ruckus, a hubbub, busyness. . . . Socrates doubted that one is a human being by birth; to become human or to learn what it means to be human does not come that easily.[32]

Lear forcefully argues that the contrast Kierkegaard is drawing between Socrates and the multitude is not between a reflective life and one that is unreflective. There is, in fact, a great deal that might be called crit-

---

31. Jonathan Lear, *A Case for Irony* (Cambridge, MA: Harvard University Press, 2011), pp. 37-38.

32. Lear, *A Case for Irony,* p. 5.

ical thought and reflection present in the multitude. Rather the contrast is between those who are sure they know what it means to be human and Socrates' worry he does not know what others seem sure about. In a similar fashion Kierkegaard contrasts those who seem to know what it means to be a Christian and his uncertainty about what it would mean for him to be Christian. Lear, however, argues that Kierkegaard's doubt about his Christianity is not simply whether he is a Christian but rather whether he is in a position to even know if Christianity exists. The problem of Christendom "is that it is the world of Christianity — that when it comes to Christianity there is no outside — and its success as illusion thus depends on its ability to metabolize and contain reflection on the Christian life."[33]

That the significance of irony is not captured by the contrast between the reflective and nonreflective is crucial, Lear argues, if we are to understand Kierkegaard's account of irony. Irony is not required for a well-lived life because we are surrounded by hypocrites and superficial people. Rather Lear suggests that for Kierkegaard even if someone desired to be a Christian they could do so only "by excavating Christendom — that is, engaging in reflection within Christendom — this activity, too, is an occasion for irony."[34] According to Lear, that means it is not sufficient to have only the experience of irony, important though that may be. Rather a capacity for irony is required because irony is a human excellence necessary for becoming human.

Irony understood as an excellence is possible, Lear argues, only for animals who can pretend, that is, who can present themselves to others in terms of established roles and practices.[35] Ducks cannot pretend to be ducks. When ducks waddle they are not pretending to do what ducks do but they are doing what makes ducks ducks. By contrast, humans can pretend in the sense that we can make a claim about what we are doing that may not be the case. Pretense is present in the most fundamental forms of our agency. I may be bent over and when I am asked why I might say, "I am tying my shoe," but given that my intentions are non-observational knowledge, the possibility of pretense is present.[36]

That is why the form of irony is in the form of questions such as "Among all the Christians, is there a Christian?" The significance of that question

---

33. Lear, *A Case for Irony*, p. 8.
34. Lear, *A Case for Irony*, p. 9.
35. Lear, *A Case for Irony*, p. 10.
36. Lear, *A Case for Irony*, p. 10. Lear's account of action obviously draws on the work of Elizabeth Anscombe.

can be shown by noting we think it makes no sense to ask, "Among all the ducks, is there a duck?"[37] Accordingly, irony names that aspect of our practical identity open to erotic and transcendent experiences that disrupts our practical identities. Lear compares irony, therefore, with the uncanniness of oracles that seem to come from an outside source in a manner that challenges the familiar.[38]

Yet our social roles, roles such as being a teacher, are necessary conditions for making us human beings. For example Lear argues that teachers are critical to sustaining our ability to be human. They are so because we are creatures ignorant of the world into which we are born, so we need teachers to teach us what we need to know. Because teachers have been a crucial constitutive part of human societies, there are numerous gestures and habits we associate with someone who is a teacher. If a teacher is a professor, for example, we often are able to identify them by the way they walk, the way they hold a book, the way they dress, the way they communicate. Thus is created the possibility of irony just to the extent that irony "arises when a gap opens between pretense as it is made available in a social practice and an aspiration or ideal which, on the one hand, is embedded in the pretense — indeed, which expresses what the pretense is all about — but which, on the other hand seems to transcend the life and the social practice in which the pretense is made."[39]

Lear argues that this understanding of irony, again an account he thinks owes much to Kierkegaard, depends on the refusal to caricature the forms of life that are thought to make us less than we can be. Lear observes, for example, that Kierkegaard knew well that there were people within Christendom who were self-conscious because Christendom certainly sponsored some forms of critical reflection. But Kierkegaard was not suggesting that irony is the same as critical self-consciousness. Rather for Kierkegaard irony has a far more disruptive capacity to unsettle our lives than simply having my identity as a Christian made problematic. Irony, at least the kind of irony identified by Kierkegaard, not only disrupts my presumption that I am a Christian but more fundamentally it makes me doubt I would even know what it means to be a Christian.

That is why Lear suggests that the experience of irony is a species of the uncanny. Irony makes the familiar strange and the strange familiar by

37. Lear, *A Case for Irony*, pp. 16-17.
38. Lear, *A Case for Irony*, pp. 15-16.
39. Lear, *A Case for Irony*, p. 11.

disrupting my world.[40] The familiar returns as the strange, making me doubt I can be at home in the world being born. At the ironic moment my practical knowledge, knowledge of what it means to be a teacher, is so disrupted I am unsure how to go on. As long as my identity is ensured by social pretense I know what to do, but irony creates the moment when I no longer am sure of my practical knowledge that makes possible my sense of self. So the instability that is constitutive of our practical identity makes irony possible. The social roles and practices that constitute who I am entail normative commitments that work against my presumption that I am a teacher (or Christian) if I fulfill the expectations of those roles.

Therefore, ironic existence is, for Lear, a form of life in which a capacity for irony is developed in order to be a more excellent human being. To have an ironic existence means that you have the capacity to live out a practical identity such as being a teacher, but also you are able to face challenges that come from the ways usual practices can fail to fulfill what it means to be a teacher. Thus the questions that mimic the Kierkegaard-inspired question about being Christian take the form of: "Among all the teachers, is there a teacher?" or "Among all the ironists, is there an ironist?"

Such questions make clear that to develop the capacity for irony is not simply to be called into question by standard forms of criticism but rather to be called into question by the questioning that will disrupt the very process I associate with being called into question. Such questioning, if done well, is a manifestation of the finiteness and vulnerability of the concepts we use to understand and live our lives. Lear concludes with this strong assertion, namely, that "ironic existence thus has a claim to be a human excellence because it is a form of truthfulness. It is also a form of self-knowledge: a practical acknowledgment of the kind of knowing that is available to creatures like us."[41]

Alasdair MacIntyre, in a fascinating response to Lear, challenges Lear's claim that irony is a necessary capacity to be truthful. Drawing on Lear's own example of what is required to be a teacher, MacIntyre argues that a teacher who recognizes that she is not a good teacher can be transformed to be a good teacher by experiences that are not ironic. What makes the acknowledgment of a teacher's inadequacies possible, and what makes

40. Lear, *A Case for Irony*, p. 15.
41. Lear, *A Case for Irony*, p. 31.

them possible to remedy, is not necessarily irony, but humility. Of course the virtue of truthfulness is also required, but truthfulness itself is inadequate without humility. Humility determined by truthfulness makes possible the acknowledgment of our defects and faults without exaggerating those defects and faults. To so belittle ourselves is itself a vice that Aristotle identified with irony and Aquinas with sin.[42]

MacIntyre argues, therefore, that the self-discovery and self-amendment necessary to become a teacher can be achieved without irony. Instead, "what can be said ironically can be said non-ironically and for the moral shock therapy of ironic experience we can substitute the moral shock therapy effected by plain, truthful, harsh words, spoken with humility." Irony isolated from truthfulness and humility threatens to be vicious in a manner that corrupts how it might be a means to sustain our ability to be truthful and humble. MacIntyre does not deny that without irony some would not be shocked into truthfulness, but concludes that "not everyone needs a capacity for irony to be truthful — when Kierkegaard said that 'no genuinely human life is possible without irony,' he confused being human with being Kierkegaard."[43]

In response to MacIntyre, Lear acknowledges that a world without irony may be possible; but a world without irony, he argues, would be a world without norms. Norms make us vulnerable to the uncanny because we are anxious creatures with erotic longings that manifest our commitment to and responsibility for what the goodness of a whole way of life consists of. It is senseless to ask whether there can be a world without irony, because given the way the world is, some will find it impossible to avoid the experience of irony. For Lear, irony begins with the familiar but exposes us to the transcendent, and devoid of the transcendent we have no possibility of being disillusioned from our illusions.[44]

Lear, however, observes that he and MacIntyre are in fundamental agreement that irony, when deployed well, is itself a manifestation of truthfulness and humility. However, he argues that humility is itself a manifestation of truthfulness. So we do not need to say that truthfulness is insufficient without humility because humility is already constitutive of a fulsome account of truthfulness. This means, from Lear's perspective, MacIntyre's

42. Alasdair MacIntyre, "Irony and Humanity: A Dialogue between Jonathan Lear and Alasdair MacIntyre," www.hup.harvard.edu?features/irony-and-humanity/#macintyreRem, p. 8.

43. MacIntyre, "Irony and Humanity," p. 9.

44. Lear, *A Case for Irony*, p. 12.

account of truthfulness is deficient. As a result MacIntyre fails to see how irony is a handmaid of truth once it is recognized that truthfulness is the necessary condition for the fulfillment of our desire for the good. That is why irony is in a service to our desires, desires as simple and basic as to be a good teacher.

## The Point of View for My Work as a Teacher

That is what I have been — a teacher. I have been a teacher whose subject is theology. I am also the author of books in theology. Over the years I found that writing was a necessary exercise if I was to be a good teacher. Writing is not unlike the fundamental movements the body must learn in order to play a sport well. One of the ways to learn those exercises essential to the work of theology is by reading. Reading, writing, and teaching, therefore, are not three different activities for me, but constitute inseparable disciplines that make my life as a theologian. I think those disciplines, moreover, have given me a capacity for irony that I should like to think is close to Lear's account of irony.

There is a sense in which I regard most of what I have written as ironic. I was trained to be a theologian during a time, a time in which we continue to exist, in which many Christians seemed to lose confidence in the vocabulary of the Christian faith. There are many reasons for that loss of confidence, but Wallace's account of the culture produced by television has played some role. Rorty-like understandings of the philosophical alternatives certainly played a role. Just as Rorty suggested, moreover, his philosophical position was seen as supporting liberal social orders in which tolerance and fairness were the primary virtues. If Christians were to be good citizens of democratic regimes it seemed they must assume an ironic stance toward their faith.

In light of such a world I saw one of my tasks as a teacher of theology to help Christians reclaim a confidence in our vocabulary. Theology had to be seen as doing work that could not be done in any other language. I looked for "cracks" in the world which inhabits us that might show why and how what we say as Christians is necessary to sustain forms of behavior that are otherwise unintelligible. For example, in one chapter of *Suffering Presence* I ironically asked: Should we try to prevent retardation? Of course I do not think we should try to prevent all forms of mental handicaps, but to ask the question forces the articulation of the reasons why we should not try to prevent retardation.[45] In that chapter I tried to show that the reasons we should not try to prevent retardation entail theological claims that cannot be considered provisional.

I use the same ironic strategy to force the question of why we have the description "suicide" and why it is considered wrong. Drawing on liberal presuppositions concerning the presumed right each of us has to determine the meaning of our lives, I make the strongest case I can for why we should not try to prevent suicide. If suicide is but one form of a rational choice it is unclear why suicide is seen negatively. I even raise the question as to why we persist in using the description "suicide." Why do we not simply describe what we once called suicide as "self-life taking"?

As long as we continue to use the description "suicide," the presumption that we are our own creators is produced and reproduced. By contrast, the presumption we are not our own creators invites a theological vocabulary that tells a story about our existence that provides an alternative to suicide in the form of a community.[46] I do not expect this mode of argument to change anyone's mind who does not share my vocabulary, but at least they might get some sense from such an exercise that theological convictions are not just mythological language that needs to be — and can be — put in terms that do not presuppose the metaphysical commitments the language entails.

The kinds of essays to which I have just called attention are not the only way I have employed irony to disrupt the everyday. Irony has been essential for my attempt to expose the sentimentalities I associate with the Christian attempt to make our faith compatible with the reigning presumptions of our time. For example, in a chapter in *Dispatches from the Front: Theological Engagements with the Secular,* a title that is itself meant ironically, I challenge the widespread assumption that compassion is the primary Christian stance toward life. In a chapter titled "Killing Compassion," I argue that when compassion is isolated from the other virtues it is not too difficult to logically allow such contradictions as murder being considered a compassionate act.[47]

---

45. Stanley Hauerwas, *Suffering Presence: Theological Reflections on Medicine, the Mentally Handicapped, and the Church* (Notre Dame: University of Notre Dame Press, 1986), pp. 159-81.

46. Hauerwas, "Rational Suicide and Reasons for Living," in *Suffering Presence,* pp. 100-114.

47. Stanley Hauerwas, *Dispatches from the Front: Theological Engagements with the Secular* (Durham, NC: Duke University Press, 1994), pp. 164-76.

I have also used irony in defense of Christian nonviolence by challenging the presumption that nonviolence is to be justified because it is a strategy to rid the world of war. I, of course, want to live in a world in which war is less likely, but I try to show that from a Christological perspective Christians must live with the confidence that war has been eliminated. I first began to develop this perspective in *Against the Nations: War and Survival in a Liberal Society* in a chapter titled "Should War Be Eliminated?"[48] More recently I have tried to extend that argument by asking, "If a war is not just, what is it?" That question has an ironic form meant to make defenders of just war consider again the presumption that a just war perspective can be commensurate with the realistic presumptions that shape the foreign policies of the modern nation-state system.[49]

I do not regard, however, the examples of irony I have just given to be the determinative way theology must be ironic. Rather I take it to be the case that internal to the gospel is an ironic grammar that is necessary in order to grasp what it means to be a disciple of Christ. The central exemplification of that grammar can be found in the eighth chapter of Mark, where we find Peter's confession "You are the Messiah." The irony of that confession is revealed by Jesus' rebuke of Peter for refusing Jesus the kind of death he would undergo. The use of irony in the Gospel of Mark as a means to indicate the training the disciples had to undergo that they might recognize who it is they follow I take not only to be a literary device but an indication of what is required by every Christian.

"I did not intend to be 'Stanley Hauerwas'" may be the most ironic sentence I have ever written. It is the sentence with which I begin *Hannah's Child: A Theologian's Memoir*.[50] "I did not intend to be 'Stanley Hauerwas'" is an ironic signal that the whole of *Hannah's Child* is ironic. For if, as Lear maintains, irony is a form of practical reason for the constitution of the self, *Hannah's Child* is my attempt to display what that means for my life. There are, of course, more than the one "Stanley Hauerwas" I did not intend to be, but the one that continues to be for me the most surprising and odd is the Christian Stanley Hauerwas.

---

48. Stanley Hauerwas, *Against the Nations: War and Survival in a Liberal Society* (Minneapolis: Winston Press, 1985), pp. 169-208.

49. See, for example, my *War and the American Difference: Theological Reflections on Violence and National Identity* (Grand Rapids: Baker, 2011).

50. Stanley Hauerwas, *Hannah's Child: A Theologian's Memoir* (Grand Rapids: Eerdmans, 2012), p. ix. This is the paperback edition that ends with an "Epilogue" in which I respond to reviews and reactions to the book.

Lear is right, I believe, to associate irony as a mode of truth with the disruption of the uncanny. But what could be more disruptive than the declaration, as I argue in a commentary on the Gospel of Matthew, that Jesus' conception begins a new creation?[51] Such a claim is appropriately called "apocalyptic," requiring, as Ben Dillon suggests, a double vision that at once affirms God's presence in the world but not as part of the world. Dillon observes that this means the distinction between God and the world is not adequately grasped by the dualism between the material and spiritual matter. The irony of God's presence "is only intensified when God enters creation in Jesus Christ, for the divinity of Jesus transpires silently, behind the scenes; it makes no appearance in itself but is identifiable only in and from its effects."[52]

Dillon argues that these eschatological convictions must be expressed by Christians developing a double vision. It is a vision made possible by Christians learning a particular language that gives Christians the possibility of discerning what is "hidden" in history, that is, that God is at work to bring creation to consummation. It is a bold theological claim that I believe to be true, but also one that must be disciplined by the humility that comes from worshiping the One we believe is Trinity. Truth and humility, as Lear and MacIntyre suggest, require one another, but their most intimate relationship is to be found in worship.

I finally come to what I take to be the most important role of irony for the work of theology. I suggested above that I took one of my tasks as a teacher of theology to be giving students a renewed confidence in the vocabulary of the faith. Yet how can that be done without acknowledgment of my inadequate ability to live what I say? My only recourse is to pray that those I teach recognize the irony that constitutes the life of such a teacher. That is why I suspect that the most intense mode of irony finds expression in prayers that at once suggest my continuing surprise and delight that I am a Christian. Prayers like the following:

> End of all our beginnings, Lord of time, who alone makes time a gift, remind us we are creatures with a beginning. We confess we often forget we are your timeful creatures. We fear the forgetfulness our death

51. Stanley Hauerwas, *Matthew*, Brazos Theological Commentary on the Bible (Grand Rapids: Brazos, 2006), pp. 23-25.

52. Ben Dillon, "Seeing Double: Irony, Liberalism, and Christian Political Engagement," Dissertation Proposal at Duke University, 2012.

beckons. We are driven frantically to work, thinking we can ensure we will not be forgotten, to ensure our place in time. How silly we must look to you, ants building anthills to no purpose. Help us take joy and rest in your time, Eucharistic time, a time redeemed through Jesus' resurrection, that we can rest easy in our dying. You have given us all the time in the world. May we take pleasure in it. Amen.[53]

53. Hauerwas, *Prayers Plainly Spoken*, p. 31.

# CHAPTER 9

# How to (Not) Be a Political Theologian

## Trying to Understand Where I Belong Politically

I have recently discovered I am numbered among those identified as "political theologians." I must be a political theologian because there is an article, a very good article by Rusty Reno, on my work in *The Blackwell Companion to Political Theology*.[1] Reno even begins his article with the astounding claim that "in the final decades of the twentieth century, Stanley Hauerwas articulated the most coherent and influential political theology in and for the North American context."[2] Rusty Reno is a theologian of rare intellectual judgment, so I assume he must know what he is talking about, but I confess for me the idea that I am a political theologian will take some getting used to.

I want to use this essay to explore why my identification as a political theologian takes, at least for me, some getting used to. To do so will require that I revisit some of the early developments in Christian ethics that shaped how I think about the fundamental political character of Christian theology. In short, I have always assumed any theology reflects a politics whether that politics is acknowledged or not. Of course the crucial question is: What kind of politics is theologically assumed? In the tradition in which I was educated it was assumed that democratic politics was normative for Christians. Because I do not share that presumption some think I have no politics.

In truth I have no stake, one way or the other, in being counted among

---

1. R. R. Reno, "Stanley Hauerwas," in the *Blackwell Companion to Political Theology* (Oxford: Blackwell, 2004), pp. 302-16.
2. Reno, "Stanley Hauerwas," p. 302.

those doing political theology. I have always resisted modifying theology with descriptors that suggest theology is the possession of certain groups or perspectives. For me nothing is more important than the fundamental task of theology to be of service to the church; it belongs to the church. I am well aware that time and place do and should make a difference for how theology is done. But too often I fear when theology is made subservient to this or that qualifier it has inadequate means with which to resist becoming an ideology.

It is true, however, that there is no "method" that can protect theologians from engaging in ideological modes of thought, even when they claim to be doing theology qua theology. Theology stands under the permanent temptation to "choose sides," which means theology can become ideological long before anyone notices. I have no objection to calling theology "Christian," but that description does not ensure that theology that bears the name will be free of ideological perversion. "Christian" is no guarantee that theology can be safeguarded against being put at the service of political loyalties and practices that betray the gospel.

I resist using the phrase "political theology" for many of the same reasons I try to avoid the phrase "social ethics." Ask yourself: What kind of ethic would not be social? In a similar fashion I assume every theology, even theology done in a speculative mode, has been produced and reproduces a politics. If theology is done faithful to the gospel it will not only be political but it will be so in a particular way. Thus John Howard Yoder's observation in *The Politics of Jesus* that appeals to Jesus as "political" too often are only slogans that fail to indicate the *kind* of politics Jesus incarnated.[3]

Whether or not I am a political theologian depends on how "political theology" is understood. It is important to remember that the nomenclature "political theology" has only recently been reintroduced into discussions in theology and political theory.[4] Indeed, as Elizabeth Phillips rightly reminds us, political theology did not originally come from Christian theology, but rather originated in Athens where politics was understood as the art of seeking the common good of the polis.[5] Phillips observes that

3. John Howard Yoder, *The Politics of Jesus: Vicit Agnus Noster,* 2nd ed. (Grand Rapids: Eerdmans, 1995), p. 3.

4. For an extremely informative overview of the history of Christian engagement with politics see C. C. Pecknold, *Christianity and Politics: A Brief Guide to the History* (Eugene, OR: Cascade, 2010).

5. Elizabeth Phillips, *Political Theology: A Guide for the Perplexed* (London: T. & T. Clark, 2012), p. 4.

the task was later taken up by Christian thinkers such as Augustine who compared and contrasted Christianity to what had been done in the name of political theology. The phrase "political theology," however, has only recently been reintroduced into political and legal theory through the work of Carl Schmitt.

Schmitt maintained that all significant concepts that constitute the legitimating discourses of modern state formations are in fact secularized theological concepts.[6] Phillips observes that this claim has given new life to diverse approaches to "the political" — not the least being the discussions and ongoing debates around Schmitt's strong claim about the totalizing character of modern politics. Accordingly political theology has become an attempt to identify how ideas concerning salvation and devotion to God migrated from Christian theology to the nation-state. Schmitt's work is quite controversial not only because of his association with the Nazi party but because of his Hobbes-like contention that the sovereign is known by the one who decides on the exception.

Paul Kahn argues that Schmitt's understanding of sovereignty has structured an inquiry into the political that is a kind of mirror image of the political theory of liberalism. For Schmitt it is not the law but the exception, not the judge but the sovereign, not reason but decision, that determines the character of the political. Kahn argues that Schmitt's inversion of liberal presuppositions about politics is so extreme, one "might think of political theology as the dialectical negation of liberal political theory."[7] Given my identification as a critic of liberal political theory, some, with some justification, might think I am rightly described as a political theologian.

I doubt, however, that I deserve such a description. I confess it is tempting to claim this identity as a way to counter the oft-made criticism that I am a "sectarian, fideistic tribalist" who is trying to get Christians to abandon the task of securing justice through participation in politics.[8] It is true, moreover, that I find much of the work being done in political

6. Carl Schmitt, *Political Theology: Four Chapters on the Concept of Sovereignty* (Chicago: University of Chicago Press, 1985), p. 36.

7. Paul Kahn, *Political Theology: Four New Chapters on the Concept of Sovereignty* (New York: Columbia University Press, 2011), p. 31.

8. For a summary of James Gustafson's description of my work as well as my response, see the "Introduction" to my book *Christian Existence Today: Essays on Church, World, and Living In-Between* (Grand Rapids: Brazos, 2001), pp. 1-21. This book was originally published in 1988.

theology to be quite congenial with the way I think about the political challenges facing Christians in contexts such as America. But the path I have taken for how I understand the political stance Christians should assume in the world in which we find ourselves is quite different from that of those who now identify themselves with "political theology."

In order to explain that "path," as well as how I now think about the politics of Christian existence, I need to provide an account of how Christians in America became convinced they had a moral obligation to be political actors in what they took to be democratic politics. The expression "the politics of Christian existence," which I use to describe my position, indicates my distance from the story I have to tell about how Christians came to ask themselves what political responsibilities they had as Christians. That question would often produce investigations into the relation of Christianity and politics. From my perspective that way of putting the matter — that is, "What is the relation between Christianity and politics?" — is to have failed to account for the political reality of the church.

My point is not unlike John Howard Yoder's argument concerning the inadequacy of H. Richard Niebuhr's "method" in *Christ and Culture*. Yoder argues that the very way Niebuhr posed the problem of the relation of Christ to culture failed to be properly Christological just to the extent that the Christ who is Lord is separated from Jesus of Nazareth. Yoder argues that Niebuhr's account of Christ as the exemplification of radical monotheism failed to give adequate expression to the full and genuine human existence of the man Jesus of Nazareth. That Christological mistake from Yoder's point of view shaped the problematic character of Niebuhr's typology because recognition of Jesus' full humanity is necessary to recognize that Jesus himself is a "cultural reality." As a result, the Christ of *Christ and Culture* was assumed to be alien to culture qua culture, thus creating the problematic that shapes Niebuhr's book.[9]

9. John Howard Yoder, "How H. Richard Niebuhr Reasoned: A Critique of *Christ and Culture*," in *Authentic Transformation: A New Vision of Christ and Culture,* by Glen Stassen, D. M. Yeager, and John Howard Yoder (Nashville: Abingdon, 1996), p. 68. Yoder's critique of *Christ and Culture* is often dismissed as Mennonite prejudice, but Robert Jenson, who is certainly no Mennonite, has criticized Niebuhr in terms very similar to Yoder. He observes, for example, that Niebuhr's title presupposes Christ is one thing and culture another, but Christ is a title meaningful only in a particular culture. That culture is called Israel, which means that to isolate Christ from culture results in a Christology that threatens Docetism. See Robert Jenson, *Theology as Revisionary Metaphysics* (Eugene, OR: Cascade, 2014), pp. 181-88.

What I must now try to do is to tell the story of the "and" that created the question of the relation of Christianity *and* politics. I hope to show that just as Yoder suggests the "and" between Christ and culture reproduced a Christ who was less than fully human, so the "and" between Christianity and politics assumes a church that is fundamentally apolitical. Because I have been so influenced by Yoder I am often accused of tempting Christians to withdraw from participation in politics. Yet neither Yoder nor myself have assumed it possible to "withdraw" from the world, or, even if withdrawal was possible, that it would be a "good thing." Admittedly, as I will suggest in due course, Yoder changes how as Christians we are to understand "the political," but he does so because of how he understands "the politics of Jesus."[10] To show the difference Yoder makes I need to provide a brief account of how Rauschenbusch and Niebuhr understood democracy as the politics that is definitive for Christians.

## How Christians Became "Political" in America

The story I have to tell is not unlike the story I planned to tell by writing a book on the development of Christian ethics in America. In a chapter in *A Better Hope* titled "Christian Ethics in America (and the *Journal of Religious Ethics*): A Report on a Book I Will Not Write," I explain why I did not write the book.[11] I did not write the book because I did not want to write about a tradition I thought had come to an end.[12] That the tradition had come to an end had everything to do with what I took to be the storyline of the book. The storyline is that the subject of Christian ethics in America was first and foremost America. That such was and still remains the case means: just to the extent Christians got the politics they had identified as Christian, that is, democratic politics, they seemed no longer to have anything politically interesting to say as Christians.

Put differently, I suggested that the book I did not write would ask the dramatic question of how a tradition that began with a book by Walter Rauschenbusch titled *Christianizing the Social Order* would end with a

10. For a fascinating reading of the implications of Yoder for political theology see Daniel Barber, *On Diaspora: Christianity, Religion, and Secularity* (Eugene, OR: Cascade, 2011), pp. 117-22.

11. Stanley Hauerwas, *A Better Hope: Resources for a Church Confronting Capitalism, Democracy, and Postmodernity* (Grand Rapids: Brazos, 2000), pp. 55-70.

12. Hauerwas, *A Better Hope*, p. 67.

book by James Gustafson titled *Can Ethics Be Christian?* The story I sought to tell was meant to explore how that result came to be, by concentrating on people such as Reinhold Niebuhr, H. Richard Niebuhr, Paul Ramsey, Jim Gustafson, and John Howard Yoder. Yoder, of course, did not stand in the same tradition as those from Rauschenbusch to Gustafson, but that was just the point — namely, that only an outsider could offer the fresh perspective the mainstream theological tradition so desperately needed.

It is not quite true that I did not write the book I had planned. I did write a number of essays on Rauschenbusch, Reinhold and H. Richard Niebuhr, Paul Ramsey, and Jim Gustafson that developed some themes that the proposed book was to be about.[13] What I failed to do, and the failure was intentional, was to bring these essays and chapters together in one book. I do not regret that decision, but that I did not write the book means I can use this opportunity to make explicit how the development of Christian thinking about politics resulted in the loss of the politics of the church.

A strange claim to be sure. The social gospel was, after all, largely a movement of churchmen to convince their fellow Christians that they had a calling to engage in the work of social reconstruction. Of course the central reality for the social gospel was not the church but the kingdom of God. Yet Rauschenbusch claimed that the church is the social factor in salvation. The church is so because it "brings social forces to bear on evil. It offers Christ not only many human bodies and minds to serve as ministers of his salvation, but its own composite personality, with a collective memory storied with great hymns and Bible moral feelings, and with a collective will set on righteousness."[14]

Rauschenbusch appealed to Schleiermacher and Josiah Royce to emphasize that the church is the social organism that makes it possible for

---

13. See, for example, the chapter on Rauschenbusch titled "Walter Rauschenbusch and the Saving of America" in *A Better Hope*, pp. 71-108. I follow that chapter with a chapter on John Courtney Murray and his role in drafting the Vatican II encyclical *Dignitatis Humanae*. Murray and John Ryan are part of the story I wanted to tell about Christian ethics as they represented the Catholic alternative to the mainstream Protestants. I wrote numerous essays on Reinhold Niebuhr, but the two that are most relevant to this essay appear in my book *Wilderness Wanderings: Probing Twentieth-Century Theology and Philosophy* (Boulder, CO: Westview, 1997), pp. 32-62. That book also includes my essays on Jim Gustafson and Paul Ramsey. The essays I have written on Yoder are too numerous to list.

14. Walter Rauschenbusch, *A Theology for the Social Gospel* (Nashville: Abingdon, 1917), p. 119.

us to share in the consciousness of Christ. According to Rauschenbusch, the individual is saved by membership in the church because the church is necessary to make Christ's consciousness the consciousness of every member of the church. It is not the institutional character of the church, nor its continuity, nor its ministry, nor its doctrine that saves, but rather the church provides salvation by making the kingdom of God present.[15]

According to Rauschenbusch the kingdom of God is the heart of the revolutionary force of Christianity. It was the loss of the kingdom ideals that put the church on the path to abandon her social and political commitments. As a result the movements for democracy and social justice were left without religious backing. In the process many Christians lost any sense that social justice might have something to do with salvation. Absent the kingdom, Christians failed to emphasize the three commitments that the kingdom entails: (1) to work for a social order that guarantees to all personalities their freest and highest development; (2) to secure the progressive reign of love in human affairs so that the use of force and legal coercion becomes superseded; and (3) to freely surrender property rights, which means the refusal to support monopolistic industries.[16]

All of which can be summed up by Rauschenbusch's claim that the social gospel is the religious response to the historic advent of democracy. For Rauschenbusch the social gospel sought to put the democratic spirit that the church inherited from Jesus and the prophets once more in control of the institution of the church.[17] Another word for salvation, Rauschenbusch asserts, is democracy, because Jesus' highest redemptive act was to take God by the hand and call him "our Father." By doing so Jesus democratized the conception of God, and in the process he not only saved humanity but "he saved God."[18]

The Christian's task is to work to extend this democratic ideal. Rauschenbusch thinks the ideal has been largely achieved in the political sphere, but now the same democratic ideals must be applied to the economic realm. That means Christians must work to see that the brotherhood of man is expressed in the common possession of economic resources of society. They must also seek to secure the spiritual good of humanity by ensuring that such a good is set high above the private profit interests of

15. Rauschenbusch, *A Theology for the Social Gospel*, p. 129.
16. Rauschenbusch, *A Theology for the Social Gospel*, pp. 142-43.
17. Rauschenbusch, *A Theology for the Social Gospel*, p. 5.
18. Rauschenbusch, *A Theology for the Social Gospel*, pp. 174-75.

all materialistic groups.[19] Rauschenbusch was convinced, moreover, that these were not unrealizable ideals, but possible achievements Christians could bring to fruition if the gospel was recognized to be a social gospel.

It is tempting to dismiss Rauschenbusch as hopelessly naïve, but that would be a mistake. His rhetoric invites the judgment that he is far too "optimistic," but it should not be forgotten that after Rauschenbusch it was assumed by most people in mainstream Protestant denominations in America that Christians had a responsibility to be politically active in order to extend democratic practices. Reinhold Niebuhr would criticize Rauschenbusch for failing to account for the necessity of conflict and coercion for the establishment of justice, but Niebuhr never called into question Rauschenbusch's fundamental insight that Christians have to make use of politics to achieve justice. Though critical of the social gospel, Niebuhr simply assumed that Christians must be politically responsible. Niebuhr's chastened realism to be sure was a critical response to Rauschenbusch's far-too-optimistic presumption that justice was achievable, but in many ways Niebuhr's criticisms of the social gospel were made possible by the achievement of that movement.

Of course it was sin that determined Niebuhr's fundamental perspective on the necessity of politics. Because we are sinners justice can be achieved only by degrees of coercion, as well as resistance to coercion. Thus his oft-made claim that "the political life of man must constantly steer between the Scylla of anarchy and the Charybdis of tyranny."[20] These alternatives, anarchy or tyranny, Niebuhr often confidently declared were our only choices if we did not strive to sustain democratic life and institutions. Thus his remark, a remark I think he borrowed from Churchill, that democracy is the worst form of government other than all other forms of government. Democracy is so because democracy provides an alternative to totalitarianism or anarchy.

For Niebuhr, Christians have a stake in democratic societies because, given the realism that the Christian understanding of sin requires, Christians know "that a healthy society must seek to achieve the greatest possible equilibrium of power, the greatest possible centers of power, the greatest possible social checks of the administration of power, and the

---

19. Rauschenbusch, *A Theology for the Social Gospel*, p. 224.

20. *Reinhold Niebuhr on Politics*, ed. Harry Davis and Robert Good (New York: Scribner's Sons, 1960), p. 182. This is a volume that organizes Niebuhr's writing on politics in an extraordinarily helpful way.

greatest possible inner moral check on human ambition, as well as the most effective use of forms of power in which consent and coercion are compounded."[21] Democracies at their best are, therefore, able to achieve unity of purpose within the conditions of freedom and to maintain freedom within the framework of order.

It is particularly important to note that for Niebuhr democracy is a system of government that does not require the governed to be virtuous. Rather it is a form of social organization that limits self-interested people to pursuing their interests in a manner that does not destroy community. Of course a too-consistent pessimism concerning our ability to transcend our interests can lead to absolutist political theories. So Niebuhr is not suggesting that democracies can survive without some sense of justice. Rather he is reminding us that, as he puts it in what is probably his most famous epigram, "Man's capacity for justice makes democracy possible; but man's inclination to injustice makes democracy necessary."[22]

The task of social Christianity for Niebuhr is not to advocate particular solutions for economic or social ills, but to produce people of modesty and humility regarding what can be accomplished given our sinful condition.[23] It is equally important that the same modesty be applied to the church, which is no less under the power of sin. In fact, from Niebuhr's point of view the sins of the church may even be more destructive given the temptation to identify religious politics with the politics of God. For Niebuhr the task of the church is "to bear witness against every form of pride and vainglory, whether in the secular or in the Christian culture, and be particularly intent upon our own sins lest we make Christ the judge of the other but not of ourselves."[24]

The contrasts between Rauschenbusch and Niebuhr are clear, though

21. *Reinhold Niebuhr on Politics*, p. 182.

22. *Reinhold Niebuhr on Politics*, p. 186. This famous epigram is from Niebuhr's *Children of Light and Children of Darkness*, a book he wrote after World War II to chasten what he regarded as the uncritical celebration of democracy.

23. It is to Charles Mathewes's great credit that he develops what I take to be a Niebuhrian theme by suggesting that Christian engagement in politics is itself a discipline for the shaping of the Christian life. Christians must have virtues that will prepare them politically, but those same virtues will be honed through political engagement. I am sure Mathewes is right about that, but I suspect the "ambiguity" that is according to Mathewes intrinsic to political involvement can be learned from singing in the church choir. I suspect Mathewes would agree. See his *A Theology of Public Life* (Cambridge: Cambridge University Press, 2007).

24. *Reinhold Niebuhr on Politics*, p. 205.

they share more than is immediately apparent. In particular, democracy plays a very similar role in their respective positions. The question of the relation of Christianity and politics is fundamentally resolved for Rauschenbusch and Niebuhr if the politics the Christian is to presume as normative is a democratic politics. Rauschenbusch and Niebuhr are vague about what makes a democracy democratic, but I hope enough has been said to show how the language of democracy became their way to assure Christians in America that they must "be political."

## The Difference Yoder Makes

I simply assumed, as I suspect almost anyone who did work in Christian ethics in the second half of the twentieth century assumed, that Rauschenbusch's and Niebuhr's different understanding and justification of democracy was a given. Yet even before I had read Yoder I was beginning to explore issues in democratic theory that would make me worry about the assumption that democracy is normative for Christians. For example, in the earliest article I wrote on Christianity and politics, "Politics, Vision, and the Common Good," I began to worry about issues intrinsic to democratic practice and theory.[25] The civil rights movement, the protest against the war in Vietnam, and questions of economic inequality made me question pluralist justifications of democratic processes. Drawing on the work of Robert Paul Wolff, Ted Lowi, and Sheldon Wolin, I began to explore what alternatives there might be to Niebuhr's "realism."

The article on politics and the common good was paired with another chapter in *Vision and Virtue* titled "Theology and the New American Culture."[26] "Theology and the New American Culture" is probably best described as an attempt at theological journalism. Reinhold Niebuhr was the master of this genre, as he ably helped us see how what seemed to be quite theoretical issues in political theory had concrete manifestations. In "Theology and the New American Culture" I was trying to suggest that the cultural despair that was so evident among many in the 1960s was not accidentally related to some of the fundamental presumptions of liberal democratic theory and practice. Drawing on Philip Slater's *The Pursuit of Loneliness,* I tried to show there was a connection between our isolation

25. Stanley Hauerwas, *Vision and Virtue* (Notre Dame: Fides Press, 1974), pp. 222-60.
26. Hauerwas, *Vision and Virtue,* pp. 241-60.

from one another and our inability to discover goods in common through the political process.

Somehow, and it may have come from reading the Social Encyclicals, I began to think there was a deep tension between liberal political theory and accounts of politics that appealed to the common good. Niebuhr's political realism, expressed in terms of interest-group liberalism, at best can give you an account of common interests. For Niebuhr, as well as more secular accounts of liberal democratic theory, there are no goods in common that can be discovered and at the same time serve democratic politics. The democratic state, as Ernst-Wolfgang Bockenforde has argued, is an order of freedom and of peace rather than an order of truth and virtue necessary for the recognition of common goods.[27] Accordingly, defenders of liberal democracies seek to establish institutions that make possible the achievement of relative justice without people themselves being just.[28]

I observed above that I was beginning to explore critical questions internal to issues in democratic theory. That way of putting the matter is, I think, important because it indicates I was not calling into question the presumption that some account of democracy is important for Christians if we were to be politically responsible. *A Community of Character: Toward a Constructive Christian Social Ethic,* a book published in 1981, included a chapter titled "The Church and Liberal Democracy." In that essay I began to try to distinguish democratic practice from liberal political theory.[29] Drawing on the work of C. B. Macpherson, I tried to show how

27. This is Martin Rhonheimer's characterization of Bockenforde's views in Rhonheimer's sophisticated book, *The Common Good of Constitutional Democracy* (Washington, DC: Catholic University of America Press, 2013), pp. 74-75. Rhonheimer, who many would regard as a very conservative Catholic moral theologian, argues against Bockenforde by suggesting that modern democratic states' attempt to secure peace is itself a good in common. Rhonheimer does not contest Bockenforde's contention that truth is not the aim of democratic constitutionalism, but argues that constitutional democracies rightly seek to secure a minimum morality to ensure people can live together in peace. The institutions of societies are so ordered, Rhonheimer argues, to compensate for the deficit in individual morality. Rhonheimer's is a powerful argument, but I remain doubtful that peace is possible without truthfulness.

28. Some may think this an unfair characterization, but John Rawls is admirably candid that his project is an attempt to give an account of justice that does not require those who enjoy the system of justice so created to be just. See *A Theory of Justice* (Cambridge, MA: Harvard University Press, 1971), pp. 54-65.

29. I am quite well aware that a phrase like "liberal political theory" does not do justice to the many forms of liberal theory. For the best account I know of the diversity of liberal theory see Paul Kahn, *Putting Liberalism in Its Place* (Princeton: Princeton University Press,

liberalism, particularly in its economic modes, subverted the democratic commitment to sustain a common life necessary to make possible lives of virtue.[30] Accordingly I argued that just to the extent the church is or can be a school for virtue, Christians can be crucial for the sustaining of democratic social and political life.

By the time I wrote *A Community of Character* I had read and begun to absorb the work of John Howard Yoder. What I learned from Yoder meant I was to be labeled a sectarian, fideistic tribalist because I was allegedly tempting Christians to withdraw from political engagement. Nothing could have been further from the truth. In fact the attempt to distinguish democratic practice from liberal political theory reflected my conviction that Christians could not and should not withdraw from serving their neighbor through political engagement. Some suggested the book I wrote with Rom Coles, *Christianity, Democracy, and the Radical Ordinary: Conversations Between a Radical Democrat and a Christian,* represented a more positive approach to the political than my previous work.[31] That

---

2005). Kahn argues that liberalism's greatest deficit is the failure by liberal theorists to account for the significance of the will (and thus love) in the politics of modern nation-states. Kahn distinguishes between a liberalism of interest and a liberalism of reason. The former emphasizes the centrality of the market while the latter attempts to ground political life in a compelling foundation comparable to the sciences. But both forms of liberalism, Kahn argues, fail to do justice to the will as the source of love necessary to ground politics. See Kahn's chapter, "The Faculties of the Soul: Beyond Reason and Interest," pp. 145-82.

30. Stanley Hauerwas, *A Community of Character: Toward a Constructive Christian Social Ethic* (Notre Dame: University of Notre Dame Press, 1981), pp. 72-88. I cannot believe I used the phrase "social ethic" in the title of this book. The use of that phrase is problematic because it cannot help but reproduce the presumption that there is another area of ethics that is not social. I am aware that Macpherson's account of "possessive individualism" has been the subject of aggressive critique. I remain convinced, however, that the main lines of his argument remain valid. For an insightful analysis of the question of the relation of democracy and liberalism in my work as well as Stout's critique of my identification of democracy with liberalism see William Cavanaugh, "A Politics of Vulnerability: Hauerwas and Democracy," in *Unsettling Arguments: A Festschrift on the Occasion of Stanley Hauerwas's 70th Birthday* (Eugene, OR: Cascade, 2010), pp. 89-111. In his *The Mystical as Political: Democracy and Non-Radical Orthodoxy* (Notre Dame: University of Notre Dame Press, 2012), Aristotle Papanikolaou observes that I have never "really taken the time to nuance what I mean by liberalism" (p. 135). I do not think that a fair characterization. The problem is not that I have not taken the time to give more nuanced accounts of liberalism. The problem is, I have done so too occasionally. I should say I am quite sympathetic with Papanikolaou's emphasis on the importance of spirituality for democratic politics, and in particular the politics of truth.

31. Stanley Hauerwas and Romand Coles, *Christianity, Democracy, and the Radical Ordinary: Conversations Between a Radical Democrat and a Christian* (Eugene, OR: Cascade,

may be true of the tone of the book, but I understood the conversation between Coles and myself to be the continuation of my attempt to find a way to talk about forms of democratic life that were not shaped by liberal presuppositions.

That is not to say, however, that Yoder did not make a difference in how I thought about Christian political engagement. Prior to reading Yoder I had the sense that my emphasis on the virtues meant that the church was a crucial polis for the formation of virtuous lives. The church became the polis that Aristotle knew had to exist but, in his case, did not. Accordingly Yoder's ecclesiology supplied the politics I needed to make intelligible the stress on the virtues. That meant, as Dan Bell argues, that I had to resist any politics that portrays the church as apolitical in a manner that leaves the formation of the body, i.e., the church, to the state. I refused any reduction of politics to statecraft in order to emphasize the political character of the church as a political space in its own right.[32]

From such a perspective the moral emptiness at the heart of liberalism could be construed as an advantage for Christians if the church was capable of producing lives that are not empty. Liberalism as a practice for organizing cooperative arrangements between moral strangers could be good for Christians, though I think it bad for liberals. Indeed I thought my critiques of liberalism were charitable because my criticisms were an attempt to suggest to liberals that there are alternatives to a liberal way of life. Of course, one of the difficulties with that way of conceiving the political mission of the church is that too often Christians had policed their Christianity to make it compatible with liberal tolerance. The other difficulty is that the alleged indifference of liberal states concerning formation of "citizens" was anything but "neutral." In fact, the liberal state is quite good at the formation of people who possess virtues that sustain war.

---

2008). For a very enlightening analysis of the relation of liberal political theory and democracy see Alan Ryan, *The Making of Modern Liberalism* (Princeton: Princeton University Press, 2012), pp. 21-107. Ryan rightly identifies liberalism as a "theory of the good life for individuals that is linked to a theory of the social, economic, and political arrangements within which they may lead that life" (p. 15). He suggests that Rawls failed to finally separate his account of liberalism from a view of the good life. Ryan's account of liberal anxiety is particularly telling: "Liberals suffer a self-inflicted wound: they want the emancipation that leads to disenchantment, but want the process that emancipates us to relocate us in the world as well. Nietzsche and Weber are only the most eloquent among the voices that say it cannot be done in the way the liberal wants" (p. 78).

32. Dan Bell, "State and Civil Society," in *The Blackwell Companion to Political Theology*, pp. 433-34.

I do not mean to suggest that Yoder's influence on me made little difference. In fact it made all the difference. Thus his claim:

> To ask, "What is the best form of government?" is itself a Constantinian question. It is representative of an already "established" social posture. It assumes that the paradigmatic person, the model ethical agent, is in a position of such power that it falls to him to evaluate alternative worlds and to prefer the one in which he himself (for the model ethical agent assumes himself to be part of "the people") shares the rule.[33]

Yoder's challenge, interestingly enough, made me wonder — given my interest in exploring issues in democratic theory — whether, in fact, rather than being a "sectarian" I did not continue to be a Constantinian.

Of course, if Alex Sider is right, and I certainly think he is, it is very hard to avoid being Constantinian. That it is hard to avoid being Constantinian is clear because, as Sider argues, even Yoder was unable to avoid that fate. According to Sider, Constantinianism is not so much a "problem" as it is a totalizing discourse. That means that the resources one has for mapping a way out of Constantinianism will themselves likely be implicated in Constantinianism.[34] In short, Constantinianism conditions the possibility for its own investigation just to the extent that it determines what is to count as history.[35] That is why Sider argues that more fundamental than the distinction between transcendental and empirical uses of the description "Constantinianism" is the distinction between historicist and eschatological discourse. That means for Yoder "the true meaning of history is in the church. And this history is, at least in part, one of disavowal and apostasy."[36] But the very narration of Constantinianism as apostasy reproduces a Constantinian view of history.

Sider's account of the unavoidability of Constantinianism makes clear how, in spite of what I have learned from Yoder, I have in many ways remained a Constantinian. Yet I have never pretended that everything associated with Constantinianism is to be rejected.[37] Certainly Yoder did not

---

33. John Howard Yoder, *The Priestly Kingdom: Social Ethics as Gospel* (Notre Dame: University of Notre Dame Press, 1984), p. 154.

34. Alex Sider, *To See History Doxologically: History and Holiness in John Howard Yoder's Ecclesiology* (Grand Rapids: Eerdmans, 2011), p. 120.

35. Sider, *To See History Doxologically*, p. 121.

36. Sider, *To See History Doxologically*, p. 121.

37. In a number of essays I have tried to suggest the alternative between Constantinian-

think such a rejection was warranted or required, because he often saw much good in some developments associated with Christendom arrangements. It is important, moreover, to observe that Yoder's remark about the question, "What is the best form of government?" is one made in the context of his chapter, "The Christian Case for Democracy." With his usual analytical power Yoder explores in that essay the limits and possibilities of appeals to the rule of the people, observing that it is by no means clear why rule by the people is a good; and how would we know it to be good if the people did rule?[38]

Yoder worries that the glorification of democracy as the rule of "the people," as well as the presumption that democracy represents a form of government that does not suffer from the disabilities of other forms of government, results in uncritical support of wars fought in the name of democracy. So his strategy in the chapter on democracy can almost be described as Niebuhrian just to the extent that he seeks to humble the rhetoric surrounding the uncritical celebration of democracy by Christians. Yet he argues that if Christians accepted our minority status in societies like those in North America, we would be free to hold rulers to account by asking them to rule consistent with the rhetoric they use to legitimate their power. What we dare not forget, however, is that the assumption that "we" the people are governing ourselves is actually not the case. We are governed by elites. Democracies are no less oligarchic than other forms of government, but it is true, according to Yoder, that democratic oligarchies tend to be the least oppressive.[39]

For Yoder the task is not to justify "democracy." Rather he simply accepts the fact that we are told we live in a democracy. He is not convinced we know what that entails. But drawing on A. D. Lindsay's argument in his *The Modern Democratic State,* that the origins of democracy were in Puritan and Quaker congregations where the dignity of the adversary made dialogue not only necessary but possible, Yoder argues that the church

---

ism and non-Constantinianism is often not very helpful if we are to discern how Christians must attempt to find ways to serve the neighbor. Several chapters in *A Better Hope: Resources for a Church Confronting Capitalism, Democracy, and Postmodernity* (Grand Rapids: Brazos, 2000) were attempts to defy the assumption that anti-Constantinianism meant Christians have nothing useful to say to the alternative politics of the world. *The State of the University: Academic Knowledges and the Knowledge of God* (Oxford: Blackwell, 2007) may be even more relevant.

38. Yoder, *The Priestly Kingdom,* p. 151.

39. Yoder, *The Priestly Kingdom,* pp. 157-58.

can serve democratic orders in a similar fashion by being a community that continues to respect the adversary both within and outside of the church. From Yoder's perspective, the church best serves the social orders that claim to be democratic by taking seriously the internal calling of the church rather than "becoming tributary to whatever secular consensus seems strong at the time."[40]

That is the strategy I have tried to adopt in my work. It is a strategy that makes any identification as a "political theologian" doubtful. There is much to learn from work in political theology, but the way I think about Christian political engagement is less grand than most of what is identified as work in political theology. For example, I think calling attention to the work of Jean Vanier has a political purpose. For it must surely be the case that the existence and support of the work of Vanier to secure homes for the mentally disabled indicates the kind of moral commitment necessary to sustain a politics capable of recognizing the dignity of each human being.[41] But to hold up the work of Vanier as politically significant I am sure seems to many simply a way of avoiding the primary political challenges before societies like the United States of America. That may be the case, but that is the way I have learned to think theologically about politics.

In his *The First Thousand Years: A Global History of Christianity,* Robert Wilken observes that Christianity is a culture-forming religion. Consequently the growth of Christian communities led to the transformation of the cultures of the ancient world, which meant the creation of several new civilizations. At the heart of that process was language, because, as Wilken suggests, "culture has to do with the pattern of inherited meanings and sensibilities embedded in rituals, institutions, laws, practices, images, and the stories of people."[42] Wilken's description of the conceptual revolution that was Christianity rightly directs attention to the significance of

---

40. Yoder, *The Priestly Kingdom,* p. 168.

41. I have written about Vanier a number of times, but I was honored to write with him *Living Gently in a Violent World: The Prophetic Witness of Weakness* (Downers Grove: InterVarsity, 2008). I suspect, however, the work my students do is more indicative of how to go on than anything I have done. See, for example, Charles Pinches, "Hauerwas and Political Theology: The Next Generation," *Journal of Religious Ethics* 36, no. 3 (September 2008): 513-42. Pinches directs attention to Cavanaugh, Long, Toole, Bell, McCarthy, Shuman, Lysaught, and Johnson as representatives of this way of doing "political theology."

42. Robert Wilken, *The First Thousand Years: A Global History of Christianity* (New Haven: Yale University Press, 2012), p. 2.

language as the heart of politics. That is why I resist any attempt to suggest that the church is one thing and politics something else.

Luke Bretherton puts this just right when he suggests that doing church and doing politics are both about the formation of shared speech and action that form a common world. Therefore, according to Bretherton, politics and ecclesiology name two mutually constitutive locations where a *sensus communis* can be forged.[43] I take it that one of the characteristics of the culture currently described as democratic is its loss of elegant speech. It is not simply the loss of elegance, but the fact that the language used in politics is intended to obscure rather than illumine. If, as Bretherton suggests, ecclesiology is politics by another name, the church can serve the world in which we find ourselves by attending to our speech. Well-formed sermons may turn out to be the most important contribution Christians can make to a politics that has some ambition to be truthful. To so conceive Christian witness may seem insignificant and requiring a patience we do not have, but that is why Jean Vanier is so important. He is the culture Christianity produces.

## The Church as Foot-Dragging

I am aware that these last suggestions may seem far too abstract, so let me try to suggest the kind of concrete politics I think they entail, at least the kind of politics for Christians in advanced capitalist societies, by calling attention to James C. Scott's recent book, *Two Cheers for Anarchism: Six Easy Pieces on Autonomy, Dignity, and Meaningful Work and Play.*[44] I am well aware that to identify with Scott's account of anarchism will only confirm for many that I am a "sectarian, fideistic tribalist," but I have long given up on any attempt to counter that charge. That I am directing attention to Scott's book is not meant to suggest that he provides the only way to think about the political character of the church. In fact, I am quite sympathetic with Luke Bretherton's more robust account of what a Christian politics might look like.[45]

43. Luke Bretherton, "Coming to Judgment: Methodological Reflections on the Relationship between Ecclesiology, Ethnography, and Political Theory," *Modern Theology* 28, no. 2 (April 2012): 177.

44. James C. Scott, *Two Cheers for Anarchism: Six Easy Pieces on Autonomy, Dignity, and Meaningful Work and Play* (Princeton: Princeton University Press, 2012).

45. Luke Bretherton, *Christianity and Contemporary Politics* (Oxford: Wiley-Blackwell,

One of the attractions of Scott's account of anarchy is his reticence about any account of anarchy that tries to be comprehensive. Accordingly he describes his "method" as an "anarchist squint" that is intended to help us see what we might otherwise miss.[46] Scott does not deny that Pierre-Joseph Proudhon's description of anarchism as "mutuality or cooperation without hierarchy or state rule" certainly captures some of what may pass as anarchy, but that description may not adequately suggest the anarchist tolerance for confusion and improvisation that accompanies social learning.[47] Scott has no reason to try to nail down a definition of anarchism, being content to use anarchism to describe a defense of politics, conflict, and debate, along with the perpetual uncertainty and learning they entail. That means that, unlike many anarchists, Scott does not believe the state is always the enemy of freedom.

Scott's project might be called an exercise in small politics. For example, he tells about his stay in Germany when he was trying to learn German by forcing himself to interact with fellow pedestrians in the small town of Neubrandenburg. He tells the story of crossing the street to get to the train station in obedience to lights that indicated when it was legal to cross the street. He reports that fifty or sixty people would often wait at the corner for the light to change even though they could see no traffic was coming. He reports that after five hours of observation he saw no more than two people cross against the light. Those two who would cross against the lights had to be willing to receive from those that waited gestures of disapproval. Scott reports he had to screw up his courage to cross the street against their disapproval. He did so, justifying his law-breaking performance by remembering that his grandparents could have used more of the spirit of breaking the law in the name of justice. But because they had lost the practice of breaking small laws they no longer knew when it really mattered to break the law. Scott calls such practice of law-breaking "anarchist calisthenics," implying that Germans could use the practice.[48]

---

2010). Indeed I think much of what Bretherton does in his book is compatible with Scott's understanding of anarchy. For example, commenting on the significance of "ordinary time," Bretherton observes that attention to "ordinary time enables the valuation of the micro-political as just as important for conceptualizing faithful political witness as the set-piece relationships between church and state, and ordinary political actors as just as significant as 'heroic' figures such as Martin Luther King" (p. 213).

46. Scott, *Two Cheers for Anarchism*, p. xii.

47. Scott, *Two Cheers for Anarchism*, p. xii.

48. Scott, *Two Cheers for Anarchism*, pp. 3-7.

Scott observes that under authoritarian regimes, subjects who are denied public means of protest have no recourse but to resort to "foot-dragging, sabotage, poaching, theft, and, ultimately, revolt." Modern forms of democracy allegedly make such forms of dissent obsolete. But Scott argues that the assumed promises of democracy that make "foot-dragging" no longer necessary are seldom realized in practice. He argues that what needs to be noticed is that most of the political reforms that have made some difference for democratic change have been the result of disruption of the public order. Accordingly, Scott argues that anarchism at least is a reminder that the cultivation of insubordination and law-breaking are crucial for political developments we call democracy.[49]

Yet Scott observes that proponents of liberal democratic theory seldom attend to the role of crisis and institutional failure that lead to political reform. That liberal democracies in the West are generally run for the top 20 percent, for those who possess wealth, is no doubt one of the reasons that inequity of income and the crisis that can result from such inequity is hidden from view. Indeed Scott observes that the greatest failure of liberal democracies is the lack of protection they give to the economic and security interests of their least advantaged citizens. As a result, Scott argues, the contradiction between the renewal of democracy by major episodes of extra-institutional disorder and the promise of democracy as the institutionalization of peaceful change is seldom noticed.[50]

Scott's book is an account of episodes of foot-dragging and disruption. In particular he directs attention to matters not often considered "political" to illumine our political landscape in advanced industrial societies. For example, he pokes fun at the use of quantitative measures of productivity in the academy in order to show how democracies like the United States have embraced meritocratic criteria for the elite selection and distribution of public funds to create "a vast and deceptive 'antipolitics machine' designed to turn legitimate political questions into neutral objective administrative exercises governed by experts."[51] This strategy to depoliticize protest masks a lack of faith in the possibilities anarchists and democrats have in the mutuality and education that can result from common action.

Scott's defense of anarchy, therefore, turns out to be a defense of politics. He observes that "if there is one conviction that anarchist thinkers

---

49. Scott, *Two Cheers for Anarchism*, pp. 16-17.
50. Scott, *Two Cheers for Anarchism*, pp. 18-19.
51. Scott, *Two Cheers for Anarchism*, p. 111.

and non-demagogic populists share, it is faith in the capacity of democratic citizenry to learn and grow through engagement in the public sphere."[52] Yet he argues that the formation of bodies wrought through populist politics is often defeated by something as simple as the SAT exam. For that exam serves as a way to convince middle-class whites that affirmative action is a choice between objective merit and favoritism. As a result the SAT robs us of the public dialogue we need to have about how educational opportunity ought to be allocated in a democratic and plural society. Cost-benefit analysis often functions in a similar way to make the conflict needed seem petty.[53]

Scott ends his book by directing our attention to the role of "history" in modern politics. The purpose of such histories is to summarize major historical events by making them legible by a single narrative. As a result, the "radical contingency" of history is domesticated in an effort to underwrite the assumption that the way things turned out is the only way they could be. Such condensations of history, the needs of elites to project an image of control, create a blindness to the fact that the "emancipatory gains for human freedom have not been the result of orderly, institutional procedures but of disorderly, unpredictable, spontaneous action cracking open the social order from below."[54]

I confess it is with some hesitancy that I use Scott's account of anarchy to exemplify what a Christian politics might look like. I worry that "anarchy" may suggest that I have no use for institutions that inevitably involve hierarchies of authority. I assume it is never a question of whether hierarchies of authority should or should not exist, but rather how authority should be understood as an aid for the discovery of the common good of a community. Indeed I am in deep agreement with Victor Lee Austin's argument in *Up with Authority* that because the common good of communities is not one isolated goal, "authority is needed because it is desirable that particular goods should be taken care of by particular agencies."[55] The irony is that such an account of authority stands as a challenge, a challenge that may appear to threaten anarchy, in a liberal social order in which common goods by design are reduced to common interest.

---

52. Scott, *Two Cheers for Anarchism*, pp. 121-22.

53. Scott, *Two Cheers for Anarchism*, pp. 123-24.

54. Scott, *Two Cheers for Anarchism*, p. 141.

55. Victor Lee Austin, *Up with Authority* (London: T. & T. Clark, 2010), p. 31. The quoted sentence is from Yves R. Simon's *A General Theory of Authority* (Notre Dame: University of Notre Dame Press, 1980), p. 72. Austin's account of authority draws quite rightly on Simon.

The church is rightly a hierarchical institution. It is so because the church is a community that believes the truth matters. Accordingly the saints and martyrs stand as authorities who test the changes that may be necessary if the church is to remain faithful to the gospel. Those singled out for the offices in the church to ensure that the church attend to the saints must recognize that the exercise of their authority can never be an end in itself. But it is "political" in the most basic sense of what it means to be political, and accordingly can serve as an example for the exercise of authority beyond the church. If that is a Constantinian strategy, then I am a Constantinian.

Above I referred to Sider's suggestion that Yoder's anti-Constantinianism is best expressed in terms of the church being the true meaning of history. That is an extraordinary claim, requiring a people to exist who know how to drag their feet when confronted by those who think they know where history is headed. Which, I hope, is one way to say that the church does not have a politics, but rather the church is God's politics for the world. If Christians are well formed by that politics they hopefully will serve the world well by developing an "ecclesial squint." By doing so they might just be able to serve their neighbor by helping us see "it did not have to be." That, moreover, is the most radical politics imaginable.

CHAPTER 10

# How to Think Theologically about Rights

## What Is Right about Rights

I am usually identified with those who have reservations about the language of rights. That I am so identified is not without reason, but allow me to begin by saying that in no way do I want to discount how the appeal to rights has been a means to protect those who have no protection in the world in which we find ourselves. For many, claims to "rights" express the hope that something like a human community exists, making possible declarations that all people deserve to have their dignity recognized. From a theological perspective, rights so understood can be regarded as an expression of the Christian eschatological hope that all people are to be ultimately united in common worship of God.

It is hard to understand how anyone, at least anyone who cares about human suffering, could possibly be against the use of "rights" language. Yet even this very positive account of rights as an expression of human dignity is not free of controversy.[1] For example, David Gushee suggests in his book *The Sacredness of Human Life: Why an Ancient Biblical Vision Is Key to the World's Future* that human dignity functions simultaneously to ground the concepts of human rights as well as the content of specific

1. Steven Pinker has called into question the appeal to dignity itself in his article "The Stupidity of Dignity," *The New Republic,* May 28, 2008. For a well-argued defense of the appeal to dignity see Gilbert Meilaender, *Neither Beast nor God: The Dignity of the Human Person* (New York: New Atlantis Books, 2009). I am indebted to Brian Volck and Joel Shuman for reminding me of the controversy Pinker's article occasioned. I have benefited from their yet unpublished paper, "Dignity and the Body: Reclaiming What Autonomy Ignores."

rights.[2] John Milbank, however, has challenged the yoking of human dignity to human rights. Milbank acknowledges that one can understand how in the face of totalitarian suppression of human freedom and the brutal treatment of certain classes of human beings, human dignity and human rights were thought to be mutually implicated when in fact they represent two fundamentally opposed traditions of political and ethical thought. Human rights are correlative of the liberal political tradition embodied in the American Constitution, whereas human dignity derives largely from the Catholic tradition.[3]

Though I am sympathetic with Milbank's genealogy, I should like to think his account of the origins of rights language means that all appeals to rights do not carry the implications he finds so deleterious. I will have more to say about the questions of origins further on, but my primary purpose in this essay is to provide a more modest defense of right-making claims that can sustain the moral commitments associated with the acknowledgment of our mutual humanity. As a way to begin that effort, however, I need to revisit what I have said about rights in the past.

In her book *The Ethics of Human Rights: Contested Doctrinal and Moral Issues,* Esther Reed calls attention to my early reservations about appeals to human rights to sustain moral judgments and arguments. She provides an extensive quote from my essay titled "Rights, Duties, and Experimentation on Children." This was an essay originally written for a government committee charged with the duty to investigate the moral constraints on experimentation on children. That essay was later published in my book *Suffering Presence: Theological Reflections on Medicine, the Mentally Handicapped, and the Church.* I call attention to the essay's origin because, as I observe in the essay, given the charge before the committee, the language of "rights" would prove particularly attractive for those trying to develop general policies on matters such as experimentation on children. It turned out I was right that the committee would find it impossible to avoid using the language of rights to explain the moral possibility that children could be used as experimental subjects.

In an effort to summarize my reservations about rights, Reed provides this selective quote:

2. David Gushee, *The Sacredness of Human Life: Why an Ancient Biblical Vision Is Key to the World's Future* (Grand Rapids: Eerdmans, 2013), pp. 19-20.

3. John Milbank, "Dignity Rather Than Rights" (unpublished paper available on the Center for Theology and Philosophy website).

An appeal to rights cannot provide the kind of basic moral presuppositions needed for the social and political life of a good society. When rights are assumed to be basic there seems to be no way to avoid an arbitrariness in the list of alleged rights and/or how conflicts of rights can be adjudicated. . . . When rights are taken to be the fundamental moral reality we are encouraged to take an ultimately degrading perspective on society. No real society can exist when its citizens' only way of relating is in terms of noninterference. The language of "rights," especially as it is displayed by liberal political theory, encourages us to live as if we had no common interests or beliefs.[4]

Reed's summary quotation does not quite do justice to my worries about appeals to rights developed all too briefly in my testimony before the investigating committee. In particular I did not abjure all appeals to rights for moral argument, but argued that if rights were to be intelligible "they must be correlative to specific contexts and institutions we believe serve a common good. If families, for example, have rights they do so because such rights are the means to protect the goods we believe constitutive of the family."[5] I suggested that rights language is peculiarly relevant for adjudicating relations between strangers, but just to the extent rights serve that function the language of rights is inappropriate for determining the relationship between parents and their children. I also raised the problem of whether children possess the moral and psychological characteristics that allegedly right-bearing creatures must have to claim the rights due them.

I call attention to Reed's identification of me as a critic of rights language because I assume that many regard me as a representative of those most modern of atheists, namely, those who do not believe in rights. I take it to be a mark of our times that a theologian may have worries about

---

4. Esther Reed, *The Ethics of Human Rights: Contested Doctrinal and Moral Issues* (Waco, TX: Baylor University Press, 2007), p. 29. The quote comes from *Suffering Presence: Theological Reflections on Medicine, the Mentally Handicapped, and the Church* (Notre Dame: University of Notre Dame Press, 1986), p. 130.

5. Of course one of the crucial questions is whether a family can have rights. I have always thought John Rawls's understanding of the family has not received the attention it deserves because Rawls with his usual clarity and honesty saw quite clearly that the family "may be a barrier to equal chances between individuals" in a well-ordered society shaped by the two principles of justice. *A Theory of Justice* (Cambridge, MA: Harvard University Press, 1971), p. 301. That such is the case does not mean that right-making claims are antithetical to a commitment to the family, but neither can it be denied that there may be a tension between claims to have rights and how the moral status of the family is understood.

whether God exists, but we cannot call into question the status of rights. For as Reed suggests, the language of rights came into its own after World War II in response to the absence of any unifying political ideologies or religious belief systems necessary to bind the majority of individuals together. Rights are, therefore, as I suggested above, regarded as a source of ethical and political value that was and is capable of binding people together without violence. The language of rights became and remains the language of the high humanism many think necessary to sustain moral peace in a fragmented world.[6] To be a critic of rights, therefore, is close to putting oneself on the side of terrorism.

In fact Reed calls attention to the 1987 Convention against Torture and Other Cruel, Inhuman, or Degrading Treatment or Punishment as a crucial example of the importance of the development of rights language. If we did not have the language of rights we might, it seems, lack the necessary moral presuppositions for the condemnation of torture. She notes that governmental and nongovernmental agencies make frequent appeals to this Convention in support of political prisoners and their families around the globe. Accordingly rights as ideals and principles form a basis for liberal democracies that have assumed a value and authority without precedent in the history of the world.[7] It is hard to imagine why anyone, particularly someone like me who is committed to nonviolence, would have any hesitations concerning appeals to rights.

Yet I do have reservations, which interestingly enough involve how one thinks about torture. I will develop my worries below, but I can put the matter succinctly: if you need a theory of rights to know what torture is, or if you think you need rights to ground your judgment that torture is morally wrong, then something has clearly gone wrong with your moral sensibilities. What follows is my attempt to defend that remark, but before doing so I at least need to make clear that I have not called into question all appeals to rights. In fact, in my Oxford Amnesty International Lecture in 2008 I acknowledged that I have no difficulty with "rights" claims that express social and legal duties.[8] Indeed I assume the law is rightly regarded

6. Reed, *The Ethics of Human Rights*, p. 23.

7. Reed, *The Ethics of Human Rights*, p. 22.

8. This lecture, which was titled "Pentecost: Learning the Languages of Peace," can be found in my book *War and the American Difference: Theological Reflections on Violence and National Identity* (Grand Rapids: Baker, 2011), pp. 117-34. The observation about rights is on p. 122. I am, of course, aware that Nicholas Wolterstorff has argued that rights cannot be grounded in duties. I will not, however, address his argument directly because I am not sure

as the source and proper context for claims of rights because the law expresses well-established social and political expectations.[9]

While I find very interesting the current debates about how the history of rights is best understood, my worry about rights language is not whether that language began in the Enlightenment or in earlier canon law, but rather what that language is now doing.[10] In that respect I do have a number of worries about appeals to rights that I will try to make explicit. These worries may be due to what I can only regard as the overuse of appeals to rights that may be due to liberal political and social habits, but that is not my primary worry. Rather my primary concern is that rights language has become too powerful. By that I mean that appeals to rights threaten to replace first-order moral descriptions in a manner that makes us less able to make the moral discriminations that we depend upon to be morally wise.

I cannot hope to give an adequate philosophical or theological justification concerning my worries about rights language, but I at least need to try to provide an account of what I take to be my primary concerns. Yet I feel the need to begin by naming the difficulties I see with claims about rights in general. By doing so I hope to show — or at least suggest — how my worries about rights are interrelated. So what follows is a broadside critique of what I can only regard as the overdependence on rights lan-

---

why rights need a "grounding" in the first place. It is not clear to me also if what I mean by a duty is what Wolterstorff means by obligation. See his *Justice: Rights and Wrongs* (Princeton: Princeton University Press, 2008), pp. 264-84.

9. I must acknowledge, however, that given Wolterstorff's distinction between right-order accounts of rights and inherent rights I remain firmly in the former category. To explore that distinction as well as to defend a right-order position would make it impossible for me to ever get around to my worries about rights. See *Justice: Rights and Wrongs,* pp. 21-43. For an extremely informative, at least informative for me, account of my interactions with the law see John Inazu, special editor, "Theological Argument in Law: Engaging with Stanley Hauerwas," *Law and Contemporary Problems* 75, no. 4 (2012). I am indebted to the authors of the essays that make up this issue, and, in particular, I owe John Inazu much for planning the conference in which the papers were delivered. All the essays are interesting, but I think many would find the essays by Inazu and Stephen Carter relevant to the central issues at the heart of *The Work of Theology.* I responded to the essays in *Law and Contemporary Problems* in an essay titled "Hauerwas on 'Hauerwas and the Law': Trying to Have Something to Say," pp. 233-51.

10. For a good overview of these debates see David Gushee, *The Sacredness of Human Life,* pp. 214-59. John Milbank provides a spirited response to Wolterstorff's genealogy of rights in his "Against Human Rights," *Oxford Journal of Law and Religion* 1, no. 1 (February 2012).

guage in our culture. Once that task is completed I hope to defend how right-making claims can and should be used by attending to the work of Simone Weil and Rowan Williams.

## What Is Wrong about Rights

I can illustrate what I mean when suggesting that rights language has become too powerful by calling attention to a remark of someone whom I believe was in the Department of Justice during the civil rights campaign in Mississippi. Several civil rights workers had been killed. The spokesman for the Department of Justice was appropriately outraged. But in order to express his outrage he resorted to the moral vocabulary in which I assume he most felt at home. He said that those who had been killed had had their rights violated. When rights become a more basic moral description than murder, you have an indication that your language has gone on a holiday.

Of course one cannot help but have some sympathy for the Department of Justice representative. He was using the most powerful language he knew to indicate what a horrible moral crime had been committed. Yet the very appeal to the violation of rights as the fundamental moral description may indicate a profound worry about such a morality. For if confidence in the language of rights is lost it is not clear what the alternative to nihilism would be.

I worry, therefore, that for no doubt many reasons some are trying to make the language of rights do more work than it can do. Not very long ago one of the fundamental issues that characterized that strange activity called meta-ethics was whether "right" or "good" was the primary ethical notion on which all other ethical judgments were to be justified. That fruitless debate was, of course, an attempt to choose between Mill and Kant on strictly logical grounds. The challenge to that way of understanding ethics was represented by philosophers such as Bernard Williams, Iris Murdoch, Philippa Foot, Alasdair MacIntyre, and Raimond Gaita, who directed attention to words such as "kindness," "honesty," "gentleness" as descriptions at least as — if not more — important than "big words" such as "right" and "good." I am trying to make a similar point about rights.

Not unrelated to the overdetermination of rights language in our current moral vocabulary is my worry that once the language of inalienable rights is introduced there is no way to control their multiplication. Once rights are divorced from the practices that they depend upon for their intelligibility, they multiply faster than rabbits. I may well think I have a right to my body, but it is not clear how that claim can be commensurate with a people who think suicide is wrong. If I have a right to my body does that mean, as some seem to think, that I have a right to die?

Not only does the unlimited scope of rights language seem uncontrollable once the cat of inalienable rights is let out of the bag, but there is also no way it seems to adjudicate mutually exclusive right claims. The assumption that I have a right to my body is not very different from someone who thinks they have an unlimited right to their money. The moral life conceived primarily in terms of rights turns out to produce people who end up shouting at one another by claiming that their rights have been violated.

John Milbank observes, for example, if rights for women only mean that women are to receive their respective shares of *ius* in relation to men and children then the notion of a woman's right as self-possession can rebound to further oppression of women. For example, if only women have "rights" over the fetus, Milbank suggests, then "men as men will naturally exercise their implied equivalent rights to have nothing to do with childbearing or the nurture of children."[11]

My other concern about "rights" language is the moral psychology that is often presupposed by those who use that language. It was not by accident that I raised this issue when testifying before a committee charged with assessing the legitimacy of experimentation on children. In *A Theory of Justice* John Rawls had admirably acknowledged that, at least in relation to animals, his account of justice did not require that those lacking a capacity for a sense of justice were owed strict justice.[12] Rawls is clearly making a point about his understanding of justice, but many draw a similar conclusion about the capacity that must be present in order to claim rights.

Questions concerning the moral psychology that is necessary to claim rights are particularly important for how one thinks about the morality of abortion. If the "fetus" lacks the characteristics necessary to be a "person" and is, therefore, not capable of being a rights-bearer, does that mean that abortion does not need to be justified? Or even more radical, if the fetus lacks the capacity to claim rights, do we need the language of abortion at all? "Termination of pregnancy" is a description that seems perfectly adequate if the fetus has no rights. Of course "termination of pregnancy"

---

11. Milbank, "Against Human Rights," p. 29.

12. John Rawls, *A Theory of Justice* (Cambridge, MA: Harvard University Press, 1971), p. 512.

suggests that this is purely a "medical procedure" that raises no moral questions.

Finally I worry that the language of rights has not been thought through theologically. In particular it is not clear what the implication of the language of rights has for our relationship to God. Rights seem to suggest that we may well have a standing over against God that betrays what it may mean to be a creature. Such a stance may not be without theological justification, but it surely demands more reflection than it has been given. It is to Nicholas Wolterstorff's great credit that he has addressed this issue straight on by arguing that the *imago Dei* entails the claim that because we are loved by God we have a bestowed worth that grounds our claim to have rights, even if we seem to lack the capacity for such a claim.[13] Wolterstorff may well be right that no purely secular account of rights is possible, but I find his correlative claim, namely, that God has rights, to be an odd claim.[14]

Such is my bill of particulars against the language of rights. I need to emphasize again that I am not calling into question all appeals to rights. There is no question that claims about human rights have served to challenge forms of human oppression. David Gushee is surely right to suggest that Christians should celebrate recent advances in international human rights law in which the "smallest" individual has been given protection from the "greatest" ruler.[15] Yet even that achievement is not without problems because it is not clear that a claim to have a right makes sense without a mechanism that can enforce that claim.

## Simone Weil on Rights

I described the above as a broadside attack on rights. In order to defend that broadside I want to call attention to Simone Weil's account of rights. In particular I want to direct attention to a set of her remarks about rights in her remarkable essay "Human Personality." This essay, like all her work, was published after her death in 1950, but it seems to have been written in 1943. It now appears in her *Selected Essays: 1934-1943*.[16] She begins the essay by observing that something is amiss with the vocabulary of personalism

13. Wolterstorff, *Justice: Rights and Wrongs*, pp. 352-60.

14. Wolterstorff, *Justice: Rights and Wrongs*, p. 306.

15. Gushee, *The Sacredness of Human Life*, p. 376.

16. Simone Weil, *Selected Essays: 1934-1943*, trans. Richard Rees (London: Oxford University Press, 1962), pp. 9-34.

just to the extent that what is sacred in each of us is not our personhood, but that we are who we are and not someone else.[17] What makes us and others sacred is not our human personalities, but everything about us, the whole of us, our arms, our thoughts, our eyes.

This understanding of the sacred character of our lives is the background that makes intelligible Weil's remarks about rights that I think are particularly important. She says:

> If you say to someone who has ears to hear: "What you are doing to me is not just," you may touch and awaken at its source the spirit of attention and love. But it is not the same with words like "I have the right . . ." or "you have no right to . . ." They invoke a latent war and awaken the spirit of contention. To place the notion of rights at the centre of social conflicts is to inhibit any possible impulse of charity of both sides.
>
> Relying almost exclusively on this notion, it becomes impossible to keep one's eye on the real problem. If someone tries to browbeat a farmer to sell his eggs at a moderate price, the farmer can say: "I have the right to keep my eggs if I don't get a good enough price." But if a young girl is being forced into a brothel she will not talk about her rights. In such a situation the word would sound ludicrously inadequate. Thus it is that the social drama, which corresponds to the latter situation, is falsely assimilated, by the use of the word "rights," to the former one. Thanks to this word, what should have been a cry of protest from the depth of the heart has been turned into a shrill nagging of claims and counter-claims, which is both impure and unpractical.[18]

What I find particularly interesting about these remarks is Weil's examples. The farmer has every right not to sell his eggs. His claim to possess such a right depends on the thick network of relationships and habits that make him the farmer he is. He does not have to sell his eggs because his neighbors will understand why he refuses to sell at a reduced price. To claim his right not to sell is to locate the farmer in a network of relations and the narratives that give intelligibility to the farmer's practices. It is the very mediocrity, Weil's word, of the rights to which the farmer appeals that makes his declaration to have rights intelligible.

---

17. Weil, *Selected Essays,* p. 9.

18. Weil, *Selected Essays,* p. 21. I am indebted to Rai Gaita for calling my attention to this passage in Weil.

Yet the mediocre character of the appeal to rights by the farmer, according to Weil, is the reason that an appeal to rights by a young girl being forced into a brothel does not do justice to the seriousness of the wrong being done to her. It does not help, according to Weil, to try to raise the stakes by suggesting that her "personal rights" are being violated. Indeed to add the word "personal" to "rights" is only to make matters worse. It is not, Weil argues, her personality that is being violated but her very being.

Weil expands her remarks about the "personal" by suggesting that to add the language of "personal" to qualify rights only makes the cry of the oppressed even meaner than bargaining. It does so because it inflects the call of justice with the tone of envy. She observes that "to the dimmed understanding of our age" the claim that all should have an equal share of privilege does not seem odd. Yet the claim is both absurd and base, absurd because privilege is by definition a matter of inequality, and base because what is claimed to be worth having is not worth having. In fact, the kinds of people who formulate such claims are in a privileged position, which makes them presume they have a monopoly on the language of rights. They are the last people, therefore, who should say that privilege is unworthy to be desired.[19]

Weil is no defender of injustice. It is important to remember Weil's profound sympathy for those who work in factories. In fact she closely identified with those who worked at such tasks, even trying to join them in similar work. But she argued that to put in the mouth of the afflicted words she describes as coming from the "vocabulary of middle values," words such as "democracy," "rights," and "personality," is to offer the afflicted that which can bring them no good and will inevitably do them much harm. It is the language of truth, beauty, justice, and compassion that they need — not the language of rights.[20]

Weil's worry about the use of rights language by those she identifies as the "afflicted" is based on her judgment that the notion of rights is linked with notions of exchange and measured quantity. In short, the language of rights has a commercial ring that is evocative of law courts and arguments. Accordingly rights are colored with the tone of contention. Such a tone, however, if it is to be serious, must rely on force if a claim to rights is not to

19. Weil, *Selected Essays,* p. 22. If Weil seems to be operating in a Wittgensteinian key on these matters, that may well be the case, at least if Peter Winch is right. See his "Introduction" to Simone Weil, *Lectures on Philosophy* (Cambridge: Cambridge University Press, 1978), pp. 1-23. Winch makes some fascinating comparisons of Weil and Wittgenstein.

20. Weil, *Selected Essays,* pp. 23-24.

be laughed at. That rights depend on force is but a reminder that rights are originally the creation of the Romans and, in particular, Roman property owners. It is important, moreover, to remember that the "property" the Roman owners owned was other human beings.[21]

Weil is not denying that rights have some moral standing. Rather her worry is that rights, which she identifies as being launched into the world in 1789, have proved unable to fulfill the role assigned to them. They have been unable to secure the sacredness of each human being, because the sacred can only be secured by the good. "This profound and childlike and unchanging expectation of good in the heart is not what is involved when we agitate for our rights."[22] There is, therefore, no guarantee for the protection of life against collectives unless the disposition of public life understands how life itself manifests a relation to the higher good.[23]

What I find so compelling about Weil's understanding of rights is her refusal to turn rights into abstractions. The language of rights has its place, but that place requires the display of thick human relationships. Weil begins her great book *The Need for Roots* by observing that "the notion of obligations comes before that of rights."[24] Obligations come before rights because for a right to be effectual it cannot spring from the individual who possesses it. Rather the efficacy of a right depends on other people who consider themselves to be under certain obligations toward the one who claims the right. An obligation that goes unrecognized is still an obligation, but a right that is unrecognized by anyone is, Weil wryly observes, "not worth very much."[25]

Weil argues it is nonsense to say that we have rights and obligations as if those "possessions" have the same status. The relation between obligations and rights is that between object and subject, which means that a person considered in isolation only has duties, some of which will be duties to herself. A person left alone in the universe would have no rights, but she would still have obligations. She would have obligations because obligations, unlike rights, are independent of conditions in which they are expressed. By contrast, rights are always to be found related to certain conditions. That is what the revolutionaries of 1789 did not recognize, namely,

---

21. Weil, *Selected Essays,* pp. 19-20.

22. Weil, *Selected Essays,* p. 10.

23. Weil, *Selected Essays,* p. 34.

24. Simone Weil, *The Need for Roots,* trans. Arthur Wills (New York: Harper & Row, 1952), p. 3.

25. Weil, *The Need for Roots,* p. 3.

they failed to see the contradiction entailed by their asserting their rights and yet at the same time wanting to postulate absolute principles. In effect they confused that which is eternal and unconditioned with that which is conditioned by facts.[26] From Weil's perspective we have been paying the moral and political price for that confusion by trying to make rights do more than they are able to do.

For Weil, respect for another human being cannot be grounded in rights, but rather is a reflection of the obligations that make us human. The object of any obligation is the human being as such because the very reason such an obligation exists is because we are just that, namely, human beings. Such an obligation has no foundation, but is verified in the common consent found in our behavior toward one another. The recognition of such an obligation in particular cases can be expressed, to be sure, in a confused and imperfect way by what are called positive rights.[27] The recognition of such obligations, however, depends not on claims to possess rights but on the recognition of our common human needs.

The introduction of the language of "needs" makes clear that Weil and most defenders of rights in our time have radically different anthropologies. For Weil the "need for roots" is basic because as creatures destined for eternal life we will discover that destiny through needs as basic as order, liberty, obedience, responsibility, equality, hierarchism, honor, punishment, freedom of opinion, security, risk, private property, collective property, and truth. For Weil, the basic needs of our bodies create the condition that makes possible our being rooted in forms of life that enable respect for ourselves and the other.

From her perspective, therefore, the right to choose divorced from the rules that make life together possible can result in the loss of the enjoyment liberty should provide. That loss means people "must either seek refuge in irresponsibility, puerility, and indifference — a refuge where the most they can find is boredom — or feel themselves weighed down by responsibility at all times for fear of causing harm to others."[28] As a consequence some may even, Weil suggests, conclude that liberty is not to be desired.

So concludes my account of Weil on rights. I have ended with her observation about the effect an overemphasis on the expression of rights as "freedom of choice" can have, because I fear she describes the lives of

26. Weil, *The Need for Roots*, p. 4.
27. Weil, *The Need for Roots*, pp. 4-5.
28. Weil, *The Need for Roots*, p. 13.

many in the world as we now find it. Of course one must be careful when making such claims. Whatever may be the pathologies that possess our lives it would surely be a mistake to attribute those pathologies exclusively to an overemphasis on rights. In fact, I suspect that for many the appeal to rights that has been at the heart of the call for the integration of African Americans into American life; the struggle of women to be recognized as full moral agents; and the gay and lesbian challenge to prejudices against them has provided for many a moral identity otherwise unavailable.

One cannot help but admire those who have migrated from one cause to another in the pursuit of securing the rights of those who have been unfairly treated — if not oppressed — in our society. They are people who have made the pursuit of rights a way of life. In a morally confused world, lives so constituted are very attractive. The problem, however, is that lives determined by the pursuit of rights require the constant pursuit of a cause. Such a pursuit may postpone the boredom Weil suggests can be the result of unlimited choice, but it is not clear that lives so conceived can have the staying power of a life well lived.

In that respect I find it quite interesting that some of the people I deeply admire, people like Jean Vanier, as far as I can determine, never use the language of rights. Vanier is committed to being with those who are said to be mentally disabled. You might think the language of rights would be the natural language he would use to defend and protect those with whom he lives. Yet he does not utilize that language. I suspect he does not use the language of rights because that language may prevent him from recognizing the full bodily reality of the human beings who share their lives with him.

### Rights as the Expression of Our Need for Bodily Communication

I want to conclude by elaborating on this last remark about the importance of the body for disciplining the language of rights. I do so partly because I am aware that Simone Weil is regarded by many as a brilliant but eccentric thinker. Yet I think her emphasis on the bodily needs that ground our regard for one another is crucial if the language of rights is to be appropriately used for helping us better understand the moral character of our lives. I have, I should like to think, a weighty ally in support of that claim, namely, Rowan Williams, who has argued in a manner quite similar to Weil that because our bodies are not reducible to being an object among other objects, due regard for the body is foundational for our recognition of the rights of others.[29]

Williams develops this understanding of rights in response to Mac-Intyre's claim in *After Virtue* that human rights, like unicorns, simply do not exist.[30] Williams thinks MacIntyre is surely right that the standoff between rights and utility in our culture has resulted in a managerial account of political life in which "experts" are now given authority in a manner that inhibits the arguments we need to have to discover the goods in common. But Williams does not think that means all rights-talk is to be left behind exactly because rights is now one of the resources we have for challenging the assumption that the modern state can do what it pleases.

In defense of rights language Williams calls attention to the uneasy relationship of Christians with slavery. Slavery was not condemned in scripture, and the early church obviously included in the ranks of the church slaveowners as well as slaves. But the relationship between the slaveowner and the slave, Williams observes, was complicated by baptism. Because of baptism Christians could not view their bodies or the bodies of their fellow Christians as "property." Indeed the body became the medium of the meaning. For what it means for us to have a soul is that the body is "the medium in which the conscious subject communicates, and there is no communication without it."[31]

Sounding very much like Simone Weil, Williams argues that the recognition of a body as a human body is fundamental for the recognition of another's rights. It is so because to recognize the body of another as a human body, a body that roots us in life, is to recognize the body as a vehicle of communication.[32] Though he does not reference Herbert McCabe, Williams's focus on the significance of the body is quite similar to Herbert McCabe's stress on the significance of the body to make communication

---

29. Rowan Williams, *Faith in the Public Square* (London: Bloomsbury, 2012), p. 152.

30. MacIntyre's declaration about the nonexistence of rights is in *After Virtue,* 3rd ed. (Notre Dame: University of Notre Dame Press, 2007), p. 69. MacIntyre argues that rights and utility, which are thought to be the moral alternatives to an ethic of the virtues, are fictions that hide from agents that we lack an account of the rationality of our morality.

31. Williams, *Faith in the Public Square,* p. 152. In "Against Human Rights," John Milbank criticizes Williams for grounding rights on the idea that we are our speaking bodies because to do so reproduces the liberal subject that assumes we own our body rather than receive our bodies as gifts. I do not think Williams makes that mistake, for no other reason than I do not think Williams is trying to "ground" the doctrine of rights at all.

32. Williams, *Faith in the Public Square,* pp. 152-53.

possible. For example, McCabe observes that "it is because I have this sort of body, a human body living with a human life, that my communication can be linguistic. The human body is a source of communication."[33]

I call attention to the similarity between Williams and McCabe because both insist that the body is not an instrument of communication, but rather the human body is intrinsically communicative. Accordingly ethics is but the study of human behavior as communication. Williams argues that this understanding of the communication that the body makes possible has the advantage of not grounding rights in accounts of human dignity in which dignity is associated with having certain capacities. Such accounts, as I observed above, cannot but have the result of excluding some from being regarded as deserving recognition because they lack the appropriate characteristics.[34]

That the body as a human body is a system of communication that is by no means rational or even verbal, Williams argues, is basic for why we should want to speak of rights at all. For constitutive of the routine act of communication is the doctrine of our shared obedience to Christ based in our bodily nature. That doctrine affirms that the body of every person is related to its maker and savior before it is related to any human system of power. Accordingly we have an identity that cannot be taken over by any other person's will. This holds true, moreover, of those who lack the means to communicate with their body.[35]

Williams, therefore, maintains that if he is right about the communicative character of our embodiment, then it is the inviolability of the body that is the basis for thinking about rights. Rights do not belong only to the person who has a rational capacity, but rather rights can be attributed to any organism that can be recognized as a human body. This view of the body, moreover, draws on the Christian presumption that as a communicative being a bearer of a message cannot be silenced. The dignity accorded to others is not in recognition that they may be better than they seem, but rather is in recognition that what they have to say may be a gift of God.[36]

Williams argues, therefore, that the language of rights is not a language that lends itself to resolution in purely secular terms. For in secular terms the language of rights cannot help but become a supreme and noncon-

---

33. Herbert McCabe, *Law, Love, and Language* (London: Continuum, 2003), pp. 90-91.
34. Williams, *Faith in the Public Square*, p. 153.
35. Williams, *Faith in the Public Square*, p. 154.
36. Williams, *Faith in the Public Square*, p. 156.

testable concept that overwhelms the concepts we need for communication. Appealing to Sabina Lovibond's use of Wittgensteinian-inspired arguments in her book *Realism and Imagination in Ethics,* Williams argues that there comes a point when argument comes to an end and we recognize that a level has been reached that is basic if we are to think at all. To speak of non-negotiable rights is the attempt to say that we have not chosen these commitments but rather they make our very ability to speak to one another possible.[37]

Williams concludes that it is unlikely that the political and legal philosophy used to sustain the language of rights will converge with his theological framework for understanding rights. At the very least this means we should not presume that claims about inalienable rights have a firm foundation. As an alternative Williams suggests that the language of human rights should be regarded as an aspect of culture. Such a culture might be called the culture of dignity, indicating the outworking of a habit of accepting a wider acknowledgment of belonging.[38] For Williams the language of human rights becomes confused and possibly dangerous when it is divorced from the question of belonging and recognition. Those questions, moreover, cannot be explored in the abstract but must be explored in the concrete give-and-take between bodies rooted in particularistic histories and traditions.

## Final Confession of a Rights Atheist

I see no reasons, therefore, why Christians should refrain on a selective basis from using rights language as part of our moral toolkit. We do so, however, with modesty. For the appeal to rights depends on concrete practices that are more determinative than when right-making claims are used as ends in themselves. Rights, I think, are best understood as reminder claims to help us remember the thick moral relationships our bodies make possible and necessary.

I do not think, however, that the language of rights needs to be justified or grounded theologically. If we do not need to justify or ground the use of a concept such as kindness for helping us name how Christians should live, why should it be assumed that an appeal to "rights" needs to be

37. Williams, *Faith in the Public Square,* p. 158.
38. Williams, *Faith in the Public Square,* p. 165.

"grounded"? That would only be the case if rights are mistakenly assumed to be more basic than the kindness that should be constituent of the virtue of charity. The question is not: Can a Christian appeal to rights? Rather the question is whether our moral vocabulary is in good enough condition that such an appeal does not threaten to determine all we have to say. And that is all I have to say about rights.

# CHAPTER 11

# How to "Remember the Poor"

*"They asked only one thing, that we remember the poor, which was actually what I was eager to do."*

PAUL THE APOSTLE (GAL. 2:10)

## The End of Charity

I begin with Paul's report of what he was asked to do by the church in Jerusalem as a reminder that to be asked to remember the poor is an ongoing Christian obligation. Yet as Bruce Longenecker makes clear in his thorough analysis of the early Christian commitment to care for the poor, it is by no means clear who the poor were that Paul was to remember. Nor was *how* the poor were to be remembered made fully explicit. Money was to be collected from Gentile Christians to support the church in Jerusalem, but that collection does not seem directed to the poor as such.

In particular, Longenecker argues that any attempt to construe "remember the poor" as a "church politics" strategy separated from the gospel itself is problematic. In other words "remember the poor" was not in itself a way to deal with the tension between Jewish Christians and non-Jewish Christians. There is little evidence, according to Longenecker, that the Jerusalem followers of Jesus were known as "the poor." Therefore Longenecker argues that the followers of Jesus in Galatia would not have recognized Paul's reference to the poor as referring exclusively to the followers of Jesus in Jerusalem.[1]

---

1. Bruce Longenecker, *Remember the Poor: Paul, Poverty, and the Greco-Roman World* (Grand Rapids: Eerdmans, 2010), p. 202.

Longenecker's careful analysis of the ambiguities surrounding Paul's commitment to the care of the poor, or perhaps better put, the ambiguities surrounding who would count as someone who is poor, does not call into question the presumption of the early Christians that they had an obligation to care for the poor. Indeed he argues that, though economic assistance to the poor was not exhaustive of the good news of Jesus, neither was it peripheral to that good news. "Care for the poor was thought by Paul to be a necessary hallmark of the corporate life of Jesus followers who lived in conformity with the good news of the early Jesus movement."[2]

I call attention to Longenecker's account of the commitment to the poor by the early followers of Jesus to remind us of the commonplace presumption by Christians that we are a people of charity. We are supposed to care for those less well off. Almsgiving is constitutive of what it means to be a Christian. Yet how Christians have cared for those who have less has recently come under severe criticism. I want to explore that critique and hopefully provide a constructive response.

One of the reasons I am intent to address questions surrounding what it means to remember the poor, or in other terms, why charity is at the heart of Christian living, is that I do not think I have adequately dealt with the challenge that Christians must be a community of the poor that cares for the poor. Claims such as "the first task of the church is not to make the world more just but to make the world the world" may seem to suggest that justice toward the poor by Christians is not a high priority for me. I certainly do not think that to be the case, but the question of *how* Christians care for the poor is all important. I think it may well be true that I have not sufficiently emphasized or explored that "how" in my work.

One of the reasons I have tried to spell out what it means to "remember the poor" is that I am not sure how best to do that without turning the poor into objects. I am quite suspicious of the phrase "the poor."[3] That is not

2. Longenecker, *Remember the Poor,* p. 1.

3. Luke Bretherton quite helpfully argues that attempts to provide technical definitions of poverty fail to grasp the moral claims underlying that phenomenon. Any account of poverty, he observes, must be located within a broader discursive context, which for Christians the Bible supplies. Bretherton suggests, therefore, that in the Old Testament four primary meanings of poverty are to be found, that is, poverty in scripture is associated with destitution, powerlessness, affliction, and humility. Bretherton provides an extremely informative analysis of each of these ways of understanding poverty. See his "A Preferential Option for the Poor or the People? Theological Reflections on the Nature of Poverty, Power, Privilege," in *Climate, Consumption, and the Common Good* (forthcoming).

quite accurate. I am highly suspicious of that phrase as produced by capitalist economies. "The poor" cannot help but become an abstraction because capitalists need "the poor" to secure their own identity. In other words, the production of "the poor" as a general category reproduces and legitimates those that have benefited from capitalism. Concern for the poor becomes an ideology but like any ideology cannot be acknowledged as such.[4]

I will try to address these matters below but I cannot pretend to give them the kind of attention they deserve. You would need to know more about modern economics than I do to get at these issues adequately, but one of the characteristics of capitalist economies is the production of economics as a mathematical field that makes those outside the field amateurs.[5] However, just as it is said that war is too serious to be left to the generals, so it is that economics is too important to be left to economists.[6] I am happy to report, moreover, that though I may have not engaged modern economics practice and theory sufficiently I have had students who have done so. Much of what follows is deeply indebted to them.[7] Before exploring the *how* of remembering the poor, however, I need to indicate why so many now seem to think charity has become so problematic.

In fact we seem to be living in a time in which people have lost confidence in giving. This is true of secular forms of giving, but it is also a conclusion drawn by many Christians who once were committed to charity toward the poor. A vast literature, a literature written by people who often had been agents or at least supporters of aid to poor countries, now exists in which such programs are seen to have produced little good or, even

---

4. I am indebted to conversations with Luke Bretherton for helping me articulate these worries.

5. For an extremely instructive account of the development of economics as a mathematical science as well as some of the problematic aspects of that development see E. Roy Weintraub, *How Economics Became a Mathematical Science* (Durham, NC: Duke University Press, 2002).

6. For an account of as well as a critique of modern economics for disembedding economic relations from social and political realities, see Luke Bretherton's *Resurrecting Democracy: Faith, Citizenship, and the Politics of Common Life* (Cambridge: Cambridge University Press, 2015), chapter 8.

7. I am thinking primarily of Daniel Bell's *Liberation Theology After the End of History: The Refusal to Cease Suffering* (London: Routledge, 2001); Kelly Johnson, *The Fear of Beggars: Stewardship and Poverty in Christian Ethics* (Grand Rapids: Eerdmans, 2007); Christopher Franks, *He Became Poor: The Poverty of Christ and Aquinas's Economic Teachings* (Grand Rapids: Eerdmans, 2009); and Kathryn Blanchard, *The Protestant Ethic and the Spirit of Capitalism: Christians, Freedom, and Free Markets* (Eugene, OR: Cascade, 2010).

worse, have been deeply harmful.[8] There are four primary reasons given for the failure of aid to poorer countries.

First and foremost, aid is said not to work because the aid given was not effectively planned. Money was simply thrown at a problem with little idea of how the money could be best used to make a positive response to a definite need. As a result the aid did not get to the people who actually needed it but instead was virtually stolen by those in power.

Second, it is argued that even when aid is more carefully planned it does not achieve its objectives because aid is inherently a negative process. Aid creates a dependency that cannot easily be rectified in those who receive the aid.

Third, aid simply is a bandage on a wound that is much deeper than aid can address. Aid, it is argued, simply cannot overcome the chronically unjust international economic systems. Globalization is but another name for capitalism in which those who have will continue to have and those who do not have can do little to counter the power of the "haves."

Finally, it is argued that aid does not work because it was not designed to work. Indeed it is not even clear what it would mean for aid to work. The poor are poor for numerous reasons, but the bottom line is the poor got left out of the development of advanced economies and there is little one can do to rectify that reality.

Some have countered these critiques of aid by arguing empirically that it can be shown that aid has made a difference, because without aid there would be more people in poverty now than in fact there are if aid had not been given. That claim, however, is hard to sustain as an empirical generalization. It can be asked, for example: How could you know how many would now be in poverty if aid had not been given? In effect, this is an argument from silence that the critics of aid find unpersuasive.

It is important to note, however, that critics of aid seldom argue against emergency aid to peoples or countries that have experienced cataclysmic events. So it is assumed that aid should be given when people are suffering from floods, earthquakes, and wars. Yet even this kind of aid is criticized

---

8. See, for example, William Easterly's *The White Man's Burden: Why the West's Efforts to Aid the Rest Have Done So Much Ill and So Little Good* (Oxford: Oxford University Press, 2007), or Thomas Dicter, *Despite Good Intentions: Why Development Assistance to the Third World Has Failed* (Amherst: University of Massachusetts Press, 2003). More controversial is Dambisa Moyo, *Dead Aid: Why Aid Isn't Working and How There Is a Better Way for Africa* (New York: Farrar, Straus & Giroux, 2009). For a more positive view see Jeffrey Sacks, *The End of Poverty: Economic Possibilities in Our Time* (New York: Penguin, 2005).

by some on the left as a form of United States imperialism. This general distrust by poorer countries of the United States is not limited to those who represent the forms of governmental aid but also has increasingly been directed at those who work for nongovernmental organizations (NGOs). Even though an NGO is allegedly independent of the government, those who work for an NGO report that they are inevitably viewed as agents of the foreign policy of the State Department.

I have briefly reviewed the debate about international aid because many of those same considerations seem to have found a home among some Christians who are having second thoughts about Christian charity. I am thinking in particular of books like Robert Lupton's *Toxic Charity: How Churches and Charities Hurt Those They Help*.[9] What makes Lupton's critique of charitable endeavors by Christians so compelling is that he is not a representative of conservative political or economic interest. In fact he has been an enthusiastic participant in the kind of mission enterprises he now so effectively criticizes. He has, moreover, spent many years working with urban poor in Atlanta as well as around the world. In short, he is a person who has experienced what he now criticizes.

One of the most interesting questions raised by Lupton, a question I noted is also explored by Longenecker, is how the poor are identified as well as what makes them poor. Failure to address these questions is often the reason so many attempts to address poverty fail. For example, Sam Wells reports he learned from being a vicar at an estate in Norwich, England, that poverty is not primarily about money. Money no doubt plays a role, but according to Wells he discovered as part of a government-funded regeneration process that poverty is "about having no idea what to do and/or having no one with whom to do it."[10]

Wells's observation is the heart of Lupton's worries about Christian charity. Lupton fears — and his fears have been schooled by extensive engagement with programs designed to "help" the poor — that too often with the best will in the world Christians have robbed those they wished to help of the imagination necessary to sustain the community processes that offer a new way of life. Lupton is particularly critical of mission trips, which may make those who have made the trip happy but effect no lasting

---

9. Robert Lupton, *Toxic Charity: How Churches and Charities Hurt Those They Help* (New York: HarperCollins, 2011).

10. Samuel Wells, *God's Companions: Reimagining Christian Ethics* (Oxford: Blackwell, 2006), p. 7.

change for those who have been the subject of the kindness of strangers. Such trips almost become a parody of themselves when those returning look more like tourists who have been on holiday than people worn out by hard work.[11]

Lupton's concern about such trips, however, is not primarily about what the trips mean for those who go on "missions," but the effect it has on those who they go to "help." He fears not only that no lasting change is enacted, but that those who have been the subject of such charity may even be harmed. Too often the help provided weakens those they serve by introducing technologies that cannot be sustained after those who have brought the technologies leave. Even more disturbing, such trips invite and foster forms of dishonest relationships by inviting those who are allegedly being helped to be "grateful" for these intrusions into their lives. Finally, mission trip interventions can erode the work ethic of those being helped with the result that their dependency is deepened.

According to Lupton these results are often unavoidable given the presumption of those who go on such trips that they are trying to help by doing something for the poor. Lupton argues, however, that the challenge is *to be with* the poor. To be with the poor means one must first learn to listen to the poor and by listening to discover that the poor are not without resources for survival. That means, at the very least, if you want to be with the poor a commitment of time is required for the building of trust necessary to sustain honest relationships.

Such relationships will often depend on the willingness of those who have gone to serve the poor to be served by the poor. I have seen university students transformed by such trips. As Lupton suggests, they went on the trip to do some good, but they soon discovered that they lacked the linguistic and everyday skills to survive in the villages in which they landed. As a result they had to depend on the poor for survival. That they, the rich, had to be cared for by the poor gave them a whole new perspective on what it means to be "of help." They learned to observe and listen. Their survival depended on it.

Lupton's understanding of the form charity must take to avoid degrading the recipient of charity draws on the wisdom of the organization

---

11. I once had an encounter with a very influential Southern Baptist seminary president whose office was filled with the heads of wild animals he had killed in Africa after he had been on mission trips to that continent. I hope I may be forgiven for being a bit cynical about his motivations for such trips given his love of killing the animals of Africa.

committed to organizing the poor called the Industrial Areas Foundation. In particular Lupton's position seems quite similar to what the IAF calls the "Iron Rule."[12] That rule is quite simple: "Never do for the poor what they have (or could have) the capacity to do for themselves."[13] Indeed most of Lupton's positive recommendations mimic the work of community organizers who are seeking, as Wells suggests, to discover imaginative alternatives through the building of community.[14] How this can be a form of charity that is not toxic I now want to explore.

## Why Charity Is an Obligation for Christians

To be a Christian is to be obligated to be charitable. This is true whether you are rich or poor, healthy or ill, old or young, male or female, oppressed or free, established or disestablished. Indeed it is particularly important that Christians who are poor understand that they too must be charitable. To be poor does not mean you lack the means to extend charity to another. You may lack money or food but you have the gift of friendship to overwhelm the loneliness that grips the lives of so many. That all Christians must exercise charity, of course, has everything to do with Matthew 25:31-46, in which we are told: "Truly I tell you, just as you did it to one of the least of these who are members of my family, you did it to me" (v. 40).

That Christians believe we meet Christ in the poor means charity for us is not just another way to be kind to someone less fortunate than ourselves. As Gary Anderson argues in his book *Charity: The Place of the Poor in the Biblical Tradition,* the kind of charity found in the Bible is not simply

12. For an extremely insightful account of the IAF see Jeffrey Stout, *Blessed Are the Organized: Grassroots Democracy in America* (Princeton: Princeton University Press, 2010). Stout provides a wonderful account of how anger can be and often is a resource for social change. He also stresses the importance of political action being concrete. He is quite critical, therefore, of the utopian visions often associated with Christian social commitments, which, as Stout wonderfully puts it, end up "unwittingly assisting actual lions in the destruction of actual lambs" (p. 42). For Stout on the "iron rule," see pp. 136-37.

13. Lupton, *Toxic Charity*, p. 8.

14. Wells provides an insightful diagnosis of poverty as fundamentally isolation, which means, according to Wells, that the most appropriate intervention is not doing for the poor but learning to be with the poor. Wells develops this insight in his soon-to-be-published book *A Nazareth Manifesto* (Oxford: Blackwell, forthcoming). In this book Wells develops an extraordinary argument about the significance of the phrase "being with" as crucial for our understanding of God as Trinity, as well as crucial for how we discover our common life.

compassion. Rather charity in the Bible, Anderson argues, is nothing less than a declaration about the metaphysical structure of the world. It is so because charity is "not just a good deed but a declaration of belief about the world and the God who created it."[15] Anderson argues that charity must be at the heart of what it means to be a Christian because charity is the very heart of God.

That charity is a claim about the very character of all that is, Anderson attributes to Israel's discovery that there is an intrinsic connection between the worship of God and the care of the poor. In particular he calls attention to Moses' speeches in Deuteronomy in which Moses links the practice of bringing the first fruits of the harvest to the temple along with the "tithe for the poor" in Deuteronomy 26:12-16. Accordingly the tithe for the poor becomes part of the sacrificial practice that is the heart of Israelite worship. That sacrifice and caring for the poor were interrelated is the necessary practice that shaped the people of Israel's understanding that what they gave to the poor was in fact a "loan" to God. They did so because they understood that even if the one who owed the money might never be able to pay back the loan, the loan will be paid back by God himself. The obligation to care for the poor, therefore, was understood by Israel as a loan first and foremost given to God. That is why Proverbs 19:17 became the central text shaping the people of Israel's practice of caring for the poor. In Proverbs we are told, "Whoever is kind to the poor lends to the Lord, and will be repaid in full."[16]

Anderson stresses the importance of this way of understanding charity because it makes clear that to give to the poor is not "just another act of charity," but rather an encounter with God. Loans can be joyfully given to the poor because who could imagine a better guarantor of a loan than God? Anderson draws on a contemporary example, Mother Teresa, to exemplify this mode of charity. Mother Teresa's refusal to establish any endowment for her order to survive, Anderson suggests, exemplifies her presumption that the order she founded must always necessitate that members be ready to give one's whole self to the poor. She sought to establish an order in which the sisters were committed to live in total reliance on God because to learn reliance on God is necessary if you are not only to help the poor but to be with the poor.

15. Gary Anderson, *Charity: The Place of the Poor in the Biblical Tradition* (New Haven: Yale University Press, 2013), p. 4.

16. Anderson, *Charity*, p. 30.

Anderson develops his account by focusing on Ben Sira and the book of Tobit to show how almsgiving in Judaism was often compared to the sacrificial offering enacted in the temple. Ben Sira is particularly important because, according to Anderson, he taught that acts of charity toward the poor were equivalent to temple sacrifice even when the temple was no longer standing. The reason this is so significant is that it makes explicit the relation between charity to the poor and sacrifice. Charity is more than a horizontal action involving a donor and recipient; rather the sacrificial character of charity makes clear that charity also has a vertical dimension. To give alms was and is to perform an act of worship of God. Anderson even goes so far as to describe acts of charity as sacramental.[17]

Anderson's use of the language of "sacrament" suggests that, although he is making a historical argument about the continuities between Tobit, Sirach, rabbinic Judaism, and early Christianity, he is also making a theological point not only about how charity has been understood by Christians but also about how charity should be understood by Christians. Quite simply, Anderson believes that charity to the poor has the power to save because one meets Christ through the concrete showing of mercy. The poor are quite literally sacramental because they are mediators of the Godhead. Anderson supports this way of understanding charity by quoting Pope Leo the Great (d. 461) who claimed that almsgiving is "so important that, though the other virtues exist without it, they can be of no avail. For although a person be full of faith, and chaste, and sober, and adorned with other still greater decorations, yet if he is not merciful, he cannot deserve mercy. For the Lord says 'blessed are the merciful for God shall have mercy on them'" (Matt. 5:7).[18]

Anderson also draws attention to the observation by Basil the Great that when one assists the poor a gift is offered but in the form of a loan. It is a gift, according to Basil, "because of the expectation of no repayment, but a loan because of the great gift of the Master who pays in his place." Anderson suggests that Basil's observation supports the sacrificial character of charity. It does so because such a view of charity challenges the presumption that charity is primarily for the poor person. That the gift is in the form of a loan, Anderson suggests, means that the natural interpretation of the giving of the loan assumes God will provide the appropriate reward.

But Anderson argues that would be a misinterpretation of how Basil

---

17. Anderson, *Charity*, p. 105.
18. Anderson, *Charity*, p. 9.

understands almsgiving. Basil, according to Anderson, means quite literally that God receives the gift given to the poor. Anderson supports this reading of Basil by calling attention to Basil's admonition that Christians should "give the money, since it is lying idle, without weighing it down with additional charges, and it will be good for both of you. That will be for you (the donor) the assurance of the money's safety because of God's custody; for (the poor) who receives it, there is the advantage of its use. And, if you are seeking additional payment, be satisfied with that from the Lord. He Himself will pay the interest for the poor. Expect kindly acts from Him who is truly kind."[19]

Bruce Longenecker in his *Remember the Poor* provides a compelling understanding of Paul's concern that the poor be remembered that supports Anderson's account. In particular he argues that Paul's mission to the Gentiles, as well as his encounters with Greco-Roman urbanites, suggests that Paul embodied and exemplified the interconnections between Eucharistic action and the care for the poor. Paul understood the care of the poor as the outworking of divine grace found in Christ, but Longenecker argues this did not distinguish the Jesus movement's understanding of these matters from Judaism. According to Longenecker the only difference between the Jewish and Christian understanding of charity was the Christian inclusion of Gentiles as recipients of charity.[20]

That is why 1 Corinthians 11 is so important for Longenecker, because there we see explicitly how Eucharistic action and the poor were linked by the cruciform character of Christ's gift of himself. Longenecker observes that the poor lay at the heart of Paul's theology because "caring for the poor lies at the heart of the identity of Jesus-followers, because it lies at the heart of the story of Jesus who is proclaimed as Lord and at the heart of the story of the sovereign deity who judges all. For Paul, remembering the poor was to lie at the heart of the eschatological identity of communities he had founded, and was itself a practice integral to an embodied proclamation of the good news."[21]

This becomes particularly important because it helps us better understand the political implications of the Jewish and Christian understanding of the obligation to care for the poor. For what was so startling about that commitment, at least what is so startling if the likes of Peter Brown and

---

19. Anderson, *Charity*, p. 31.
20. Longenecker, *Remember the Poor*, p. 206.
21. Longenecker, *Remember the Poor*, pp. 154-55.

Bruce Longenecker are right, is that the commitment to care for the poor was unknown by the Romans.[22] To be sure some Romans were benevolent, but they gave to the poor primarily as a way to be recognized as important people to whom honor is due rather than as an expression of care for those in poverty.[23]

Indeed Peter Brown even suggests that Christian bishops invented "the poor."[24] They did so not simply by urging wealthy Christians to give to the poor, but by claiming that the community as a whole — represented by the office of the bishop — had a responsibility to care for the poor.[25] To claim to have such a responsibility meant the poor could be identified as a class of people who had a claim on the church. As a result "the poor" were singled out as an entity in a manner that was simply unknown in the ancient world.[26] According to Brown the bishops seem to have understood that care for the poor represented a power that gave them social standing otherwise unavailable. Brown even suggests that charity toward the poor was one of the main reasons Christianity became the established religion of Rome.

Brown's point can be nicely supported by the famous episode in which the emperor Julian tried to force pagan priests to give alms to the poor in the hope that they could outdo the Christians. As Longenecker observes, Julian sought to trump the generosity of Christians so that pagan religions might reclaim their influence in Rome. Julian, it seems, recognized a real enemy when he saw it. Thus his claim that "the impious Galileans support not only their own poor but ours as well" — and he did not mean it as a compliment.[27]

By calling attention to Anderson's and Longenecker's accounts of charity I have tried to show what an extraordinary thing it was for Christians to continue Israel's presumption that to care for the poor cannot be

---

22. Longenecker provides an extensive treatment of the Roman treatment of the poor in *Remember the Poor*, pp. 60-107.

23. Longenecker, *Remember the Poor*, p. 107.

24. Peter Brown, *Poverty and Leadership in the Later Roman Empire* (Hanover, NH: University Press of New England, 2002), pp. 8-9.

25. Robert Wilken makes this point in his *The First Thousand Years: A Global History of Christianity* (New Haven: Yale University Press, 2012), pp. 156-57.

26. Brown, *Poverty and Leadership in the Later Roman Empire*, pp. 6-9.

27. Longenecker and Anderson report on the Emperor Julian's attempt to reestablish pagan religion through generosity. See Longenecker, *Remember the Poor*, pp. 86-87, and Anderson, *Charity*, p. 17.

separated from their worship of God. But we dare not forget that it is whom we worship as Christians. That means how Christians unders charity may not be the same as how that practice is understood in Judaism. Yet I hope I have made clear that whatever the difference may be, the common commitment is stronger yet. The Gospels make clear that those who were poor and vulnerable were of particular significance in Jesus' ministry. But just as important is the recognition that the one who said "you will always have the poor with you" was poor.[28] That is the one we meet in prison, who is hungry and sick; that is the one with whom we eat when we share his body and blood.

## Charity in the World of Capitalism: Some Christian Responses

I began by recounting contemporary worries and doubts about aiding the poor by secular as well as Christian agents. Charity from such a perspective seems to do more harm than good. But now I have given you an account of charity that makes it obligatory for Christians. Does that mean we must do what cannot help but be a failure in the name of serving our God? How do we go on?

I will have some suggestions about how to go on, but first I have to make matters even more complex by engaging questions about charity in modernity. One of the reasons, and it may well be *the* reason, charity has become problematic in our day is the transformation of our lives by what is generally known as capitalism. I cannot, even if I were competent to do so, provide an account of that multi-splendored thing we call capitalism. But what I need to do is at least suggest how some aspects of Adam Smith's account of capitalism have implications for how we understand and practice charity.

I need to warn you this is not a diatribe against capitalism. Indeed my primary purpose is to give an account of what I take to be the great moral project that shaped Smith's account of capitalism. That purpose can be put very simply. Smith sought to do nothing less than to give an account of emerging economic relations that would eliminate the poor. He wanted to make begging a thing of the past. Through the division of labor and the

---

28. For my reflections on this claim see my sermon titled "The Appeal of Judas," in my *A Cross-Shattered Church: Reclaiming the Theological Heart of Preaching* (Grand Rapids: Brazos, 2009), pp. 94-98.

establishment of a free market he sought to show how a system was possible in which wealth would be created sufficiently to make every person self-sufficient.

Smith was, of course, a great moral philosopher, having written *The Theory of Moral Sentiments* prior to writing *An Inquiry into the Nature and Causes of the Wealth of Nations.*[29] Kelly Johnson, whose work I am indebted to for the account of capitalism I am about to give, describes questions about the relation of these two books as the "Adam Smith problem." The problem, according to Johnson, is that *The Theory of Moral Sentiments* has "sympathy" at the center of Smith's ethics, but *Wealth of Nations* seems to assume we are self-interested agents because if we were not self-interested, competition as the organizing principle of social organization could not be sustained. What seems to be a contradiction between these two perspectives Johnson argues is a deep mistake. It is so because the way Smith understands sympathy is not opposed to what seems to be an underwriting of self-interest in *Wealth of Nations.*[30]

Sympathy, for Smith, is the key to our moral lives. It is so because sympathy makes possible the imaginative possibility that I can imagine, even against my own will, other people's situations and lives. We are people affected by other people, making possible our ability to understand lives quite different from our own. Smith saw no tension between sympathy and self-interest, given the fact that I am only able to know myself by seeing myself reflected through the eyes of others. Smith's account of this process is very complex, but suffice it to say that Smith sought to give an account of our dealings with one another that makes possible our ability to take an impartial perspective that is equivalent to reason itself.

Once the significance of sympathy is recognized as the heart of Smith's understanding of the moral life, the importance of the division of labor can be appreciated not only because it makes wealth possible but also because it forces us to sympathetically — to imaginatively — enter the lives of others. The "system" is meant to create a world in which I can desire the admiration of others because I have the ability to admire others. That, however, is why Smith has such a problem with beggars. Because beggars do not seek to be admired, they become parasites. Johnson observes that

---

29. Adam Smith, *The Theory of Moral Sentiments,* ed. D. D. Raphael and A. L. Macfie (Oxford: Clarendon, 1976); Adam Smith, *An Inquiry into the Nature and Causes of the Wealth of Nations,* ed. R. H. Campbell and A. S. Skinner (Indianapolis: Liberty Classics, 1981).

30. Johnson, *The Fear of Beggars,* p. 102.

Smith thought people rightly despised beggars because they do not want to feel, as they will be tempted to do, any sympathy with those who refuse to be self-sufficient. Beggars are morally corrupt because they refuse to "see" themselves rightly by entering into the perspective of the impartial spectator. Instead beggars use their suffering to coerce others to be in sympathy with them.[31]

Smith distinguished, however, between the poor and beggars. The poor could be subject to our sympathy as long as they sought to be like those who were not poor. Yet it was Smith's hope that capitalism as a system for the production of wealth would provide an alternative that would eliminate poverty. Indeed one way to think of Smith's vision is to see capitalism itself as a system of charity. No longer will individual acts of charity be required, because the system itself will raise all the boats as the water rises. Capitalism so understood is an extraordinary utopian project.

Of course the difficulty with such projects is they invite the illusion that though things may not be working out, i.e., we still have the poor among us, all we need is more time and the system will take care of itself. The other alternative is to blame those who have not become self-sufficient by suggesting they lack some essential virtues to make the system work. As a result the poor get blamed for being poor. I hardly need to mention that the poor are often subject to such judgments in advanced capitalist societies.

It did not take long for those deeply influenced by Smith to recognize that the poor were not going away. The inequality of wealth as well as the continuing existence of beggars made it clear that the poor, particularly the poor in England and America, were not simply an anomaly. What would be the Christian response? The name of the response, a name that is still quite prominent among those who want to do "something about the poor," is called stewardship. Johnson, interestingly enough, credits John Wesley as the originator of this response to poverty. Thus the Methodist slogan: Make all you can, give all you can.

Though Kelly Johnson credits Wesley with the idea of stewardship as a way for Christians to care for the poor, it was Archbishop Sandy who was

---

31. Johnson, *The Fear of Beggars*, p. 106. Johnson notes that there is a shift in Smith's views of beggars from the *Theory of Moral Sentiments* to *The Wealth of Nations*. In the former beggars are by definition ignoble, but in *The Wealth of Nations* begging is but one form of exchange that commercial life depends on (p. 109). The difficulty, of course, is that beggars are not productive, but then neither are most priests. Smith, of course, was not that happy with priests.

the first to state the fundamental idea that defined stewardship. According to Sandy, "The rich man is a servant to the poor, to relieve and comfort him as he is able; for that is right and to that end God hath made him rich, that he as a faithful steward may bestow rich blessings upon the family and household of God."[32]

According to Johnson the problem with this strategy as a response to poverty is that it conflates two claims, that is, only God is the true owner of my wealth, yet the wealth is a gift given to a person; who therefore has an uncontestable right to do what they wish with the money?[33] Moreover stewardship gives far too much control over our assumed private "property." As a result, Johnson observes, stewardship as a way to negotiate wealth occludes other theological questions about matters such as just wages or the ethics of usury.[34]

There was another alternative in response to the kind of poverty capitalism produces. It was called the social gospel. The social gospel was a movement in the late nineteenth century in response to the economic depression and poverty that were devastating the industrial cities of the United States. Those associated with the social gospel saw that it was not sufficient to care for the poor through charitable acts, for the problem of poverty was systemic. Christians should continue to be charitable, but far more important was addressing the social conditions that made people poor in the first place.

As the social gospel developed its language, "justice" began to displace charity as a description of how Christians should respond to poverty. Charity sounded too much like philanthropy and philanthropy was seen to be part of the problem. It was part of the problem because too often what was given the poor served to mask from the giver and receiver the structural injustices that kept people in poverty. Reinhold Niebuhr was the great name associated with this turn toward justice.

In particular Niebuhr's book *Moral Man and Immoral Society,* a book that Niebuhr understood to be quite critical of the moral idealism of the social gospel, represented the turn toward justice as crucial for addressing questions of poverty and inequities.[35] In particular Niebuhr was quite critical of what he took to be the political naïveté of the social gospel. What the

32. Quoted in Johnson, *The Fear of Beggars*, p. 80.
33. Johnson, *The Fear of Beggars*, p. 88.
34. Johnson, *The Fear of Beggars*, p. 98.
35. Reinhold Niebuhr, *Moral Man and Immoral Society* (New York: Scribner, 1932).

representatives of the social gospel missed, from Niebuhr's perspective, was the role of power for the achievement of justice. For Niebuhr the only way to do something substantive about poverty was to use the technologies of power available to the dispossessed to challenge the often-hidden power of the established order.

Yet when the poor used strikes and other forms of direct confrontation they were often described as being unreasonable at best, and at worst it was said they threatened violence. Those who benefit from the way things are always call for peace or, once confronted by those they have oppressed, say they cannot respond to violence. What those who benefit from the way things are cannot recognize is "when collective power, whether in the form of imperialism or class domination, exploits weakness, it can never be dislodged unless power is raised against it."[36] For Niebuhr, therefore, if you want justice you must recognize that conflict and possibly violence will be necessary.

Crucial for Niebuhr's position was the presumption that democracy was the most preferable form of government for the achievement of more nearly-just social orders. It is so because democracy allows that open-ended conflict be part of the social organism. Niebuhr knew well, as he acknowledges in *Moral Man and Immoral Society,* that democracies are the creature of and the servant to commercial classes, but he argued that though democracy was subject to ideological perversion it is the best alternative we have if we want to achieve justice for the poor.

But that means a commitment to justice requires those so committed to abandon any presumption that justice can be achieved without the use of force. Thus Niebuhr's forceful claim that "once we have made the fateful concession of ethics to politics, and accepted coercion as a necessary instrument of social cohesion, we can make no absolute distinction between non-violent and violent types of coercion or between weapons used by governments and those used by revolutionaries."[37]

I think it fair to say that Niebuhr changed the world in terms of how Christians, particularly in America, understood how the poor were to be served. Rather than focusing on individual acts of charity, Christians now tried to imagine social policies that would make the poor no longer poor. Niebuhr's extraordinary ability to imagine and support policies that offered some care for the poor was remarkable.

36. Niebuhr, *Moral Man and Immoral Society,* p. xii.
37. Niebuhr, *Moral Man and Immoral Society,* p. 179.

Christians, under the influence of Niebuhr, became more concerned with trying to make the government the agent of care for the poor rather than "remember the poor." For the political realm was seen as the way social goals could be used to qualify the excesses of capitalism. As a result Christians increasingly came to believe that their obligation to care about the poor could be met by voting for the left wing of the Democratic Party — a vain ambition given the fact that there is now no left wing of the Democratic Party left.

The result of these strategies was nicely articulated by Peter Maurin in one of his *Easy Essays*.[38] Maurin, Dorothy Day's great friend, observes:

> In the first centuries
> of Christianity
> the hungry were fed
> at a personal sacrifice,
> the naked were clothed
> at a personal sacrifice,
> the homeless were sheltered
> at personal sacrifice.
> And because the poor
> were fed, clothed and sheltered
> at a personal sacrifice,
> the pagans used to say
> about the Christians
> "See how they love each other."
> In our own day
> the poor are no longer
> fed, clothed and sheltered
> at a personal sacrifice,
> but at the expense
> of the taxpayers.
> And because the poor
> are no longer
> fed, clothed and sheltered
> the pagans say about the Christians
> "See how they pass the buck."

---

38. Peter Maurin, *Easy Essays* (Eugene, OR: Wipf and Stock, 2010), p. 110.

It would be unfair to suggest that Niebuhr is the person responsible for the results Maurin finds so regrettable. Yet Niebuhr, in many ways still a child of the social gospel, legitimated the presumption by many Christians that the best way to express our obligation to the poor was by being on the correct side politically. There is nothing wrong with thinking it important to be on the correct political side, but lost in that way of trying to fulfill our obligation to the poor is how we find in the face of the poor the face of Christ. Missing in Niebuhr is any understanding of the relation between worship and charity that Anderson so helpfully articulates.

I am not in any way trying to belittle or leave behind the commitment to justice for the poor that the social gospel and Niebuhr represented. I worry, however, when that way of understanding the Christian obligation to be with the poor overwhelms concrete acts of charity. Interestingly enough, I suspect the social gospel and Niebuhr's way of trying to create more just societies was a quite appropriate response to capitalism. But I fear too often the attempt to defeat an enemy may make us a mirror image of what we oppose.

## A Plea for Charity

As I noted above, I am often criticized for my claim that the first task of the church is not to make the world more just but to make the world the world. Given the account of charity I have tried to develop, I hope that claim may not appear so self-satisfied. For it is only when the church is a community of charity that the world has some means of recognizing itself. Though the world may often appear to be more charitable than the church, it is crucial to remember that for the church the care of the poor cannot be separated from the worship of God. Worship makes possible the time Christians have to be with the poor. Put even more strongly, in and by worship Christians can imagine being poor.

"World" names the impatience with the poor for their inability to imagine not being poor. The world does not have time to be with the poor, to learn with the poor, to listen to the poor. To listen to the poor is an exercise of great discipline, but such listening surely is what is required if charity is not to become a hatred of the poor for being poor. We must listen to the stories the poor have to tell because only by listening to such stories do we have the means to know how to go on.

If we do not learn, as Sam Wells argues, to be with the poor we will continue to be caught on the unhappy choice of *either* being a church whose identity is primarily constituted by worship of God *or* being a church that is fundamentally about "social action." By calling attention to Anderson and Longenecker I have tried to provide an account that is an alternative to that unhappy choice. Worship and charity are inseparable. The challenge is to know what that might look like. What does learning to be "with" look like?

I suspect most rich Christians, filled as we are with anxiety about our wealth, try to do something for the poor before we have listened to their story. Of course listening, being with, and working with the poor are not mutually exclusive activities, but I fear we often want to help the poor without getting to know who the poor may be. I suspect we do so not from some ideology against the poor, but we prefer to do for the poor rather than be with the poor because the poor scare the hell out of us.

As an alternative I think as Christians we need to know how to be with the poor in such a manner that the gifts the poor receive do not make impossible friendship between the giver and the recipient. For friendship is the heart of the matter if we remember that charity first and foremost names God's befriending of us. If the poor are not befriended there is no way to avoid the problems I sketched at the beginning of this essay. I do not mean to suggest that friendship is some kind of magical relation that will make the dependencies associated with aid less likely. Friendships, at least superficial friendships, are just as likely to produce dependency as direct aid.[39]

But genuine friendship depends on people being truthful with one another. There is no substitute for people being honest. The poor should not be romanticized. It may be the case that because the poor have nothing to lose they may be more likely to tell the truth, but the poor like the rich are human beings. That means they, like all of us, often find it hard to distinguish the lie from the truth. If they lie, moreover, they must be held accountable, for if they are not held accountable they are robbed of having lives worth living.

I cannot help but conclude that Christians now owe our poor brothers and sisters the truth. That truth is quite simple. It is, as Pope Francis suggests in his Apostolic Exhortation *Evangelii Gaudium,* that

---

39. For a beautiful book that displays how important friendship is if we are to avoid paternalism see David Rhode, *Faith in Dark Places* (London: SPCK, 2013).

God's heart has a special place for the poor, so much so that he himself "became poor" (II Cor. 8:9). The entire history of our redemption is marked by the presence of the poor. Salvation came to us from the "yes" uttered by a lowly maiden from a small town on the fringes of a great empire. The Savior was born in a manger, in the midst of animals, like children of poor families. . . . When he began to preach the Kingdom crowds of the dispossessed followed him, illustrating his words: "The Spirit of the Lord is upon me, because he has anointed me to preach good news to the poor" (Luke 4:18). He assured those burdened by sorrow and crushed by poverty that God has a special place in his heart: "Blessed are you poor, yours is the kingdom of God."[40]

Pope Francis continues, observing that the option for the poor by the church is first and foremost a theological category rather than a cultural, sociological, political, or philosophical one. He obviously does not think these categories are mutually exclusive, but the theological emphasis is significant because, as he puts it, he wants "a Church which is poor and for the poor. They have much to teach us. Not only do they share in the *sensus fidei*, but in their difficulties they know the suffering of Christ. We need to let ourselves be evangelized by them" (198).

Pope Francis's rhetoric can invite sentimental construal of what it means to be poor, but he indicates he understands how what he is calling for will demand much of those called to befriend and be befriended by the poor. Though he does not discount the importance of activities or programs to assist the poor, his primary emphasis is how, under the guidance of the Holy Spirit, we can become attentive to the poor. Such an "attentiveness is the beginning of a true concern for the person which inspires in me effectively to seek their good. This entails appreciating the poor in their goodness, in their experience of life, in their culture, and in their way of living the faith. True love is always contemplative, and permits us to serve the other not out of necessity or vanity, but rather because he or she is beautiful and beyond mere appearances" (199).

There is nothing naïve about Pope Francis's call for the church to attend to the poor. From his perspective it is not sufficient to do something for the poor. Rather they must be included in work we are all called to perform for the common good. Pope Francis seems to understand that friendship with the poor is more likely when we have work to do in com-

---

40. Pope Francis, *Evangelii Gaudium*. Paragraph numbers will appear in the text.

mon. So it is not us and them, but rather how we become one in that work that is rest; it is called the worship of God. Charity so understood surely has some chance of being with the poor in a manner that avoids the dishonesty and dependency associated with charity aimed at doing something for the poor.

For in truth the deepest problem is that most of us want to be agents of charity without having to receive charity. But the truth is, our very being depends on our learning to receive the gift of Christ. Pope Francis suggests that perhaps the greatest failure of the church's care of the poor is the lack of spiritual care for the poor. He observes that the majority of the poor have a special openness to the faith, but they need God — and the church cannot fail to offer them God's friendship. Such an offer begins with basics such as sharing with one another the celebration of the sacraments (200).

Pope Francis does not make any specific recommendations about policy for state agencies to do something about poverty. But he is quite explicit that "thou shalt not kill" applies to what he describes as economies of exclusion and inequality. When an elderly homeless person dies of exposure we should rightly call that murder. We simply cannot stand by when food is thrown away while people are starving (53). Nor can we wait for "trickle-down theories" to work because they will never work. Rather what must be acknowledged is that "the culture of prosperity deadens us" (54). Accordingly he uses strong language, arguing that "not to share one's wealth with the poor is to steal from them and to take away their livelihood" (57).

Like Paul we are asked to do one thing — remember the poor. Such a remembrance turns out to be a challenge for no other reason than that it will force us to identify not with the abstraction "the poor" but with this very person who is suffering a loss. As I suggested at the beginning of this essay, locating the poor is no easy matter, but it has to start somewhere because there is no anywhere. There is an elderly couple who have run out of money who sit in the pew in front of me every Sunday. That is not a bad place to start if we, rich or poor, are to know how "to remember the poor."

# CHAPTER 12

# How to Be Theologically Funny

*Analyzing humor is like dissecting a frog. Few people are interested and the frog dies of it.*

E. B. WHITE[1]

---

1. The E. B. White quote is taken from Matthew Hurley, Daniel Dennett, and Reginald Adams's *Inside Jokes: Using Humor to Reverse-Engineer the Mind* (Cambridge, MA: MIT Press, 2011), p. 289. For those interested, this book will tell you more than you want to know about how humor developed in the evolutionary process. To their credit the authors resist any reductive analysis of humor, and along the way they make some enlightening suggestions about the role of humor for our lives as human beings. I call attention to their book as a way to indicate I am not trying to do what they have done.

---

I have dedicated this essay to my good friend Peter Ochs. I have many friends, but Peter is special. He is special because he is Peter Ochs. By that I mean few can match his intellectual energy and powerful personality. There is also the little matter that he is a Jew and I am a Christian. That difference makes our friendship different, but not in the way some might think. For it turns out, I often find Peter and I share more judgments than I share with other Christians. Of course, Peter knows more about Christianity than many Christians. I only wish I knew Judaism as well as Peter knows Christianity. I hope some of the remarks I make about the differences between Jews and Christians when it comes to humor are relevant to Peter's work. Peter is a funny guy and humor pervades his work. Therefore, I hope this essay pays due honor to this funny and profound man who honors me by claiming me as friend.

## Can or Should Theology Be Funny? Beginning with a Joke

It seems that John XXIII commissioned an archeological expedition in the Holy Land. They made a great discovery that the head of the expedition thought presented certain theological problems. He called John XXIII, announcing that he had some good news and some bad news. The good news was they had discovered the tomb in which Jesus was laid after the crucifixion. The bad news was that the body was in it. The head of the expedition thought he ought to alert John XXIII to the findings before they were generally known because it might entail some theological rethinking. John XXIII thanked the head of the expedition for letting him know because he did need to pray and think about this news. So he prayed and thought but was unsure what to say. Finally he said to himself, "My old friend Rudy Bultmann has thought long and hard about these matters. I will call him to see what he thinks." He called Bultmann, explaining that he had some quite momentous news that he feared might upset Bultmann, but he needed Bultmann's help. John XXIII explained about the archeological expedition and the finding of the tomb. He then again warned Bultmann that what he had next to tell him he might find deeply disturbing, but he had to tell him the truth if he was to get his help. So he said, "The body was in the tomb." There was a long silence on Bultmann's end. John XXIII waited and waited, fearing that Bultmann's faith had been shattered. Bultmann finally responded, "So he really existed."

This was the joke we told as seminarians at Yale Divinity School in 1965. At the time the joke certainly needed no "explaining." Bultmann was the New Testament historian/theologian we read. His presumption that we had little evidence to secure knowledge of the "historical Jesus" dominated discussions of New Testament scholarship. That Bultmann might be upset, or at least have to reconsider his views, if the body was found, we thought to be quite funny. I confess I still find the joke not only funny but a nice commentary on the scholarship surrounding the New Testament when I was in seminary.

I suspect the story is not nearly so funny for current generations of seminarians. Bultmann simply does not dominate New Testament scholarship the way he did when I was a student. Indeed he can be read as a deeply conservative thinker about questions surrounding Jesus, given developments in New Testament scholarship since he wrote. Better put, theologically

Bultmann never doubted that Jesus matters. But I suspect that for the joke to "work" for current students they will need some explanations that inform them about Bultmann and his scholarship. This raises a familiar but often forgotten point about attempts to "be funny," that is, humor is profoundly contextual, depending as it does on common presuppositions and habits.

I begin with an example of a joke, but I take as my task in this essay to explore a more general question than the joke may suggest. I want to try to understand the role of humor in theology. Most of those who practice Christian theology think they are engaged in a serious science. That it is so should not be surprising given the reality that at the center of Christian theology is a crucified savior. Moreover any theology that is doing the work of theology well must deal with the fundamentals of life, that is, life, death, and all the stuff in between. Stuff like love and the betrayal of love. These subjects not only are serious, but, if truthfully addressed, sentimentality and superficial nostrums must be avoided. Humor can be one of the ways that sentimentality and superficiality can be defied.

M. A. Screech observes in his erudite and wise book *Laughter at the Foot of the Cross* that "man is a laughing animal."[2] He traces that claim to Aristotle and Aquinas — a claim, I might add, I think to be more basic than the general characterization that the distinguishing character of being human is our rationality. I call attention to Screech's observation, an observation he develops by attending to the work of Erasmus and Rabelais, in order to distinguish the question of whether and how theology can and should be funny from the question concerning the task of theology to provide an account of our humanity that entails our being funny. These questions are obviously interrelated, but they are not the same question. In this essay I am primarily concerned with the former.

By beginning with a joke, as well as using the description "funny," I mean to distinguish what I am about from attempts to characterize Christian theology in general by using genre categories such as tragedy or comedy. I have no reason to deny that general characterizations of Christianity as comedic can be quite informative. For example, in *The Comedy of Redemption: Christian Faith and Comic Vision in Four American Novelists,* Ralph Wood argues quite persuasively that the Christian vision of the world is fundamentally comic. Drawing on the insights of Karl Löwith, Wood observes that because Christians do not, as the ancients did, regard the universe as eternal or divine but as created, comedy is made possible by the acknowledgment of

2. M. A. Screech, *Laughter at the Foot of the Cross* (London: Penguin, 1997), p. 3.

the sheer contingency of all that is. According to Wood, "what the Christian faith confesses is that God, in the Jews and Jesus, has perpetrated the most outrageous of tricks, a joke to end all jokes, a surprise beyond all surprises. He has upset our tragicomic equilibrium. In Israel and Christ he acts unilaterally to deliver the human race from its dialectical enslavement."[3]

I find Wood's account of the comic character of the Christian narrative to be quite insightful. I worry, however, that the use of tragedy and comedy to characterize the Christian worldview runs into the problem of diverse understandings of tragedy or comedy. The concepts of tragedy and comedy depend so heavily on the literature they are meant to characterize that it is unclear how helpful those descriptions are when turned into general designations. Greek tragedy may have some resemblances to the tragedies of Shakespeare, but the difference Christianity makes for Shakespeare's "tragedies" means that to characterize the plays of the Greeks and Shakespeare as tragic may not be instructive but misleading.[4] I say this as someone who titled an early book *Truthfulness and Tragedy: Further Investigations into Christian Ethics*.[5] In my defense I was using tragedy to avoid "lesser of two evils" arguments. I still think there may be something to that proposal, but that is a subject for another day.

Yet I do think, in spite of the considerable evidence to the contrary, that theology can and should be, in some of its modes, funny. Theology done right should make you laugh. Chris Huebner, in a recent article on my work titled "Make Us Your Laughter: Stanley Hauerwas's Joke on Mennonites," makes some insightful comments about my use of laughter that I find extremely informative.[6] For example, he calls attention to my poking fun at Mennonites in a sermon such as "On Milk and Jesus" as my way to help Mennonites recognize what a funny people they are.[7] Huebner observes

---

3. Ralph Wood, *The Comedy of Redemption: Christian Faith and Comic Vision in Four American Novelists* (Notre Dame: University of Notre Dame Press, 1988), p. 32.

4. For example Sarah Beckwith, drawing on Stanley Cavell, suggests that Shakespeare's tragedies are the result of failures in acknowledgment due to the terrifying reality that to be loved as well as to love risks being known by another. *Shakespeare and the Grammar of Forgiveness* (Ithaca, NY: Cornell University Press, 2011), pp. 6-7.

5. Stanley Hauerwas, *Truthfulness and Tragedy: Further Investigations into Christian Ethics* (Notre Dame: University of Notre Dame Press, 1977).

6. Chris Huebner, "Make Us Your Laughter: Stanley Hauerwas's Joke on Mennonites," *The Mennonite Quarterly Review* 84 (July 2010): 357-74.

7. "On Milk and Jesus" can be found in my *Disrupting Time: Sermons, Prayers, and Sundries* (Eugene, OR: Cascade, 2004), pp. 142-48. It was a sermon delivered at the installation of Dr. Gerald Gerbrandt as President of the Canadian Mennonite University in 2003.

that my use of laughter is my attempt to practice theology in a manner that refuses the attempt to manage the world. In short, my use of laughter is "an appropriate theological antidote to the Constantinian desire for control."[8]

Huebner argues it is important to note that my use of laughter does not mean I lack an appropriate seriousness. He suggests, I think rightly, that there is no contradiction between something at once being serious and funny. I do, however, have a deep distaste for the cloying seriousness associated with some forms of pietism. But my use of laughter to counter what I regarded as feigned profundity is my attempt, as Huebner puts it, to offer "a response to the idolatrous temptation to take ourselves more seriously than God."[9]

Huebner calls attention to my self-designation as a "high church Mennonite" to illustrate how I use humor to make a serious theological point. He rightly suggests that I use that description as a joke. He doubts it is all that funny, but credits my use of the description as a way to raise theological questions about how we define our identities. Huebner argues I am trying, probably not very successfully, to call into question our preoccupation with identity. My use of "high church Mennonite" is but one expression of my general concern that "preoccupation with neatness tends to generate models of theological discourse that are methodologically egoistic."[10] Without laughter, our speech about the strange, surprising, and funny God we worship threatens to become speech about ourselves.[11]

By calling attention to the importance of humor and laughter in theology I am trying to suggest that theology should be done in an entertaining manner. Humor is not the only mode of entertainment the discourse of theology can take, but it is surely the case that we — and the "we" means most people — are often attracted to speech and writing that is funny. This is an observation that calls into question the presumption by some that if you want what you have to say to be entertaining then what you have to say cannot be serious. I have tried to defy that presumption by attempting to do theology in a manner that "tickles" the imagination.

For example, some years ago I wrote an essay titled "A Tale of Two

---

8. Huebner, "Make Us Your Laughter," p. 362.

9. Huebner, "Make Us Your Laughter," p. 365.

10. Huebner, "Make Us Your Laughter," p. 146.

11. Huebner suggests that Mennonites may not get the joke I am about, but Yoder did. For a fascinating analysis of the relation of humor and hope in Yoder, see Jonathan Tran, "Laughing *with* the World: Possibilities of Hope in John Howard Yoder and Jeffrey Stout," in *The New Yoder*, ed. Peter Dula and Chris Huebner (Eugene, OR: Cascade, 2010), pp. 253-70.

Stories: On Being a Christian and a Texan."[12] The essay begins by acknowledging that I want to entertain my reader while doing what I take to be serious intellectual work. I wrote the essay first and foremost to honor my parents in the hope that if they read the essay they would recognize how deeply I valued the way they had formed me to be a Texan without regret.[13] I assumed such training was the necessary condition to be a human being. I also wrote the essay for my own amusement because in it I was able to use William Humphrey's great novel, *The Ordways,* to elicit what it means to be a Texan. The novel, moreover, is filled with stories of Texans trying to make it in a hard land, stories that are at once humorous and sad.

The serious intellectual work the essay was meant to do was to respond to the criticism that a focus on narrative as a basic grammar of Christian speech fails to appropriately acknowledge that no one narrative can or should constitute our lives. "On Being a Christian and a Texan" was my way to show how different stories work to shape our lives. I also wanted to show how the different stories that possess us can be judged more or less truthful by suggesting how the narrative(s) generally recognized as Christian makes how the stories of Texas must be told as well as lived. The great trick is how the injustice that is inherent in the stories that are Texas can be remembered without their being justified. I should like to think not only that "A Tale of Two Stories" is entertaining but that it is so exactly because it is serious theology.

Then, of course, there is my semi-famous essay, "Why Gays (as a Group) Are Morally Superior to Christians (as a Group)."[14] That short essay was meant to be funny by reframing the question of gay relationships in terms of their (at the time) doubtful status in the military. By raising the question about why Christians could not accomplish the feat of being banned from the military as a group I was trying to suggest how arguments about gays depended on the accommodated character of contemporary Christianity in America. But if Christians as followers of Christ found

12. The essay is the first chapter in my book *Christian Existence Today: Essays on Church, World, and Living in Between* (Durham, NC: Labyrinth Press, 1988), pp. 25-45. I am grateful to Brazos Press for reprinting the book in 2001, though I continue to have the impression that the book is not widely read.

13. For a fuller account of my parents see my memoir, *Hannah's Child: A Theologian's Memoir,* with a new Afterword (Grand Rapids: Eerdmans, 2012). *Hannah's Child* was originally published in 2010.

14. The essay first appeared in my *Dispatches from the Front: Theological Engagements with the Secular* (Durham, NC: Duke University Press, 1994), pp. 153-55.

themselves banned from the military as a group then arguments about gay participation in the church would be quite different.

But enough about me. There is much more to be said about why theology needs to be funny. In particular I want to call attention to the theologian I think may be the "funniest" in the Christian tradition, namely, Karl Barth. Before doing so, however, I need to prepare the ground for Barth's humor by calling attention to a philosophical analysis of jokes. For by paying close attention to jokes we will be better able to understand that jokes are no joking matter.

I had once thought to title this essay "How to Tell a Theological Joke," but jokes are a more specific category than a story that is funny. Jokes are funny, but not everything that is funny is a joke. However, by attending to an analysis of jokes I hope to throw more light on what it means for theology to be funny. There is also the question of the relation between jokes, what is funny, and irony. It is probably the case that irony is a more inclusive category than either jokes or what is funny. Jokes often employ irony, but irony is not always in the form of a joke, nor is it necessarily funny. There is no reason to assume, nor is it crucial for the case I want to make, that these conceptual questions must be settled. I am content if the analysis of jokes I now provide helps illumine what it means for theology to be funny.

The question of the relation of theologians to their theology needs to be addressed. It is one thing to suggest that theologians need a sense of humor. It is quite something else to argue that their theology must be funny. I acknowledge the distinction, but I will maintain that not only should theologians know how to laugh at themselves but also their theology should manifest the joy that reflects the glory of God. Of course joy is not the same as what makes something funny, but what is funny depends first and foremost on a joyful recognition that God is God and we are not. The joke is on us.

## Ted Cohen on Jokes

Ted Cohen has written a very insightful and funny book on jokes. He titled the book *Jokes: Philosophical Thoughts on Joking Matters*.[15] "Philosophical

---

15. Ted Cohen, *Jokes: Philosophical Thoughts on Joking Matters* (Chicago: University of Chicago Press, 1999). Page references appear in the text.

thoughts" should not scare off any potential reader, because the kind of philosophy Cohen represents does not need to call attention to itself. For example he confesses when he first began to write about jokes he thought they could be divided into pure and conditional jokes. A conditional joke would be one that only works with specific audiences. Cohen's exploration of jokes, however, has convinced him that there is no such thing as a pure joke (p. 12). That is a philosophical point, but Cohen does not reference or elaborate the philosophical sources that clearly inform his judgment that there are no "pure" jokes.

For instance he tells a joke about the president of a small college who wants to improve the school's academic reputation. The president is told the best way to do that is to create a few first-rank departments. He first focuses on the mathematics department because he is told that increasing its quality would not be very expensive. After all, the only things mathematicians need to do their work are pencils, paper, and wastebaskets. However, the ambitious president then judges that it might be even less expensive to make the philosophy department rather than the mathematics department better, because philosophers do not need wastebaskets.

You do not need to be a mathematician or philosopher or even an academic to enjoy this joke, but you do need some understanding of mathematicians' demand for elegance as well as philosophers' presumed professional license to say what they please because there is no way to prove them right or wrong (p. 14). Cohen notes that not all jokes require specialized information or professional jargon, but they may require a little knowledge about a specific subject. He provides as an example a response of a man who is asked by a panhandler outside a theater for a handout. The man declined, saying, " 'Neither a borrower nor a lender be' — William Shakespeare." The panhandler replied, " 'Fuck you!' — David Mamet."

As I noted Cohen does not, as he might have done, call attention to philosophical accounts of rationality that would support his argument that there is no such thing as a "pure joke," but he does rightly argue that every attempt to provide a general theory of jokes turns out to be wrong (p. 43). Of course some jokes draw on what we assume is general knowledge of the human condition, such as jokes about death and illness. But that some jokes seem "to work" on the basis of such knowledge Cohen argues is not sufficient to ground a general theory about jokes. Thus the "method" of his analysis of jokes depends on exemplification.

For example, the joke: "One good thing about Alzheimer's disease is that if you get it you can hide your own Easter eggs" (p. 43) might be one anyone could "get." But Cohen notes that some find such a joke disagreeable, which indicates that how illness is experienced makes all the difference for how such a joke is meant to work. The fact that those with the disease as well as those who care for them are more likely to find the joke funny is but a further indication that we do not need a general theory about jokes. Rather what we need is insight. Thus the observation that those who find the joke funny do so because the joke helps defeat the loneliness associated with the disease.

Cohen observes that he thinks what makes a successful joke successful is "the sense held mutually by teller and hearer that they are joined in feeling" (p. 25). That good jokes are concise is due to the fact that so much can go unsaid because of what the teller and the hearers know in common. Cohen even uses the language of intimacy to describe what he takes to be the effect of a good joke. By intimacy he means a shared sense of community that a joke at once reflects and creates. Members know they are in such communities, according to Cohen, to the extent they can identify (1) a shared set of beliefs, dispositions, prejudices, preferences — in short a common outlook on the world, and (2) shared feelings (p. 28).

According to Cohen these two conditions of community that make jokes possible can be cultivated and realized without jokes, but with jokes our shared feelings are enhanced by our common outlook about the way things are. When we laugh at the same thing something important is happening. That we laugh at all is, he suggests, noteworthy. This is true even when we laugh alone, but when we laugh together we experience the satisfaction of "a deep human longing, the realization of a desperate hope. It is the hope that we are enough like one another to sense one another, to be able to live together" (p. 29). Cohen argues, therefore, that when a joke is successful there is nothing to point to but the joke itself.

That is why you know if you have to explain a joke something has gone wrong that cannot be fixed by the explanation. When a joke is unsuccessful you cannot show that the joke is really an example of some other case that should be acknowledged as funny. The joke either works or it does not, just as practical reason works or it does not. Cohen does not explicitly call attention to jokes as exemplifications of practical reason, but his account of how jokes work I take to be a compelling exemplification of how practical reason, at least practical reason as understood by Eugene Garver, works.[16]

---

16. Eugene Garver, *For the Sake of Argument: Practical Reasoning, Character, and the Ethics of Belief* (Chicago: University of Chicago Press, 2004).

Jokes can be understood rhetorically as one of the means we have to make "common knowledge truly common."[17]

Just as practical reason extends its range by engaging problems that would not exist without our being the kind of people we are, so jokes can be created by imaging a problem for oneself. Any subject will do. Cohen, for example, asks, "What is Sacramento? It is the stuffing in a Catholic olive" (p. 35). He acknowledges this is not a great joke, but one he and Richard Bernstein made up after having given themselves the challenge of making up a joke about pimiento. Perhaps a better example is the humor created by playing on certain words. Thus the eighty-five-year-old man's response to doubt about his claim to have sex almost every night: "For instance this week I had it almost on Monday, almost on Tuesday, almost on Wednesday . . ." (p. 36).

Cohen observes that though it is stimulating to explore new topics to joke about it is even more stimulating when the topic is extremely specific. He uses as an example snail jokes. "What does a snail say when riding on the back of a turtle? 'Whee!'" Or a turtle was mugged and robbed by a gang of snails. When asked for a description of the robbers the turtle replied, "I'm sorry, but I just don't know. It all happened so fast." Cohen suggests such jokes' limits are comparable to Stravinsky's remark that the most strict and rigid musical forms, forms like the fugue, are the most liberating for the composer because they free one from the need to worry about too many possibilities and leave the composer to exploit his talent by being inventive within the confine of the form (p. 39).

Perhaps the most fundamental role of jokes, however, is their use to comprehend the unexpected and absurd aspects of life.[18] We laugh at that which defies our ability to make sense of events in our lives. According to Cohen such "laughter is an expression of our humanity, our finite capacity, our ability to live with what we cannot understand or subdue. We can dwell with the incomprehensible without dying from fear or going mad" (p. 41). This role of jokes is particularly important for those who are

---

17. Garver, *For the Sake of Argument*, p. 39.

18. In his illuminating book *Redeeming Laughter: The Comic Dimension of Human Experience* (New York: De Gruyter, 1997), Peter Berger, drawing on Kierkegaard, suggests that the comic exploits the inherent contradictions of our lives. According to Berger, therefore, the difference between tragedy and comedy is that the tragic is the suffering of contradiction but the comical is painless contradiction (p. 27). Although, as I suggested above, I am skeptical of attempts to provide general accounts of tragedy or comedy, I suspect there is something to Berger's way of putting the matter.

under the control of others just to the extent that jokes help those in such a situation to laugh at their oppressor and, if they are lucky and the joke is very good, make the oppressor laugh at themselves (p. 44). Jokes often have a subversive character that cannot be acknowledged exactly because subversion is betrayed by being acknowledged.

Yet there is no escaping how jokes must deal with death. Death, moreover, is the subject Cohen suggests is the gateway for appreciating that particular tradition of jokes associated with Judaism. For Cohen, Jewish joke-telling reflects the Jewish acknowledgment of life's incomprehensibility.[19] Jewish jokes also manifest the sanctions internal to Judaism that are meant as a response to the incomprehensibility of life (p. 45). Cohen provides a number of long Jewish jokes that underwrite certain Jewish stereotypes of themselves. For example, there was the elderly rabbi in Brooklyn whose piety was renowned but whose faith had begun to waver. Pondering his growing spiritual crisis, he reasoned and prayed that if the Holy One wanted to strengthen the rabbi's faith he would do so by ensuring that the rabbi would win the New York State Lottery. The rabbi waits for weeks and months, continuing to pray that he will win the lottery. Finally, standing alone in the synagogue, he hears a rumbling and observes a brilliant light from which a beautiful melodious voice that seemed to come from every direction said, "So *nu,* buy a ticket" (p. 47).

Cohen thinks this kind of Jewish joke reflects the Jewish ability to laugh at absurdity as a way to negotiate the imponderables of life. Jewish humor reflects the conception of human decency found in the Hebrew Bible in which the mystification of the world is "a laughing acceptance, a kind of spiritual embrace" (p. 51). Moses is the great exemplification of this response to the world, as before the burning bush he answered "Here I am." That response is not funny, but Cohen suggests that Moses' response has a quality that pleases God. It pleases God because Moses turns aside to look at what he cannot comprehend. Cohen in a like manner argues that Abraham and Sarah's response to the announcement they would have a child is paradigmatic for the development of Jewish humor.[20]

19. Berger also provides an account of Jewish jokes that is quite similar to and compatible with Cohen's analysis of Jewish humor. See his *Redeeming Laughter,* pp. 87-98.

20. For a wonderful account of the whole Isaac narrative as comic see Joel Kaminsky, "Humor and the Theology of Hope: Isaac as a Humorous Figure," *Interpretation* (October 2008): 363-75. Kaminsky observes that there is an intrinsic connection between humor and hope exemplified in the stories of Isaac, that is, both humor and hope suggest that the everyday necessarily has the final word.

Such laughter, laughter that is a response to the incomprehensibility of the world, is nonetheless an acceptance of that same world. "The world and its inhabitants are forever doing the damnedest things. It is one Jewish mode of acceptance and appreciation to receive things in their wonder. Then this laughter may be heard as the echo of faith" (p. 60). This does not mean that Jews have a monopoly on jokes, yet there is a characteristic association of Jews with a joking spirit that Cohen argues is not accidental. It is the jokes of outsiders that exploit a deep and lasting concern and fascination with logic and language (p. 60).

The obsession with language and its logic that is characteristic of Jewish humor Cohen suggests comes from the bilingual character of Jewish existence in America. Yet he argues that bilingualism is not sufficient to explain the Jewish fascination with language. The Jewish tradition of reasoning and arguing developed in the study of Jewish texts Cohen thinks is crucial for understanding Jewish humor. For it is the character of Jewish tradition that debate is not only necessary but unending. For example, Cohen tells the story from the Talmud of the debate between scholars about whether a cooking oven of a particular kind is ritually clean. The debaters call on God to support their judgments by dramatic action, which finally climaxes with a heavenly voice speaking in support of R. Joshua. The other rabbis, however, were not impressed, observing that a voice from heaven cannot trump what is written in the Torah. It is said that God laughed, saying, "My sons have defeated Me. My sons have defeated Me" (pp. 56-57).

That much of Jewish humor is directed at themselves is an indication of the Jewish confidence in who they are. Yet Cohen raises the question of how far one can go in using humor to subvert oneself and still be oneself. Cohen thinks the Marx brothers managed to be at once Jewish but also American by making American humor Jewish. Of course it is true that nothing could be more Jewish than entertaining judgments against the Jews, but Cohen worries that the negative judgments about Jews by people like Freud, Marx, and Wittgenstein may suggest a self-hate that is anything but Jewish.

Cohen, therefore, concludes his wonderfully short book by raising the question of when, if at all, a joke is inappropriate. He observes that the widespread conviction exists that some jokes on some occasions are morally objectionable. But it is not at all clear what makes a joke have this moral defect. He thinks it unlikely that one can answer what makes a joke immoral by appealing to some moral theory. Given the "method" of his book, a method that clearly shows the influence of Stanley Cavell whom he claims as a friend, to appeal to a moral theory would betray the book. But just as important, Cohen does not think any theory could provide what is needed because theories cannot help but oversimplify the diverse character of the comedic.

Most moral theories would try to show that immoral jokes harm someone or reveal or reduce the moral character of the one who tells the joke.[21] Cohen doubts that anyone can show these results obtain. Instead Cohen gives some "friendly advice." If you feel a joke is no damned good, express your feeling of moral disapproval. If you are asked to defend your judgment by giving moral-theoretical reasons for your negative judgment, ask your interlocutor why you need to ground your judgments in theory. Rather what you must do is clarify matters for yourself and choose your words carefully, making sure that the words are really your words. We rightly feel disgust when exposed to jokes that are clearly racist, but crucial for the expression of that disgust is the availability of moral vocabulary to do the work that needs to be done (p. 83). That is why Cohen's account of jokes is so compelling.

## Theology Is Funny: The Case of Karl Barth

I have given an extensive account of Cohen on jokes because I find his analysis of jokes illuminating for thinking about why Christian theology should be funny. In particular I will try to make a case for how theology can and should be funny by calling attention to exemplifications of humor in the work of Karl Barth. I will end with a final brief look at some of my work. Before engaging Barth, however, I want to explore a question that Cohen's analysis of Jewish humor has raised for me. Why is there nothing in Christianity equivalent to Jewish humor?[22] As far as I know there is no

---

21. Screech puts the matter in as succinct a fashion as is possible when he observes "what makes laughter good or evil is its target." *Laughter at the Foot of the Cross,* p. 78.

22. I do not want to overlook that particular Christian traditions will develop their peculiar sense of humor. Martyn Percy, for example, argues that Anglicanism has developed a particular form of humor that is constitutive of Anglican ecclesiology. See his "Joking Apart: Exploring Comedy and Irony in Anglican Polity," *Ecclesiology* 1, no. 1 (2004): 75-86. Then there are the countless jokes about Southern Baptists. For example, "Why do Baptists object so strongly to premarital sex? They're afraid it might lead to drinking and dancing." Or "How do you know Adam was a Baptist? Only a Baptist could stand next to a naked woman and be tempted by a piece of fruit."

recognizable tradition of Christian humor comparable with Cohen's account of Jewish humor. Of course Christians can be quite funny, but they are seldom funny as Christians.[23] Is there something about the very content of the Christian faith that discourages Christians from having fun with our most fundamental convictions? For example consider the following:

> Jesus was walking down a dusty road when a woman ran toward him because she was being pursued by a mob of men calling her by slanderous names and bent on killing her by stoning her. As the woman approached Jesus he raised his arms, stopped the approaching men, and with eyes blazing stared at the woman's pursuers and then said, "Let him who is without sin cast the first stone." Soon one man and then another man dropped his stone and begin to retrace his steps. It seemed clear that the men would disperse. But suddenly a rock came flying out from the back of the group of men, striking the woman on the head so that she fell to the ground. Jesus said, "Mother, sometimes you really piss me off."

This is clearly not a very funny joke. I suspect many Christians would find it distinctly offensive. You just do not make fun of the mother of Jesus. Jesus may have told his parents he must be about his Father's business, but Jesus is Jesus and we are not. What is it about the Gospel narratives and the letters of Paul that seem to inhibit the Christian sense of humor? Does the dramatic character of struggle against the powers of destruction at the heart of the Gospels mean that Christians simply have no place for making fun of themselves and the world? As I suggested above, a story that has at its center a crucified savior just does not invite jocular commentary.

But there is the resurrection. I have always thought Thomas's recognition of Jesus profoundly comic. Jesus returns and offers his wounds to Thomas to touch so Thomas's demand for confirmation might be met. Thomas, and the text does not say he actually touched Jesus, says "My Lord

---

23. Greg Jones reminds me that Christians do have a tradition of jokes about heaven and hell. For example there is the story of Reverend Jones, a Methodist minister, who had faithfully served the church over the course of his life though he was appointed time after time to the worst churches in the conference. He approached Peter at the pearly gates only to be told his name was not on the books, so he must go to hell. Later Peter was doing some bookkeeping and discovered Jones's name. He sent Gabriel to get Jones, who was in a pool of brimstone up to his neck. On being told by Gabriel there had been a mistake, Jones refused to leave to go to heaven. When asked why, Jones observed that he was standing on his bishop's shoulder. This is a very Methodist joke.

and my God." What an extraordinary response. You would have thought, given his worries about Jesus' actual return, he would have said something like, "Oh! You're back. Tell me about it." But he instead confesses that Jesus is Lord. That confession surely has the ring of joy if not laughter. The world will never be the same.[24]

In an extraordinary Easter sermon titled "One Day You Will Laugh," Sam Wells observes that laughter is often used in a defensive manner to help us deal with unpleasant realities that often turn out to be other people. But laughter can also be used in an attack mode to belittle. Thus the jokes used to make us laugh *at* rather than *with* other people. By contrast Wells suggests that the laughter that is the resurrection is an infectious and irresistible laughter that overwhelms all who encounter it with joy.[25] If Wells is right about this, and I certainly think or at least hope he is, the question remains as to why Christians have failed to see the humor that pervades our scriptures and the lives of those who have preceded us.

It is not my intention to worry over this question about how the Gospel narratives may or may not inhibit or encourage what may be thought of as jokes, or at least funny stories. I certainly think Cohen is onto something by suggesting that the very character of Jewish debate around the law invites an imagination open to what might be called the grammar of the comedic. Could it be the very character of Christianity as a faith that one joins only by deep conviction inhibits a sense of humor about being a Christian? Jews do not choose to be Jews. To be a Jew simply comes with the territory known as their body. Such a stance invites a confidence that one has nothing to lose so that, given the trials Jews have gone through over the centuries, they can rightly wonder: "Is this what it means to be chosen?"

I suspect, however, far more significant for understanding the difference between Judaism and Christianity on matters comedic is Cohen's suggestion that the long history of Jews being outsiders has implanted in Judaism a distinct tradition of humor. Christians have sought to be in control of the worlds in which they have found themselves. If you desire to rule the world the incomprehensibility of the world that Cohen suggests is at the heart of Judaism must be denied or tamed. Constantinianism is but a

---

24. For my account of this passage from John, see my *A Cross-Shattered Church: Reclaiming the Theological Heart of Preaching* (Grand Rapids: Brazos, 2009), pp. 27-32.

25. Samuel Wells, *Be Not Afraid: Facing Fear with Faith* (Grand Rapids: Brazos, 2011), pp. 175-80.

name for the Christian attempt to make the world intelligible for Christian and non-Christian alike. What cannot be tolerated are forms of humor that might make the attempt to control a dangerous world absurd.

The subversive character of humor often expressed in jokes is an undeniable reality. Those who use humor to subvert the pretentions of the powerful often have little to lose. One might think the eschatological character of the Christian faith would make Christians a people who have learned to live "loose." To be able to so live is made possible by the recognition that the use of humor in a defensive or attack mode is indicative of people enslaved by their fears. Christians can risk being subversive because they believe there is a deeper reality than the world determined by fear.

There is, I believe, a close connection between the Christian justification of the use of violence to bring order in a disordered world and the absence of humor among Christians. Christian nonviolence is surely an absurd position requiring that you learn to live by your wits, which often takes the form of your ability to talk your way out of tough situations. The great surprise that Christians are called to bear witness to, the surprise that God became subject to our violence so that we might live nonviolently, is surely the basis for the Christian identification with the Jews. If, as I suspect, we are coming to the end of Christendom we may as Christians discover we have a sense of humor.

I give as evidence of the possibility of that development the work of Karl Barth. Karl Barth, the great enemy of cultural Christianity, I suspect was "naturally" funny, but his humor was also a reflection of the character of his theology.[26] Only a person with a profound sense of humor would write the *Church Dogmatics*. Surely someone as intelligent and a lover of all things human as Barth could have found other things to do with his life. He could still have been a theologian. He just would not have assumed his life needed to be dominated by the need to produce what surely must be the most massive theological work by any Christian at any time. Yet Barth, I think, rightly knew that in our time we needed to have the *Dogmatics*.

In *With the Grain of the Universe: The Church's Witness and Natural Theology* I have a footnote in which I discuss Barth's report of the exchange

---

26. I am certainly not the first to notice how funny Barth could be. For example Bernard Ramm called attention to the importance of Barth's humor in a chapter titled "The Laughing Barth," in his book *After Fundamentalism* (New York: Harper & Row, 1983), pp. 193-97. Ralph Wood also has a wonderful chapter in his *The Comedy of Redemption* titled "Karl Barth as a Theologian of the Divine Comedy," pp. 34-56. More recently Jessica DeCou has written "Karl Barth: Comic Warrior," *Word and World* 32, no. 2 (Spring 2012): 157-65.

between Harnack and Peterson in which Harnack challenged Peterson to name which dogmas in which century and for which church should have authority.[27] Deeply sympathetic with Peterson, Barth maintained that theology requires the theologian to identify with this or that confession of faith in this or that branch of the church, together with this or that presupposed affirmation of the ancient church on which the confession rests. Yet Barth acknowledges that in the present day, theology has no church behind it that has the courage to say unambiguously that this is the highest concreteness. As a result Barth observes that theologians are in a position dictated by King Nebuchadnezzar, who demanded that his wise men tell him not only what his dream meant but what he dreamed. I note that Peterson became a Roman Catholic. Barth wrote the *Dogmatics*. That he did so surely is a testimony to his profound sense of humor.

Jessica DeCou helpfully locates Barth's most extended discussion of humor in his *Ethics,* which was originally written in 1928.[28] Barth did not publish the *Ethics* during his lifetime, one suspects, because in this book he was testing how to think about ethics, the results of which would receive mature expression in the *Church Dogmatics.* But I think DeCou is right to suggest that Barth's fundamental attitude about the significance of humor in theology as developed in the *Ethics* never changed. It did not change because in the *Ethics* Barth grounded humor in the eschatological character of the Christian faith, which means it is incumbent on Christians to refuse to take the present with ultimate seriousness. Such a perspective elicits a "liberated laughter" that "derives from the knowledge of our final position — in spite of appearances to the contrary — with present reality."[29]

Barth observes that humor is fluid and flexible because it reflects what is done in time, but from the standpoint of eternity. "Humor arises when the contrast between our aeon is perceived and vitally sensed in what we do. Humor concerns the present as such with its strange connections and involvements. We cannot change the future into the present and the present into the future. We must persevere as best we can. We have humor when we do this."[30] Accordingly we must first laugh at ourselves so that we can laugh at others, making possible the final test of being laughed at

27. Stanley Hauerwas, *With the Grain of the Universe: The Church's Witness and Natural Theology* (Grand Rapids: Brazos, 2001), pp. 177-78.

28. Karl Barth, *Ethics,* trans. G. W. Bromiley (New York: Seabury, 1981), pp. 510-12.

29. Barth, *Ethics,* p. 511, quoted in DeCou, "Karl Barth: Comic Warrior," p. 158.

30. Barth, *Ethics,* pp. 510-11.

by them.[31] Barth concludes his account of humor by observing, an observation clearly meant to be funny, that a serious problem with Calvin is that he seems to have been unable to laugh.[32]

Barth does not deny that we must also live with an appropriate seriousness about the present, but we cannot take the present with ultimate seriousness. Humor that is genuine, however, is that which is appropriately serious. Thus Barth's haunting remark: "Of humor, too, one may say that it is genuine when it is the child of suffering."[33] From Barth's perspective the great trick is to learn to live as a human being with the possibilities and limits that constitute our being human. Humor is liberation because it expresses an acceptance of our limitations in the light of our eschatological future.[34]

DeCou observes that Barth's complaint about humorlessness reflects his impatience with boredom. For example Barth's objections to natural theology are well known, but it is quite interesting that one of his most profound concerns about natural theology is that too often work done in that name is "profoundly tedious and so unmusical."[35] In a similar fashion Barth found that theological work done in the liberal tradition failed to take seriously what it means to be a human being exactly because of the absence of laughter in liberal theology. To describe faith as ultimate or unconditional concern is to take a far-too-serious view about what it means to be a human creature. For Barth we are fundamentally animals who laugh.

Humor pervades the *Dogmatics,* but Barth explicitly discusses the significance of humor in his account of honor in *Church Dogmatics* III/4. Humor is a necessary attitude for any account of honor because a person can only be honorable as an expression of pure thankfulness that the honor that is due us comes from God. Accordingly the person honored by God finds himself oddly the object of such esteem. Thus Sarah laughed on being told of the birth of Isaac. Barth asks: "Is not the contrast between man himself and the honor done him by God really too great for man to take himself ceremoniously, and not to laugh at himself, in his quality as its bearer and possessor?"[36]

31. Barth, *Ethics,* p. 511.
32. Barth, *Ethics,* p. 512.
33. Barth, *Ethics,* p. 511.
34. DeCou, "Karl Barth: Comic Warrior," p. 159.
35. Barth's observation can be found in *Church Dogmatics* II/1 (Edinburgh: T. & T. Clark, 1957), p. 666.
36. Karl Barth, *Church Dogmatics* III/4 (Edinburgh: T. & T. Clark, 1961), p. 165.

In the context of his discussion of honor Barth displays his character-istic humor by recounting a story of a person who is reported to have died because of a negative review of one of his books. Barth, clearly with tongue in cheek, declares, "But he had no business to do this."[37] I do not know if Barth meant to be funny by his judgment that the man had no business to die, but it is hard to believe Barth did not recognize how funny it was for him to make such a judgment.

DeCou calls attention to John Updike's observation of Barth's "humor and love of combat" as evidence of Barth's being genuinely "indulgent of the world."[38] Perhaps nowhere is that judgment better confirmed than in Barth's love of Mozart. For example in the "Preface" to *Church Dogmatics* III/4, and often Barth's self-deprecating humor is on display in his "Pref-aces," Barth confesses that while he still enjoys debate he has "gradually acquired more and more feeling for the affirmations by and with which we can live and die." "But," and you can hear the "but" coming, Barth observes that while he has gotten used to and does not respond to the criticisms of the neo-Calvinists in the Netherlands who accuse him of being a "monist," they have finally gone too far and he must respond. Barth observes it is one thing to criticize him, but they have gone too far because they have tried to offend Barth by disparagement of W. A. Mozart. Barth observes that, of course, "in so doing they have shown themselves to be men of stupid, cold and stony hearts to whom we need not listen."[39]

Some years later in the "Preface" to *Church Dogmatics* IV/2 Barth re-turns to his conflict with the neo-Calvinists of the Netherlands. He begins by saying he needs to make some necessary amends. He observes that the wrath of a man seldom does what is right in the sight of God. Responding to the publication of Berkouwer's book on Barth's theology, a book that treats Barth so fairly, Barth says he must withdraw the ill-founded words he unleashed against the neo-Calvinists. So they will have nothing in the future to fear from Barth as long as "they do not say any more unseemly things about Mozart."[40]

Some may find Barth's love of Mozart odd given Barth's attack on all forms of cultural Christianity. But, as Ralph Wood has argued, exactly be-

---

37. Barth, *Church Dogmatics* III/4, p. 679. For my extended discussion of Barth (and Trollope) on honor see my *Dispatches from the Front: Theological Engagements with the Secular* (Durham, NC: Duke University Press, 1994), pp. 58-79.

38. DeCou, "Karl Barth: Comic Warrior," p. 163.

39. Barth, *Church Dogmatics* III/4, p. xiii.

40. Barth, *Church Dogmatics* IV/2 (Edinburgh: T. & T. Clark, 1958), p. xii.

cause Barth's theology was so sure of the victory of Christ he was free to enjoy the world. Barth, according to Wood, understood that the Bible contains the one ultimate cause for laughter and rejoicing. "Its joy is not cheap and easy but something deep-seated and lasting. Indeed, it often comes reluctantly. 'We may as well admit it,' Barth says of the believer, 'he has something to laugh at, and he just cannot help laughing, even though he does not feel like it.' "[41] From Barth's perspective Mozart, as many who are not necessarily Christian have done, "heard the harmony of creation to which the shadow also belongs."[42]

Barth was an energetic and spirited human being. Even if he had not become a theologian he would have been the kind of person you cannot help but find attractive. At least one of the reasons for such attraction would have been that he was genuinely funny. Stories abound about his humor and some of them may be true. For example, and I know this story is true, John Howard Yoder had written a very critical paper on Barth's view of war titled "Karl Barth and the Problem with War." Yoder being Yoder gave the paper to Barth a week or so before Yoder was to be examined for his Ph.D. by Barth and other faculty at Basel. Barth began the exam observing, "Herr Yoder, you Mennonites are so bellicose." Barth obviously not only respected Yoder's courage but also enjoyed the challenge.

Yet I have tried to show that Barth's humor is not a "personality quirk." Rather, the way he taught himself to do theology is itself a testimony to the humor necessary if theology is to be a free discipline. I suggested above that when Christians think they must do theology in a manner that ensures that the way things are is the way things were meant to be, the result cannot help but be the loss of humor. Barth was a free theologian because he thought theology that is a witness to God cannot help but manifest the sheer joy made possible by the recognition that we are not alone.

### Hauerwas One Last Time (at least in this chapter)

Which finally brings me back to me. A number of times, when being introduced before giving a lecture, the story is told of my encounter with a student at Harvard. It seems I was walking across Harvard looking for the

---

41. Wood, *The Comedy of Redemption*, p. 55.

42. Wood, *The Comedy of Redemption*, p. 73. The internal quote is from Barth, *Church Dogmatics* III/3, p. 298.

library. Not sure I was going in the right direction, I asked an undergraduate if he could tell me where the library is at. He responded by observing, "At Harvard we do not end sentences with a preposition." I am said to have responded, "Can you tell me where the library is at, asshole?" There is just one problem with that story: it did not happen. However, the story now seems to have reached a canonical stage, so it makes no difference whether it happened because the story confirms for many both negative and positive judgments about me.

I relate this phenomenon because the story also reflects the general presumption that I am a "funny guy." Some even think I have a gift for the one-liner. It is not for me to claim to be funny, but I do hope that I have been able to do theology in a funny manner. I think my work is funny at least in two ways. First, I hope my work is really funny in the sense that people laugh out loud about something I have said or written. I know I often laugh at what I say and I see no reason that others should not laugh with me or about me. Secondly, my work is funny because I try to find ways to "do theology" in disguise. So I push the limits of presumptions about what theology is if it is to be "serious" in the hope that the difference might make a difference for how we live.

I think I am at my best as a humorist in prayers and sermons. So I think it appropriate to bring an end to this essay with this prayer:

> Funny Lord, how we love this life you have given us. Of course we get tired, bored, worn down by the stupidity that surrounds us. But then that stupid person does something, says something that is wonderful, funny, and insightful. How we hate for that to happen. But, thank God, you have given us one another, ensuring we will never be able to get our lives in order. Order is finally no fun, and you are intent on forcing us to see the humor of your kingdom. I mean really, Lord, the Jews! But there you have it. You insist on being known through such a funny people. And now us — part of your joke on the world. Make us your laughter. Make us laugh, and in the laughter may the world be so enthralled by your entertaining presence that we lose the fear that fuels our violence. Funny Lord, how we love this life you have given us. Amen.[43]

---

43. Stanley Hauerwas, *Prayers Plainly Spoken* (Downers Grove: IVP, 1999), pp. 99-100.

# CHAPTER 13

# How (Not) to Retire Theologically

## On Retiring

On June 30, 2013, I retired from the faculty of the Duke University Divinity School. I am now an emeritus professor. I have a continuing appointment in the Divinity School at Duke as a Senior Research Fellow. That means I get to keep my office for at least two more years in exchange for being "available." Availability means if a student or colleague wants to talk to me I will be more than happy to talk with them. Not a bad deal.

It is not a bad deal, but I have to say I am increasingly coming to the judgment that I do not like to think of myself as retired. Indeed I do not like the language of retirement at all. But I was the one who decided to "retire," so I have no one to blame but myself. I woke up one morning with a sense that I was tired of preparing for class. That seemed to be a good indication that I should retire. I was, after all, in my early seventies. I had taught for over forty-five years. I had directed over seventy dissertations.[1] It seemed time to "move aside." I do not regret that decision.

But to decide no longer to teach is not equivalent to "retiring." I am a theologian. How can I retire from being a theologian? I am often asked

---

1. I was stunned when I learned how many dissertations I have directed. I have never kept count, but at a wonderful retirement event in November 2014, Dean Richard Hays reported that I had directed over seventy dissertations. The news at once made me feel extremely lucky to have had such wonderful people trust me. The news also made me feel tired. The retirement event was overwhelming with so many friends coming to celebrate the day: Jennifer Herdt, Charlie Pinches, Jonathan Tran, Peter Dula, and Sam Wells. Those papers and my response are in *The Difference Christ Makes: Celebrating the Life, Work, and Friendship of Stanley Hauerwas*, ed. Charles M. Collier (Eugene, OR: Cascade, 2015).

what I am planning to do in retirement. I can only respond: I do not have any plans for my retirement. Why should I have plans for my life in retirement when I have never had any plans for my life? I have done what people asked me to do, and as far as I am concerned that way of living has worked out well enough. Some may find my disclaimer not to have had any plan for my life doubtful because no one could have done what I have done without a plan. Not to recognize that I am a driven person is only an indication of my skill in self-deception. Yet I think it true that I never "planned" my life. Thus the claim I use to begin *Hannah's Child: A Theologian's Memoir,* "I did not intend to be 'Stanley Hauerwas.' "[2]

Of course there are many things I wanted to do. I wanted to be an academic. I discovered that I wanted to be a good teacher. I use the language of "discover" because I did not begin by wanting to be a teacher; but because I had to teach in order to think about what I thought important, I had to learn to teach and I wanted to teach well. I also wanted to write and write well, but again that was more a discovery along the way than a well-defined project with which I began. I wanted to have something to say that might be of help to me and others. In retrospect I am somewhat surprised by what I discovered I had to say.

I wanted to be an academic, a teacher, and a writer because those "roles" made it possible for me to be a theologian. I do not remember any decisions I made that might be identified with a desire to be a theologian, but I must have wanted to be a theologian even if I was not sure what it meant to pursue that task. I think one of the reasons I "wanted" to be a theologian is I thought, and continue to think, that theology is a discipline that takes over your life because the subject matter of theology is life-changing. I cannot imagine, therefore, what it might mean for a theologian to retire. I simply do not know how nor would I want to retire from being a theologian.

I write because I am a theologian, but obviously not all writers need to be theologians. Writers can and should write about much that is not directly about theology. It is, however, an interesting question if you can be a theologian without writing. I should like to think I have written well enough about theology, but I have discovered, a discovery that owed much to my writing *Hannah's Child,* that I am also a writer. I need the hard and good work of constructing sentences, paragraphs, and books about mat-

---

2. Stanley Hauerwas, *Hannah's Child: A Theologian's Memoir* (Grand Rapids: Eerdmans, 2012), p. ix. The 2012 edition has an "Afterword" in which I call attention to the importance, at least the importance for me, of the claim that I did not intend to be Stanley Hauerwas.

ters that I hope matter. I cannot imagine, therefore, what it would mean to retire from being a writer.

For these reasons, and likely for other reasons not yet identified, I do not like the concept of retirement. I confess, however, until I retired I had not thought seriously about retirement. That is not surprising because I suspect most people do not think about retirement qua retirement. Many of us may think about "retiring," but I suspect we seldom think about what retirement seems to imply in general about the ordering of our lives. Walter Reuther, the great labor leader, for example suggested retirement is the time in a person's life when they are too old to work but too young to die. That is why I suspect retirement for many seems like "a little death" due to the loss of a sense of worth associated with a job well done.

Of course, one of the frustrations of the job I have had is you are never sure that you have done it well. To be a theologian comes with a kind of ambiguity that means you are unsure whether what you have done is theology, not to mention whether it is theology done well. Nor can you ever be sure, even if you think you have done theology well, that is the end of the matter. To do theology well means you have a sense that you are never finished. I want to explore why that is the case and why that means that retirement is not a possibility for the theologian. But before doing so I want to suggest why I think the idea of retirement is not a good idea — not only for theologians but for anyone. Retirement is, of course, an idea of recent origin but that is not why I think it is "not a good idea." Many ideas of recent origin are quite helpful, but I do not think retirement to be one of them.

## Why Retirement Is a "Bad Idea"

Once there was no retirement. In the ancient world no one "retired" because "old age" was not thought to be a reason to quit working. Of course work was quite varied, but it was assumed that the elderly would continue doing what they had done most of their life. Old age became a different reality with the economic developments we call capitalism. Once work was determined by economies of money a problem was created for the elderly. That problem quite simply was how to get the elderly out of the way to make room for younger and more energetic workers.[3]

3. The following account of the history of retirement is gleaned from many sources, which may mean some of the details are not properly substantiated. I am not particularly

Retirement was the name given to social policies aimed to encourage workers to stop working in order to provide places for younger workers. Bismarck is usually given credit for making the state responsible for supporting people who had reached the age of sixty-five in their retirement. Bismarck thought this to be not only an important economic policy but also a way to instill in workers loyalty to the state. That, of course, is the kindest way to describe Bismarck's policy. For in effect he was trying to find a way to provide an alternative to the attraction of socialism among the working class in Germany. In 1882, by an act of the German parliament, workers were given the opportunity to retire in the hope they would as a result look on the state as a benevolent benefactor who cared about their lives.

It is quite interesting that the public policy that established the practice of retirement began prior to attempts to establish the contours of aging by the developing biological and psychological sciences. In 1905, however, William Osler, an extremely influential doctor and scientist of the day, identified the biological ages he thought determine our lives. According to Osler, after our youth we have before us our creative years that fall between the ages of twenty-five and forty. After forty, however, we live through what Osler called the "uncreative years" in which little can be expected from us. His "science" nicely confirmed the economic realities that were beginning to develop in which the young were given special considerations. Osler's scheme justified the social policy challenge of how to get the elderly out of the way so that those who are in their creative years can have their rightful place.

The answer, an answer pioneered by the railroads in America, to the challenge of what to do with the elderly was a social policy that paid them to retire. In 1935, for example, it was suggested that those willing to retire should be paid two hundred dollars a month. The railroad pension plans, which many thought to be quite progressive, became the paradigm for the later creation of social security. Once social security is in place retirement is no longer a lifestyle choice. Rather it is increasingly assumed that older workers have an obligation to retire.

Though social security is generally celebrated as a "good thing" it was not always regarded as a positive development even by those who might be freed from physically demanding jobs. Many who received pensions from

---

concerned about the details I relate because I think the broad narrative I develop is true. For a short but, I believe, accurate account of the idea of retirement see Mary-Lou Weisman, "The History of Retirement, From Early Man to A.A.R.P.," *New York Times,* March 21, 1999.

the railroad, as well as those who later got social security, were ambivalent about "losing their jobs." People usually want to work even if the work they have done is not all that interesting. What they often miss is not the work itself but the people with whom they worked.

The sense of loss associated with retirement was responded to by Del Webb in 1960 by creating Sun City, Arizona. Sun City was the institutional form that expressed Webb's creative idea, that is, after a life of work a person should be rewarded by leading a life of leisure. Florida and Arizona became names for the formation of cultures for the elderly that were based on play. The result not only isolated the elderly from those who "have to work," but the elderly now are identified as those who have to work very hard at playing. The resulting isolation of the elderly is an indication that we now live in a culture that believes we have no stake in developing people of wisdom and memory necessary for the sustaining of good social orders.[4]

Perhaps the climax of these developments was the creation of the American Association of Retired Persons as a lobby on behalf of the elderly. The elderly, the retired, have now become an interest group to lobby Congress to get their fair share of resources to which the young might lay claim. No longer can the elderly and retired be thought of as people who have wisdom crucial for the discovery of the common good across generations, because now the old and the young are fundamentally moral strangers to one another.

This admittedly potted history of the development of retirement as an idea and as a social policy may seem to have little implication for what it might mean to retire as a theologian. But I think it is important because it reminds us that retirement entails a politics. If a theologian cannot retire, this means the theologian is serving a very different politics than that represented by recent social arrangements.

## Some Theological Reflections on My "Retirement"

I think it quite fascinating that there is nothing in the New Testament about retirement. For example, it surely never occurred to Paul to think, "I've

---

4. For a wonderful account of what it means to grow old as well as how the old owe to those not yet old the gift of wisdom, see Johann Christoph Arnold, *Rich in Years: Finding Peace and Purpose in a Long Life* (Walden, NY: The Plough Publishing House, 2013).

done the best I can but I am never going to get those Christians in Corinth to straighten out. I am tired of traveling and controversy. I think it is time for me to retire." Nowhere in the New Testament is there a hint that the early Christians thought there was a time when they might retire as a Christian or from being a Christian. I do not think this was only due to the early death of many Christians. Rather I believe Christians could not conceive how their lives could make sense if they did not assume they had particular responsibilities and obligations as they grew old in Christ.[5]

In particular those who were lucky enough to "grow old in Christ" had as one of their responsibilities to share the vulnerability of the body with their brothers and sisters in Christ. They understood that we are creatures whose lives move always toward death. Accordingly, to grow old does not grant permission to be free of responsibility. Rather it obligates the elderly to live lives shaped by their baptism so they might help those who are not yet old learn how to grow old and even die. Often that means no more than to be bodily present, but to be so present means if you are a Christian you never get to retire.

That retirement is not an idea or practice applicable to our lives as Christians, however, may seem irrelevant for the role retirement plays in our lives given the jobs and work many have to do. No one as far as I know has suggested that anyone can or should retire from being a human being, much less a Christian. Rather retirement is only relevant to the work or job we do. Retirement can be a godsend for those who do hard physical work that is difficult if not impossible to do as we grow older. Moreover, retirement is a welcome relief for many whose jobs often seem to be quite meaningless or boring. I have no reason to deny that retirement can be a quite positive alternative in such circumstances. But I do not think that is the end of the matter.

That retirement is the only alternative for many who have jobs that give little satisfaction is surely not a sufficient response to work so conceived. Rather what is needed is a sense that even jobs such as picking up the trash can and should be "meaningful" if we remember that those who do such work are performing a vital service for the community. The problem is not that the work is "meaningless" but rather that we have no way of gesturing how important such work is for the common good.

---

5. This is a dominant theme in most of the essays in *Growing Old in Christ,* ed. Stanley Hauerwas, Carole Bailey Stoneking, Keith Meador, and David Cloutier (Grand Rapids: Eerdmans, 2003).

There is, of course, the opposite problem; that is, for many their work is so consuming that they cannot imagine a life without their work. I suspect this might be particularly true of those whose jobs are a constant challenge to the imagination. Though this state of affairs is often associated with intellectual tasks I suspect it is also true for farmers and builders. People engaged in such activities find retiring difficult because to no longer do what one has come to love, as I suggested above, can seem to be a loss of self.

Another form of this problem is associated with those whose work is generally regarded as so "significant" by others that any thought of quitting implies that the ones doing the work will lose their status. This seems true particularly of positions that make the holder of the position "well known." American politicians and entertainers seem prone to this stance. When "public figures" retire this can signal a loss of control, making it impossible to ensure they will continue to be seen. And if they are not seen they are not sure they exist. They might as well be dead. Those who have been praised for their beauty or physical stature when young may, in a similar fashion, find "growing old" to be equivalent to death. These are complex matters with a thousand variations, which suggest that retirement is no simple act.

Indeed these last observations I find particularly relevant for my retirement. For better or worse, without trying, I have become a contradiction in terms, that is, I am allegedly a famous theologian. It is not clear to me how seriously I have identified with that description, though I should like to think I have not lived in a manner that has made becoming "famous" a way of life. But I have wanted to make a difference in the world of theology and even more in the world of the church. How that can be done without taking oneself more seriously than is appropriate is not easily negotiated. Self-deception looms.

Yet I cannot deny, given my ambition to make a theological difference, that to retire can and does feel like a loss. I am not quite sure how to describe the character of the loss. I do have the modest ambition to make every Christian in America aware that as a Christian they have a problem with war. By retiring I feel like I am losing some of the power I had to enact that ambition. To be sure, the power I think I am losing I may never have had, but it does not mean the feeling I have lost power is any less real. At the very least it means I no longer have students whom I hope to try to recruit for the task of convincing Christians we have a problem with war.

Given that my retirement status is still new, it is probably natural to be perplexed by the various feelings that accompany it and could not have been anticipated. As with all feelings, we must be prayerful if we are going to sort through them and face them honestly. No matter how much I have disavowed any ambition to be recognized as a public intellectual, many persist in so designating me. I may disavow that description, but I recognize how the characterizations others place on us shape our understanding of ourselves — no matter how strongly we may try and resist. Therefore, if I am honest, it may be what I really fear is my loss of status as a public intellectual. It may not be the loss of the power to change how people think about what it means to be Christian I am really regretting, but rather it is the loss of being "known." I confess I am not sure how to discern which of these narratives may or may not be shaping my life.

What I am sure about, however, is that what I most care about is the work of theology, and I know that is work from which you cannot retire. When asked what I plan to do in retirement I usually say, "I will do what I have always done." I will get up, read a book, and write. Reading a book and writing is my way of saying I will continue to think about what I have always thought about, which is the difference God makes for the living of our lives. The exploration of that difference is never finished, which means the theologian always has something to do. I take that to be a great gift.

That the work of theology is never finished, however, does not mean that the theologian's, and in particular this theologian's, relation to that work does not change. In a wonderful sermon on the Ascension, for example, Sam Wells begins by reporting on an account of four stages of work identified by management theory. The first stage is called Unconscious Incompetence, in which, as the description implies, the ones beginning the work do not know what they do not know. Conscious Incompetence is the next stage, in which you begin to know what you do not know. The next stage is when you know what you know, making you a person of Conscious Competence who thrives in all you do. The final stage, however, is when you have forgotten what you know but remain competent. You are described as one who is Unconsciously Competent, indicating you have reached the stage when you probably need to find something else to do.[6]

I fear I may well exemplify what it means to be Unconsciously Competent even as a theologian. I do so even though, as I have indicated, it is not clear to me that anyone can ever be Consciously Competent as a theo-

---

6. Samuel Wells, "Time to God," a sermon preached in Duke University Chapel on May 20, 2007.

logian. Theology is an ongoing attempt to make connections that are at once as strong and fragile as a spider web.[7] Often you discover how to make articulate some of the connections, but you forget how the connections were made because now that the connection is made you do not need to return to the process that made the conclusion possible. Results can seem to make memory unnecessary (at least for a while) with the result that the work necessary to get the result is forgotten. The result becomes less than it was when first discovered.

That a theologian can become Unconsciously Competent may be partly due to the need to introduce the uninitiated to the work of theology. Such introductions often require, at least in the beginning, simplification. Moreover if you are lucky you are invited to give lectures in which you are asked to address audiences beyond the academy. In such circumstances you are tempted to entertain your audience with the conclusions to which you have come without making articulate the prices you have paid to come to them. For example, it is not easy to make clear how John Howard Yoder taught me to think in a manner that changed how I think about everything.

Yet I think the craft of theology, exactly because it is never finished, provides resources that help the theologian avoid becoming Unconsciously Competent. Because theologians are never sure they have competence, and competence may just be a description of what it means to have a soul, they must say the same thing again and again only differently. That means you must constantly rethink what you have thought. That what we have thought demands to be rethought has everything to do with the wonderful simplicity of what we believe as Christians; but that very simplicity requires thought. That is why theologians can never retire. They never know enough to retire, but more importantly they must think about that which they are never sure they understand. By saying just a bit about theology I hope to substantiate this claim.

## Why Theological Work Cannot Be Finished:
## The Example of Karl Barth

That theology cannot ensure its own subject matter frustrates many. After all, the subject matter of theology involves claims that put one's life at risk.

7. For an elaboration of theology as a web see the "Introduction" to my *Sanctify Them in the Truth: Holiness Exemplified* (Nashville: Abingdon, 1998), pp. 1-15.

Jesus responds to "a certain ruler" who asks him what he must do to inherit eternal life by telling him that he must not only keep the commandments, but he must sell all he has and give it to the poor (Luke 18:18-25). But he was very rich and could not do as Jesus asked. Earlier in Luke's Gospel Jesus had made it clear that no one could become his disciple unless they are willing to give up all their possessions (Luke 14:25-33). Indeed to follow Jesus means that life itself, which some count as one of our "possessions," may be lost.

This "Christian stuff" is, therefore, about life and death. It does not get more serious than that. Much is at stake, so any suggestion of the tentative character of Christian theology seems to betray what is asked of those who would be Christian. If I am going to have to contemplate the loss of life in the name of Jesus then I surely want to be certain he is who he says he is. Jesus was who he said he was, but that he was who he said he was is the reason that Christian theology must remain unfinished. For at the heart of Christianity is the avowal that in this particular man we see God.

That claim has implications that must invite thought as well as make us reconsider thoughts we thought we were sure about. It is a claim, for example, that is particularly offensive to those who believe that any ultimate judgment about our lives and the world must be grounded in what can be secured by a reason that makes what we believe certain. I suspect the deepest worry many have about Christianity is that they find it incomprehensible that all that is, and all that is includes us, could turn on the existence of a particular person called Jesus. Of course the significance of his existence is but a correlative of God's promise to Israel, but those who find difficult Christian claims about Jesus usually think claims about God's calling of Israel to be the promised people equally problematic.

That some think theological claims must be grounded in empirical proofs is based on the assumption that there is an essential tension between faith and reason. Even Christian theologians have sometimes underwritten the assumption that the faith of Christians cannot be rationally defended. However, the very presumption that reason is one thing and faith is another betrays a distorted view of reason. What Christians believe is not a "take it or leave it" choice, but rather an ongoing claim that all that is exists by God's good grace. The working out of that claim is never finished.

If the task of theology is to show that the world we experience can only make sense in the light of what has been done through the life, death, and resurrection of Jesus there is no subject foreign to the work of theology. Though theology can never aspire to be philosophy, it is equally true that much of theology is by necessity done in a philosophical mode. Of course there are diverse forms of philosophy, which means that one of the questions before theologians is what form of philosophy is most appropriate for the work theology has to do. This stance on theology means that theologians can never determine who their conversational partner may be because they must be ready to be challenged by those who do not share their convictions.

Theology is accordingly concerned to enter into conversation with those who do not share our convictions. These interactions may be described as the necessary conversation theology must have with the world. There are, however, the mandatory conversations that theology must always have with itself. For example, the question of the relation of Israel to the church is one that can never be finished. For the very question of Israel's significance for Christian theology entails a challenge to the presumption that we know how to speak of God separate from God having made himself known; that is, the presumption that we can speak about God abstracted from the calling of Israel to be his promised people.

That God is Trinity — Father, Son, and Holy Spirit — for example, involves the commitment by Christians to affirm that the God we worship is the same God who called Israel into existence as his people only to engraft the Gentiles into that reality through the life, death, and resurrection of the Son. To claim that God is Trinity is not only to make a massive metaphysical claim, but it also commits one to the ongoing and never complete task of reading the Old and New Testaments as one book. The speculative metaphysical work done by Christian theologians is important, but the fundamental form of theology remains exegetical. Through exegesis, moreover, the theologian should find pleasure and a sense of wonder in the inexhaustible nature of scripture.

Khaled Anatolios is quite right, therefore, to contend that the meaning of the doctrine of the Trinity is not to be sought in the objective reference to a set of "Trinitarian" propositional formulae but rather in the "exigencies involved in the entirety of Christian faith and life."[8] For as Anatolios observes, the doctrine of the Trinity did not emerge from some isolated insight about the being of God, but rather it was an attempt to provide a global interpretation of Christian life and faith as a correlative of the attempt to provide a Christological account of all reality. According to Ana-

---

8. Khaled Anatolios, *Retrieving Nicaea: The Development and Meaning of Trinitarian Doctrine* (Grand Rapids: Baker, 2011), p. 7.

tolios the Trinity is better understood, as George Lindbeck suggested, as a performance rather than as a set of propositions because it is an attempt to show how the entirety of Christian existence is Trinitarian.[9]

Karl Barth is surely one of the great performance artists of Christian theology. He was so because he discovered that theology cannot help but begin and end with a truth that has been given to it by God through the church. That is why, according to Barth, "theology cannot appear as a quest for truth or a philosophy of general truth. So far as theology bows to the truth of revelation, it understands that the different world views which are designated 'truth' are, at best, only relative, tentative, and limited truth."[10] Rather, for theology truth is to be found in the worship of God and in particular the sermon, which is an action that enables the church to serve the Word of God so that the world may hear time and time again the Word in this particular time and place.[11]

Barth observes that those who preach and those who hear sermons are human beings. They are people of a particular time and place. That means, according to Barth, that the problem of language is always at the forefront of theological work. It is so because the question regarding what form the Word should take so that it might be heard as the Word of God remains central to the theological task.[12] Theology must, therefore, always begin and end with revelation, with the scriptures, and not with personally achieved psychological or pedagogical assumptions, so that God becomes apprehensible.[13]

That Barth so understood the theological task helps account for his lack of concern over not finishing the *Church Dogmatics*. In the "Preface" to *Church Dogmatics* IV/4 he begins by reporting that over the last years he has been asked often about the nonappearance of the remaining parts of the *Church Dogmatics*. He responds by calling attention to the "inconsiderable bulk" of the *Church Dogmatics* that already exists as an *opus imperfectum*. He continues, noting that some of the subjects he was to treat in the proposed volumes have been given some space in earlier volumes. And he acknowledges that the *Dogmatics* will remain incomplete. Yet he notes that most of the medieval *Summae* as well as many cathedrals were never

---

9. Anatolios, *Retrieving Nicaea*, p. 8. Anatolios refers explicitly to George Lindbeck's account in *The Nature of Doctrine* (Louisville: Westminster John Knox, 1984).

10. Karl Barth, *God in Action* (Eugene, OR: Wipf & Stock, 2005), p. 47.

11. Barth, *God in Action*, p. 55.

12. Barth, *God In Action*, p. 55.

13. Barth, *God in Action*, p. 56.

finished. Even Mozart, Barth observes, due to his untimely death, was unable to finish his *Requiem.* So not to finish is a testimony to our finitude. Barth concludes by pointing out he had argued in *Church Dogmatics* II/2 that perfection or completeness is an attribute that can only be ascribed to God, which means that "it is better not to seek or to imitate perfection in a human work."[14]

In the "Preface" to *Church Dogmatics* IV/4 Barth observes that in 1962 he retired and was made "professor emeritus." Barth is clearly not sure what to make of that title, observing that "emeritus" is an amusing word. Barth acknowledges that the title indicates that his work as a university professor has come to an end, but that does not mean he retired from being a theologian.[15] Yet we should not assume we know what Barth meant when he identified himself as a theologian. For example, in an interview close to the end of his life, an interview included in a book titled *Final Testimonies,* Barth responded to a question about the relation of his theology to Mozart by declaring, "I am not ultimately at home in theology, in the political world, or even in the church. These are all preparatory matters. They are serious, but preparatory. We have to learn to stand in them, but we have also to learn to look beyond them."[16]

The interviewer, who quite understandably seems taken aback by Barth's disavowal of being at home in theology, attempts to make Barth confirm who the interviewer thinks Barth is by asking Barth to say something about "grace." Barth responds by first observing that "grace itself is only a provisional word" — a remark that only a theologian as accomplished as Barth can make. He explains, "The last word that I have to say as a theologian or politician is not a concept like grace but a name: Jesus Christ. He is grace and he is the ultimate one beyond world and church and even theology. We cannot lay hold of him. In him is the spur to work, warfare, and fellowship. In him is all that I have attempted in my life in weakness and folly."[17]

Barth retired from teaching, but he could not retire from the subject that had gripped him from the beginning, that is, Jesus Christ. Barth did not have to finish the *Dogmatics* because he had confidence that we had seen the end in Christ. Raymond Kemp Anderson reports that at a birth-

14. Karl Barth, *Church Dogmatics* IV/4 (Edinburgh: T. & T. Clark, 1969), p. vii.

15. Barth, *Church Dogmatics* IV/4, pp. vii-viii.

16. Karl Barth, *Final Testimonies,* ed. Eberhard Busch (Grand Rapids: Eerdmans, 1977), p. 29.

17. Barth, *Final Testimonies,* pp. 29-30.

day party for Barth, a "Dutch enthusiast" celebrated Barth's *Dogmatics,* which in the German edition was bound in white, as an immense finished creation comparable to the huge white whale in *Moby Dick.* According to Anderson, Barth rose to his feet protesting that description, arguing that the whole thing might be done better and quite differently. For Barth there was nothing absolute or finished about the work represented by all fourteen volumes of the *Dogmatics.*[18] That is why, moreover, Barth was a great theologian.

## Going On, or I Am Not Dead Yet

I have always regarded it as an honor to live and work in a time in which Barth lived and worked. Only God knows from where he came and what made him possible. I think it a judgment on the intellectual sterility of our culture that Barth remains largely unknown in self-identified secular disciplines. We are in Benjamin Lazier's debt for providing in his book, a book tellingly titled *God Interrupted: Heresy and the European Imagination Between the World Wars,* an account of Barth's significance for Hans Jonas, Gershom Scholem, Leo Strauss, and Franz Rosenzweig.[19] Of course none of these significant figures agreed with Barth, but they understood that any disagreements they had with Barth would be significant.

I have not had any fundamental disagreements with Barth, but I hope my agreements with him are as significant as those who disagree with him. I am, of course, not in Barth's league as a theologian. Indeed I suspect some might wonder, given the character of Barth's *Dogmatics,* if I am even a theologian. I seldom do theology "straight up" as Barth did. By "straight up" I mean how Barth displayed the interrelation of theological motifs by attending to what first needed to be said so that what is said subsequently can be said. Getting the order right is everything because, as Raymond Anderson observes, for Barth the display of God's perfections shows how each successive set of descriptions presuppose and grow out of the previous ones.[20] I take that to be a characteristic of the *Dogmatics* as a whole.

I have not done theology in the way Barth did theology, but I have

18. Raymond Kemp Anderson, *An American Scholar Recalls Karl Barth's Golden Years as a Teacher (1958-1964)* (Lewiston, NY: Edwin Mellen, 2013), pp. 13-14.

19. Benjamin Lazier, *God Interrupted: Heresy and the European Imagination Between the World Wars* (Princeton: Princeton University Press, 2008).

20. Anderson, *An American Scholar Recalls Karl Barth's Golden Years,* pp. 214-15.

tried to take seriously the need to get the order right because I think the order has everything to do with our ability to discover the difference God makes for how our lives are lived. To show the difference has been central to everything I have done, because if we are unable to show the differences we will lack the ability to know, much less show, why we believe what we believe as Christians. To show the difference does not mean that the differences that make us Christian share nothing with those who are not Christian, but it means that whatever we have in common must be discovered.

One of the ways I have suggested what it means "to get the order right" is to remember that what we believe as Christians commits us to the strong claim that the world and our lives can be and are in fact "storied." That means, I have tried to suggest, that one of the fundamental tasks of theology is the ongoing attempt to develop the tools necessary to tell truthfully the story of Jesus Christ in such a manner that his life shapes our lives. That means, however, that there is not nor can there be an end to the telling of the story, because the story is quite literally ongoing.

To try to show the difference that story makes means not only that the work of theology cannot be finished, but I find I cannot stop doing it. I suspect that is a condition shared by many others. You finally cannot stop because what you have said makes it necessary to respond to the problems that are created by what you have said. For if you have said anything well, you will discover new challenges you had not anticipated. You may not be sure how to go on but you must try. This can be very tiring, because like most people I would like to find a place to stop, or at least rest for a bit.

A form of rest is available if you understand rest to be activity in which the end and the means are commensurate. Theologically the name for rest so understood is worship. Worship, moreover, is but another word for prayer. The work of theology is a second-order activity that depends on the actual existence of a people who have learned to worship God. I fear that too often, particularly in recent times, theologians have proceeded as though theology is an end in itself. I am not suggesting that worship is immune from theological critique, but the critique will be possible only on the basis of a more truthful worship of God.

That I cannot stop doing theology given the way I have done it also accounts for the range of my work. I confess when I think about the diverse topics I have addressed it not only makes me tired but it elicits in me a sense of embarrassment. I am not smart enough to know what needs to be known in order to address questions that range from how personal identity is to be understood to the ethics of war. But I have a stake in both of those topics, and many more, if I am to do the work I take to be the work of theology. This very essay, an attempt to think theologically about something called "retirement," is an example of how theology is self-propagating if it is an outgrowth of worship. For when one worships the triune God, one becomes keenly aware of the inescapability of him; there is no sphere of human life that evades theological implication because we were made to worship him. I hope the range of my work exemplifies this conviction.

I think the way I think is not unlike the way some who identify themselves as ordinary language philosophers think. In her book *Why We Need Ordinary Language Philosophy*, Sandra Laugier, commenting on Stanley Cavell's account of J. L. Austin on excuses, observes Cavell rightly maintains that excuses, like performative utterances in general, bind acts and language together in a manner that makes problematic all attempts to "explain" or ground language by an appeal to acts qua acts. Laugier observes that this means "we do not really know what it is to *say* or *mean* something, any more than we know what it is to do something."[21]

If, as Laugier argues, one of the tasks of ordinary language philosophy is to renew a speaker's relationship to the language that possesses us, I should like to think I have been about a similar task theologically. I thought the problem, however, for Christians is how hard it is for us to be possessed by the Christian vocabulary. Accordingly my work has been one long thought experiment in trying to imagine what it would mean for Christians to be possessed by what we say or, at least, should say. That is obviously an unending task that no one person can or should hope to bring to an end. The good news, at least for me, is I am not dead yet, so I continue to have good work to do. But even more important is the fact that I have been joined by some who graciously describe themselves as "my students" who can do the work of theology far better than I have done.

The work of theology is never done. That is very good news. The work of theology can never be done alone. That is even better news.

---

21. Sandra Laugier, *Why We Need Ordinary Language Philosophy* (Chicago: University of Chicago Press, 2013), p. 104.

# By Way of a Response to Nicholas Healy's Book, *Hauerwas: A (Very) Critical Introduction*

Nicholas Healy is an estimable theologian. I have read, admired, and learned from his books.[1] He has written a (very) critical introduction to my work that deserves a considered response. I may not be happy with Healy's reading of my work, but when someone like Healy has taken the time to read and criticize you his criticisms must be taken seriously even if I think his critical reading of what I am about is off the mark. Criticisms like those Healy makes are important even if I think they are wrong because they indicate possible ways of reading what I have written that I did not sufficiently guard against.

Though most of the chapters that make up *The Work of Theology* were written before I had read Healy's book, I should like to think that much of what I do in *The Work of Theology* is a response to Healy's criticisms. By addressing Healy's understanding as well as his criticisms of what I am about I can hopefully make clear why the chapters in *The Work of Theology* all begin with "How." To be sure, the use of "How" in some of the titles is grammatically inelegant, but the "How" is meant to remind me and the reader of the essential connection between doctrine and life. It will soon be apparent that this connection is at the heart of Healy's critique of my work.

I cannot pretend to respond to all of Healy's criticisms. I confess I find some of his criticism to have the logic of the accusation "When did

---

1. Nicholas Healy, *Church, World, and the Christian Life* (Cambridge: Cambridge University Press, 2000) and *Thomas Aquinas: Theologian of the Christian Life* (Aldershot, UK: Ashgate, 2003). In *Hauerwas: A (Very) Critical Introduction* (Grand Rapids: Eerdmans, 2014) Healy calls attention to the titles of his books to suggest he has some sympathy with my attempt to deny a strong distinction between theology and ethics. Page references for Healy's *Hauerwas: A (Very) Critical Introduction* will appear in the text.

you quit beating your spouse?" It is also the case that I find his criticisms about my alleged failure to account for the "empirical" church a tired and uninteresting topic. I have no reason to resist his call for ethnographic studies of actual churches and what such studies may or may not tell us about "unsatisfactory Christians." I had never encountered that description before, but I think it a nice suggestion for how all Christians might think of our lives as Christians. Yet I do not understand why Healy thinks that if we are "unsatisfactory Christians" that is a decisive objection to my ecclesiology. Contrary to his suggestion that I do not account for God's action to sustain the witness of "unsatisfactory Christians," I cannot imagine that witness being possible if God has not, as we say in the prayer after Eucharist, "graciously accepted us as living members of your Son our Savior Jesus Christ." I assume that "us" is made up of God's "unsatisfactory" people.

What I find extremely interesting, however, is Healy's suggestion that in terms of theological "method" I am actually closer to Schleiermacher than I am to Barth. According to Healy I am closer to Schleiermacher because like Schleiermacher I rely on social-philosophical theories, to be sure theories quite different from those that shaped Schleiermacher's work, which are nontheological. As a result my theology is ecclesiocentric rather than theocentric (p. 118). Healy thinks when all is said and done the bottom line for me is the church is more important than God (p. 49). I will come back to this criticism, but I first need to address what I take to be Healy's more fundamental critique, a critique that goes to the heart of *The Work of Theology*, which is that I conflate the logic of belief with the logic of coming to believe (as well as the logic of living out our beliefs) (p. 52). As a result, in spite of what may seem to be my strong claim that theology matters for ethics, my theological work is "thin."

Healy develops his account of the distinctions between the logic of belief and the logic of coming to believe by drawing on David Kelsey's discussion of these distinctions in his massive two-volume work, *Eccentric Existence: A Theological Anthropology*.[2] In his turn Kelsey attributes his account of this distinction, that is, the distinction between the logic of belief and the logic of coming to believe, to Hans Frei in his book *The Identity of*

---

2. David Kelsey, *Eccentric Existence: A Theological Anthropology*, vol. 2 (Louisville: Westminster John Knox, 2009), pp. 683-89. Kelsey's extended discussion of the distinction between the logic of belief and the logic of coming to believe is in volume 1 of *Eccentric Existence*, pp. 80-119.

*Jesus Christ: The Hermeneutical Bases of Dogmatic Theology.*[3] I admire Frei's and Kelsey's work and find it a bit odd for Healy to put us in opposition.

I quite appreciate, however, that Healy thinks I have done exactly what Kelsey explains was Mr. Frei's primary theological worry about confusing the logic of belief, that is, the meaning and interconnection of dogmatic statements, with the logic of coming to believe. The logic of coming to believe Frei associated with the apologetic attempts to discover a universal account of the way people come to believe.[4] Frei was concerned that if the logic of coming to believe determined the logic of belief, the result too often was the creation of a Christ subject to our projections and desires. Frei worried that to focus on the apologetic task resulted in revisionist Christologies that, as Kelsey puts it, "dissolve Jesus' humanity into a divine function, perhaps associated with a historical artifact."[5] I have always thought Frei was right to refuse to subordinate doctrine to the epistemological conceits of the alleged modern subject.

So I do not think Healy is right to suggest I conflate the logic of belief with the logic of coming to believe. I remember reading *The Identity of Jesus Christ* first in a magazine whose name I no longer remember, but I do remember the lasting impression it made on me. I should like to think you can see its effect in my dissertation. The account of personal identity in that book is quite similar to Frei's account in *The Identity of Jesus Christ*. The influence of Wittgenstein, an influence Healy ignores, was too strong for me to make the mistake of conflating the logic of coming to belief with the logic of belief.

But Healy is right that I do conflate the logic of belief with what he identifies as a third logic, that is, the logic of living out our beliefs. Healy does not explain how this third logic of living out our beliefs may or may not be different from the logic of belief, but I think the logic of living out our beliefs is quite different from the logic of coming to believe. Living out the logic of our beliefs is a challenge to the narcissism that threatens all accounts of our coming to believe.

---

3. Hans Frei, *The Identity of Jesus Christ: The Hermeneutical Bases of Dogmatic Theology* (Philadelphia: Fortress, 1975), p. xii.

4. Kelsey's characterization of Frei's understanding of "coming to believe" is in *Eccentric Existence*, vol. 2, p. 684. Kelsey rightly notes that Frei was skeptical that a universal account of coming to believe was possible. Frei observed that he was persuaded there is no single road to Christianity either as a matter of principle or in practice. *The Identity of Jesus Christ*, p. xii.

5. Kelsey, *Eccentric Existence*, vol. 2, p. 688.

Healy is, therefore, right that I do try to show the relation of the logic of belief with the logic of living out our beliefs. In my terms I try to show why the "what" of what we believe cannot be separated from the "how." No doubt Healy will find the emphasis on the "how" in *The Work of Theology* to confirm his judgment that I conflate the logic of belief with the logic of coming to believe, but my emphasis on the "how" is meant to challenge that confusion. In particular it is meant to stress the how of living out the gospel and, in particular, how the how entails learning a language that is a decisive challenge to the apologetic agenda of modern theology.

My emphasis on the "how" is my way to show how the logic of belief and the logic of living out our beliefs are inseparable, particularly for considerations of what it means to claim what we believe is true. I should like to think one of the ways I have done that is to elaborate Frei's observation that the logic of religious discourse is odd because the grammar of Christian convictions combines modes of factual affirmation with claims about how we are to live. Frei elaborates this connection by noting that this is not to claim "that the self-involving quality of religious statements is the indispensable logical condition or interpretative setting for the intelligibility of the doctrine that Jesus is the crucified and risen Savior. It is to affirm very simply that, unlike other cases of factual assertion, that of the resurrection of Christ shapes a new life."[6]

If I have conflated the "logics" of belief it is not the logic of coming to believe and the logic of belief that I have confused. Rather I have tried to show how, as Frei puts it, "the resurrection of Christ shapes a new life." My "pragmatism" is but the expression of that endeavor. The focus on practices is but one way I have tried to show the practical character of Christian convictions. That emphasis is why Healy is quite right to call attention to my preference for the language of conviction rather than belief to characterize what makes us Christians. I do so because I think James McClendon was right to suggest that convictions entail a self that would not be without the convictions that make who we are who we are.[7] Accordingly convictions suggest how lives are shaped in a manner that the grammar of the concept "belief" does not.

6. Frei, *The Identity of Jesus Christ*, p. xiii.

7. James McClendon and James Smith, *Understanding Religious Convictions* (Notre Dame: University of Notre Dame Press, 1975). I continue to think this to be an extremely important but unfortunately overlooked book in philosophical theology. The way Smith and McClendon help us see Austin's importance for what we say and do not say anticipates what some younger theologians find significant in Cavell's work.

This may seem like a small matter, but it is at the heart of Healy's criticisms of how I work. For example, Healy has little use for exegetical forays and, in particular, my commentary on Matthew. He argues that my "performance" in the readings I provide of Matthew is ecclesiocentric and thus fails to be appropriately theocentric. In short, Healy finds my engagement with scripture to be evidence of the "thinness" of my theology. It would be tiresome for me to cite one passage after another in an effort to show that I am not as theologically thin as Healy suggests, but at the very least I can note that Healy ignores the fundamental theological claim that shapes my Matthew commentary, namely, that there is an intrinsic relationship between the Christology of Matthew and what being a disciple entails. Healy notes that I seem only to make brief references to the doctrine of the Incarnation in the commentary on Matthew, but I tried (perhaps, given Healy's reading, without great success) to show why what is asked by Jesus of the disciples reflects his identity as the Son of God.[8] The "what" that is Christ is inseparable from the "how" of following him.

I wonder if one of the reasons Healy finds me so theologically deficient is his general lack of sympathy with my attempt to avoid theology becoming beliefs abstracted from how we are to live. I am not a systematic theologian. Healy is quite right to note my hesitancy to be so characterized. But in truth I am more systematic than my disavowals of being systematic suggest. Indeed I find compelling Sarah Coakley's recent suggestion that system connotes the commitment that "wherever one chooses to start has implications for the whole, and the parts must fit together. However briefly, or lengthily, it is explicated 'systematic theology' must attempt to provide a coherent, and alluring, vision of the Christian faith."[9] I may not be as "systematic" as a Jenson, Kelsey, or Coakley, but I have tried to show how the "parts fit together" if they are to be lived.

I have disavowed being systematic on what I assume are Barthian grounds. Those grounds I take to be Barth's refusal to locate one central doctrine that will determine the meaning of all other doctrines. I realize Barth's Christology may seem to be evidence that I am mischaracterizing Barth's "method." But I think that is not the case if you remember that Barth's Christology is anything but the attempt to locate an essence of Chris-

---

8. Stanley Hauerwas, *Matthew: A Commentary* (Grand Rapids: Brazos, 2006), pp. 35-36.

9. Sarah Coakley, *God, Sexuality, and the Self: An Essay "On the Trinity"* (Cambridge: Cambridge University Press, 2013), p. 41.

tianity. Rather his Christology commits him to showing how everything we believe that makes us Christians is connected to everything we believe that makes us Christians. I obviously lack Barth's theological power, but I should like to think in some small way my "nonsystematic" approach bears some resemblance to what Gerald McKenny has described as Barth's "long series of nonidentical repetitions" that make the *Dogmatics* the *Dogmatics*.[10]

I have tried to show how the "parts fit together" in a way that does not abstract doctrine from ways of life in which doctrine does work. I have never attempted, nor will I ever attempt, to provide an account of the Trinity or of the Incarnation as an end in itself. I have learned much from those who have engaged in speculation on how the one God can be three, but I have not understood that to be my task. Why should I do what Barth, Jenson, and Coakley have already done?[11] That I have tried to do "doctrine" as constitutive of how we are to live may be one of the reasons that Healy finds me so theologically deficient.

Indeed I was stunned by Healy's suggestion that theology is not structured into my work (p. 10). I think one of the kindest ways to read such a judgment about my work is to think Healy is saying that I am not David Kelsey. David Kelsey is a theological craftsman and I know very well I am not in his league, but I do not think it right to suggest theology is not integral to the way I have tried to do ethics or, as I would prefer, the way I have tried to show that theology is a performative discipline.[12] I do not think that means I am theologically thin. I think it means I do not do theology in the way that Healy thinks theology, particularly as exemplified by Kelsey, should be done.

Healy has read more Hauerwas than is probably good for anyone, but I find it interesting that he seldom makes use of *With the Grain of the Universe: The Church's Witness and Natural Theology*.[13] In that book my account

---

10. Gerald McKenny, *The Analogy of Grace: Karl Barth's Moral Theology* (Oxford: Oxford University Press, 2010), p. 1.

11. I do not mean to imply that Barth's, Jenson's, and Coakley's accounts of the Trinity are in agreement, but even their disagreements suggest they share more in common than they disagree.

12. I confess I simply do not understand how Healy ignores a chapter such as "Performing the Faith: The Peaceable Rhetoric of God's Church," in *Performing the Faith: Bonhoeffer and the Practice of Nonviolence* (Grand Rapids: Brazos, 2004) when he makes the accusation that I am theologically thin. I wrote that chapter with Jim Fodor, but that does not seem to be a sufficient reason to make no reference to it.

13. Stanley Hauerwas, *With the Grain of the Universe: The Church's Witness and Natural Theology* (Grand Rapids: Brazos, 2001).

and general agreement with Barth would, I should hope, qualify Healy's judgment that in contrast to Kelsey my account of Christian practices is not sufficiently theocentric. Of course it is true that I generally avoid the language of "theocentric" because I am a determined Trinitarian. "Theocentric" sounds too much like H. Richard Niebuhr's radical monotheism which, for all my admiration for Niebuhr, I thought to be a bad idea.

I fear being too defensive in response to Healy's criticisms, because such a stance can confirm for some that there must be something right about Healy's criticisms. But I do have to say that I cannot help but wonder who Healy was reading when he characterized what I have been about as insufficiently theological. For example he observes that I do not seem to think that God acts in the world as we know it. It is true that for theological reasons I do not think the phrase "God acting" should be used without specifying what God has done. When "God acting" is used to ensure that God is not dead I fear that the God who acts turns out to be more deistic than Trinitarian.

I wonder, for example, what Healy makes of a passage from my *Performing the Faith* in which I observe that when Christians speak of God who creates and redeems they are not referring to some univocal being but to the Father, Son, and Spirit. I then suggest that because Christians think God is Trinity we understand human activity to be a response to God's action in which participation in God's very life is made possible.[14] I call attention to that passage not only because I think it a true and good one, but because it is anything but an isolated instance in my work.

I also find it odd that, given his criticism that ecclesiology trumps all other theological claims in my work, Healy pays little attention to my chapter on Jesus in *The Peaceable Kingdom*. You may well think what I did there deficient, but I worked very hard to show how the very language of "incarnation" was the way Christians emphasized that the whole life of Jesus mattered.[15] In other words, I was trying to show that the classical Christological doctrine that Christ was very God and very man is not a

---

14. Hauerwas, *Performing the Faith*, p. 86. Kelsey says very little about the relation of the logic of belief and living our beliefs. But interestingly enough he does say that "a conviction about Jesus as the image of God requires a self-involving, existentially shaping decision that, despite its ambiguity, the human life of Jesus is indeed the decisive image of the living God." *Eccentric Existence*, vol. 2, p. 907. I am indebted to Brett McCarty for calling my attention to this passage.

15. For a confirmation that Jesus matters in my work see Sam Wells, "The Difference Christ Makes," in *The Difference Christ Makes: Celebrating the Life, Work, and Friendship of Stanley Hauerwas*, ed. Charles M. Collier (Eugene, OR: Cascade, 2015), p. 22.

shorthand to say all that needs to be said, but rather a reminder that it is not accidental that the Gospels are narratives of a life. What I was doing in that chapter in *The Peaceable Kingdom* I should like to think was an attempt to follow Mr. Frei's contention that the Gospels are descriptions of Jesus' unsubstitutable personal identity.

That chapter makes clear that the distinctiveness of the church must be a reflection of the distinctiveness of Christ.[16] That distinctiveness, I suggest, must reflect the special character of the promised people, that is, the Jews.[17] I find it quite interesting that Healy nowhere credits my attempt to show how Jesus as prophet, priest, and king reproduces God's care of Israel. If I were making any criticism of my Christology I would suggest I have not sufficiently developed in other contexts the implications of those offices for the formation of the church.

I find it curious that Healy purposefully avoided discussing my "ethics," that is, how I think theologically about matters such as disability, war, life and death, singleness and marriage, and/or my reflections on being sick. For example in my reflections on a topic such as suicide I try to show the work theological claims must do if we are to make sense of why Christians believe we owe one another our suffering. Healy's bracketing my "ethics" makes me less a theologian. My "ethics" is where I do theology, because it is in those contexts that you can show how the web that is theology is constantly changing given the problems facing the church. Accordingly, I find it hard to credit Healy with trying to "introduce" how I think. To "introduce" my work would have required Healy to say much more about the kind of world, culturally and theologically, to which I have tried to respond and as a result shaped how I have come to do theological ethics.

Just as Healy ignored some of my more direct theological works, he

16. I have in several places suggested my ecclesiology is more robust than Barth's account of the church. But I have now read Kimlyn Bender's *Karl Barth's Christological Ecclesiology* (Eugene, OR: Cascade, 2013). Bender has certainly convinced me that my understanding of the church as a community that participates in the very life of Christ is not a position foreign to Barth. Bender quotes Barth from *Dogmatics* IV/2 to the effect that the "community of Jesus Christ can be that which the human nature of its Lord and Head is. . . . Jesus lives in this His earthly historical form of existence, in the community as the form of His body" (Bender, p. 150). Though methodologically Barth is on a different planet than Schleiermacher, their views of the relation of Jesus and the church can be read as complementary.

17. Stanley Hauerwas, *The Peaceable Kingdom: A Primer in Christian Ethics* (London: SCM, 1985), pp. 72-95. I footnote the second edition of the English publication because that edition has an "Afterword" that I suspect few have read but it is not irrelevant to the issues raised by Healy.

also seems to have concentrated on my more "academic" books and ig-nored my more "popular" writing. Again I acknowledge that there is too much to read by Hauerwas, but *Lord Teach Us, The Truth about God,* and *Cross-Shattered Christ* are books in which I have done some of my most determined theological reflection.[18] In those books I make the "connec-tions"[19] between our fundamental convictions as Christians and the way we should live. Accordingly I find it hard to understand Healy's contention that I have an attenuated theology.

But then what do I make of Healy's interesting suggestion that in terms of "method" I am closer to Schleiermacher than I am to Barth? This is the case, according to Healy, because like Schleiermacher I am a thoroughly modern theologian in contrast with more traditional theologians such as Barth. Healy contrasts modern with traditional theology by suggesting that the former accepts the epistemological presumptions that resulted in the turn toward the subject by modern philosophers. Once that turn was accepted, Healy argues, modern theologians understood that they could no longer talk directly about God, because God could only be talked about in terms of the "God-consciousness of the church's membership" (p. 47). For Schleiermacher the turn to the subject is a turn to the church in which the church becomes the condition of the possibility for our ability to say anything about God and/or Christ.

I have not read or studied Schleiermacher for many years, so I cannot make any judgments about Healy's characterization of Schleiermacher's theology. I have read, however, the fascinating book by Kevin Hector in which he argues that Schleiermacher and Barth are equally modern theologians who share more in common than their assumed antagonism suggests. Again, my scholarly limitations make any attempt by me to sug-gest that Hector's Schleiermacher is closer to the real Schleiermacher than Healy's Schleiermacher a judgment I cannot make. I will say, however, that I am attracted to Hector's account — an account he uses to illumine Schleiermacher's "pragmatics" — of how concepts gain their meaning to

18. Stanley Hauerwas and Will Willimon, *Lord Teach Us: The Lord's Prayer and the Christian Life* (Nashville: Abingdon, 1996); Hauerwas and Willimon, *The Truth about God: The Ten Commandments and the Christian Life* (Nashville: Abingdon, 1999); Hauerwas, *Cross-Shattered Christ: Meditations on the Seven Last Words* (Grand Rapids: Brazos, 2004).

19. I assume because the books on the Decalogue and the Lord's Prayer are jointly authored with Will Willimon, Healy thought attribution would be difficult. I suspect he thought *Cross-Shattered Christ* too "devotional." I regret neither the joint authorship of both nor the devotional character of the latter.

be extremely suggestive.[20] I mention Hector's account of language and the work that concepts do because his account bears similarities to my display of the words we use to describe what we do and do not do in several of the chapters in *The Work of Theology* as well as the earlier book *Working with Words: On Learning to Speak Christian.*[21]

Healy rightly observes that I do not share Schleiermacher's turn to the subject or Schleiermacher's attempt to show that Christianity is crucial for German civilization because what Christians believe can be construed in a manner that meets the demands of rational inquiry set by the modern university. Nor do I share Schleiermacher's defense of the church as necessary for societal and cultural progress that we might reach higher forms of human self-consciousness (p. 45). Nonetheless according to Healy I am still closer to Schleiermacher than to Barth because I use a nontheological theory, a theory Healy suggests I get from Alasdair MacIntyre, as the basis for my account of the church (p. 49). Healy argues that like Schleiermacher I posit the church as the highest form of community, which is a typical modernist move indicating my presumption that the possession of a higher God-consciousness is more important than God himself. Therefore according to Healy, like Schleiermacher, I displace doctrine as central to the church's faith by subordinating dogma to church practices (pp. 49-51).

I began my response to Healy by exploring his argument that I conflate the logic of belief with the logic of coming to believe because my alleged conflation of those logics is the basis for Healy's claim that I am reproducing Schleiermacher's method. Healy acknowledges that I reject the turn to the subject, but he fails to see that far more important is what I have learned from MacIntyre about how to avoid the epistemological presumptions that seemed to make it so important for theologians to give an account of coming to believe.

In this respect, the case MacIntyre makes for the "traditionalist" as an alternative to the "encyclopaedist" and the "genealogist" in *Three Rival Versions of Moral Enquiry* is often misunderstood. For MacIntyre the traditionalist does not begin by trying to give an account of how she knows she knows anything at all. Rather the traditionalist begins, as anyone trained in a craft must begin, by being subject to a master who trains her in the basic

20. Kevin Hector, *Theology without Metaphysics: God, Language, and the Spirit of Recognition* (Cambridge: Cambridge University Press, 2011). Hector's account of concepts is developed in chapters 2 and 3 of his book. For his account of Schleiermacher see pp. 250-59.

21. Stanley Hauerwas, *Working with Words: On Learning to Speak Christian* (Eugene, OR: Cascade, 2011).

skills necessary to achieve the good of that craft. Crucial to the acquisition of such skills is the language constitutive of the skill. Without knowing how to say what you are doing, you do not have the skill though you may appear skillful. What many fail to notice about MacIntyre's account of craft is the implication that what we do and how we say what we do shape our knowing.[22] That is the crucial presumption that distinguishes me from Schleiermacher, or at least the Schleiermacher identified as the exemplification of Protestant liberal theology, the Schleiermacher who was trying to make being a Christian intelligible without training.

Healy may object that my appeal to MacIntyre confirms his argument that I have, like Schleiermacher, used a nontheological theory as a basis for my account of the church, but surely that is to confuse apples with oranges. MacIntyre's understanding of tradition stands as a remarkable alternative to Healy's understanding of Schleiermacher's account of God-consciousness. MacIntyre does so because he refuses to begin thinking he needs to give an account of how he knows what he knows prior to his having known what he knows. In other words, MacIntyre rightly understands that you always begin in the middle. That means there is no one place to start because anywhere you start will bring you around to all the other places where you could have started.

Healy suggests that though I have written about God, "it is not something he [Hauerwas] is especially drawn to do" (p. 56). I tried to counter that suggestion above by calling attention to some places where I have written not only about God but about the difference God makes or should make in our lives. But to call attention to where I have written about God will not or cannot be convincing to Healy because he is sure that I have subordinated God to the church. There seems to be nothing I can say in my defense. The situation is made even more difficult because of David Burrell's influence on me. Burrell's work on analogy taught me that when we talk of God we only dimly know what we say.

But that is why the church, a church of "unsatisfactory Christians," is so necessary. Healy alleges that the church I seem to want — if not demand — cannot be constituted by "ordinary people" (p. 81). But everything depends on what you mean by "ordinary." By ordinary I simply mean people who keep their promises. They are ordinary people keeping ordinary promises, and it is just such people who make the church the church. For

22. Alasdair MacIntyre, *Three Rival Versions of Moral Enquiry: Encyclopaedia, Genealogy, and Tradition* (Notre Dame: University of Notre Dame Press, 1990), pp. 58-65.

as Guy Mansini, OSB, observes, "as with ordinary promises, the promise of God in Christ is a device to conquer time. . . . An ordinary promise unites past, present, and future; but God's promise depends on the one moment of eternity to which all times are present."[23] That moment is the moment when the one who is the very love of God was crucified. That is the "what" that determines the "how" of Christian lives.

Interestingly enough, I should like to think my conflation of the logic of belief and the logic of living belief is quite close to Healy's understanding of the church developed in his book *Church, World, and the Christian Life.* In that book he identifies with my claim that Christianity is distorted if it is treated as a system of belief. Healy forcefully suggests that the church can be summarily described as "a distinctive way of life, made possible by the gracious action of the Holy Spirit, which orients its adherence to the Father through Jesus Christ. By schooling its members, the church makes the orientation a present possibility. The Christian way of life is distinctive because its Lord is a particular person and because God is triune."[24] I could not have said it better.

I have wondered if my emphasis on the significance of the church worries Healy because of his worry that the "Roman church," that is, his church, is "unwilling to acknowledge that it is part of the fallen world."[25] I understand that concern because such an unwillingness can result in a romanticized ecclesiology in service to misuse of power. I suspect a romanticized ecclesiology is exactly what Healy thinks I represent. But I am not a Roman Catholic theologian. I am a theologian for a church that has trouble acknowledging it has been brought into existence and sustained by the grace of God. Given our different ecclesial positions I wonder if Healy and I are not like ships passing in the night.

Healy strikes me as someone rightly disappointed in how his church has failed to support the laity. I think he is right to be disappointed. I often observe that Catholicism has an extraordinary ecclesiology that expresses the universal character of the church. What is often missing in Roman Catholic ecclesiology, however, is any account of the church as a congregation. Healy I think is profoundly aware of the significance of the congregation, which is but my way of saying that I am more than ready to

---

23. Guy Mansini, OSB, *Promising and the Good* (Ann Arbor, MI: Sapientia, 2005), p. 123.

24. Healy, *Church, World, and the Christian Life,* pp. 4-5.

25. Healy, *Church, World, and the Christian Life,* p. 9.

join him in his endeavor to recover the significance of the everyday reality of the church.

I hope my response to Healy will, as I suggested, help the reader better understand what I have tried to do in *The Work of Theology*. Healy is certainly right that I conflate the logic of belief and the logic of living out our beliefs. I shall have to leave it to the reader's judgment whether this is or is not a deep mistake. Even more important I hope readers will discover along the way that, despite the mistakes I may have made, it is a joyful thing to be called to engage in that good work we call theology.

# Index

Action theory, 73-74. *See also* Agency, moral

Adams, Reginald, 229n

*Ad hominem* arguments, 14-15, 21, 30

*After Christendom* (Hauerwas), 23

*After the Spirit* (Rogers), 34, 40-47

*After Virtue* (MacIntyre), 74-77, 79n, 204

*Against the Nations* (Hauerwas), 167

Agamben, Giorgio, 101

Agency, moral, 8, 70-89; Bonhoeffer and, 76-77, 82-88; Bonhoeffer's poem "Who Am I?," 85-87; Farrer's account of voluntary action, 70-71, 75, 82; habits, 71-72n; Hauerwas's early work on moral character, agency, and theological ethics, 27-28, 71-77; MacIntyre on core virtues of "integrity" and "constancy," 79-82; MacIntyre on modern compartmentalized social orders, 80-82; MacIntyre on narrative history and, 77-82, 87; MacIntyre on two conditions necessary for, 78-80; MacIntyre's account of "the case of J," 77-82, 85, 87-88; MacIntyre's *After Virtue*, 74-77, 79n; our penchant for self-deception, 71; role of virtues and character, 71-74

American Association of Retired Persons (AARP), 254

*Anabaptism: Neither Catholic nor Protestant* (Klaassen), 62

*Anabaptist History and Theology: An Introduction* (Snyder), 61

Anabaptists, 60-64; and Catholicism, 54, 63; and the Lord's Supper, 62

Anarchism: Proudhon on, 187; Scott's account of democracy and, 186-90

Anatolios, Khaled, 260-61

Anderson, Gary, 214-17, 225, 226

Anderson, Raymond Kemp, 262-63

Anscombe, G. E. M., 73n

Apostles' Creed, 38

Aquinas, Thomas: metaphysics of action, 71, 74n; and Protestant ethics, 56, 64-69; and theological speech, 66-67

Arians, 43-44

Aristotle, 27-28, 182; distinction between *techne* and *phronesis*, 72; distinction between the active and contemplative life, 146; on the practical syllogism, 4, 16; and practical wisdom and the character of practical reason, 15-17, 27-28, 146; virtues, 72-73, 146

Athanasius, 44

Atheism, 5-7

279